WITHDRAWN

The Pulse of Praise

The Pulse of Praise

Form as a Second Self
in the Poetry of George Herbert

Julia Carolyn Guernsey

DELAWARE

Newark: University of Delaware Press
London: Associated University Presses

Associated University Presses
440 Forsgate Drive
Cranbury, NJ 08512

Associated University Presses
16 Barter Street
London WC1A 2AH, England

Associated University Presses
P.O. Box 338, Port Credit
Mississauga, Ontario
Canada L5G 4L8

The paper used in this publication meets the requirements of the American National Standard for Permanence of Paper for Printed Library Materials Z39.48-1984.

Library of Congress Cataloging-in-Publication Data

Guernsey, Julia Carolyn, 1960–
    The pulse of praise : form as a second self in the poetry of
George Herbert / Julia Carolyn Guernsey.
        p. cm.
    Includes bibliographical references and index.
    ISBN 0-87413-679-2 (alk. paper)
    1. Herbert, George, 1593–1633—Criticism and interpretation.
2. Laudatory poetry, English—History and criticism.   3. Christian
poetry, English—History and criticism.   4. Difference (Psychology)
in literature.   5. Split self in literature.   6. Praise in
literature.   7. Literary form.   I. Title.
PR3508.G84   1999
821'.3—dc21   99-18962
                                                          CIP

PRINTED IN THE UNITED STATES OF AMERICA

For Elizabeth, Stewart, and Gene

Contents

Preface and Acknowledgments

I<small>N THIS BOOK, I OFFER AN INTERDISCIPLINARY READING OF INTERAC</small>-tions between form and content in George Herbert's *The Temple*. Specifically, I argue that Renaissance child rearing practices, modes of social interaction, and ideas about God and the self limit the personality of Herbert's discursive speaker, yet Herbert's prosody often offers an alternative to the speaker's way of being a self in relation to God, himself, and others. At times we may even construe Herbert's form as a "prosodic subject"—a reformed self closer to the Divine Other of Herbert's poems than the "I-speaker" is. The object relations model of psychoanalyst D. W. Winnicott illuminates various senses of self and Other which Herbert's poems express discursively and formally.

Part of Chapter 3 first came out in *Essays in Literature* 22.2 (Fall 1995): 196–214 under the title "Betwixt This World and That of Grace: George Herbert's Potential Spaces."

For this book, I owe a tremendous debt to the University of Arkansas English Department as a whole—creative writers and critics alike. I want especially to thank James Whitehead, who taught me the approach to the form and theory of poetry that serves as a cornerstone for my work; Joseph Candido, who, as my dissertation adviser, encouraged me to find my own critical voice rather than seek to appropriate his; Dorothy Stephens, who read drafts of my chapters closely and sensitively and offered both needed support and astute criticism; David Hart, who helped me a number of times to decide between alternative suggestions for revision; Debora Shuger, who, having moved on to the UCLA English Department, nevertheless agreed to serve on my committee and gave constructive criticism that challenged me always to think further and harder. Also I want to thank Jonathan Perry, director of the University of Arkansas Counseling and Psychological Services, who took time from a busy schedule on a number of occasions to offer clarification of psychoanalytic concepts and suggestions regarding further psychological sources I might consider. Without any of these people, this book would be otherwise. Indeed, as I separate from the

matrix of graduate education to seek my place in the professional community at large, I am led to affirm that, in education
as in childhood, a central object relations premise, statable by
the converse of a famous Tennyson line, sums up my grounds
for optimism: all that I have met are a part of me.

Introduction

IN THIS BOOK, I ADDRESS THE MEANING AND FUNCTION OF GEORGE Herbert's poetic form from a psycho-historical perspective, and argue that close attention to prosody can contribute to critical discussions about the devices of self-representation, the dynamics of self-Other relation, and the depths of self-transformation in *The Temple.* Although these issues lie at the heart of many historical and religious studies of *The Temple,* surprisingly few critics have addressed subjectivity and inter-subjectivity in Herbert from a psychoanalytic perspective. Fur-thermore, while Herbert's critics have discussed his poetics in the contexts of Renaissance music, visual arts, theology, and other historical ideas, no one has emphasized what prosody con-tributes to Herbert's representations of self and the self-Other relationship. I draw on D. W. Winnicott's object relations model, which focuses on self-development in a relational context, to illuminate various senses of self and Other which Herbert's poems express discursively and formally.

I wish to introduce the book by offering an account of how it came to be: both the ways of thinking that shaped it and the process by which it evolved. Also, I want to touch on several issues that may arise in regard to my theoretical choices and to offer a brief precis of the chapters that will follow.

To convey the ways of thinking that have shaped my interdisci-plinary study of form-content interactions in Herbert's poetry, I might start by asking my readers to imagine that there is a God. This God is not the only and ultimate self in the universe, onto-logically justified in his bias against all that is not he; neither does this God judge from the standpoint of omniscience and moral certainty the objective rights and wrongs of creatures whom sin has separated from him. Rather, this God is one so wise, creative, compassionate, and fair that he attends simulta-neously to every human perspective, empathetically assessing each act, each intention, each motive, and the past sources of all acts, intentions and motives, as well as the present and future effects each person's actions have on others, prior to rendering

11

a verdict succinctly stated once: "Father, forgive them; for they know not what they do" (Luke 23:34 Authorized Version). The empathic God is one who forgives because he is one who knows.

I state this idea less as a theological conviction than as an indication of a metaphysical center, a point of origin out of which my intuitions have come and toward which my thoughts have tended throughout the course of this project. I believe this understanding of God has been scripted in part by Herbert's text; at the same time I do not mean to disclaim it; it is very much my own. If as poststructuralists since Derrida have argued, all critical work is grounded on metaphysical assumptions (or more recently on the negation of metaphysical assumptions), then I would characterize my metaphysical position as evolving from neither of two, perhaps equally imaginary, extremes: pure subjectivity or pure objectivity. The center, as humanly impossible to reach as the infinitely approachable zero, is in fact the intersection of all centers; it is intersubjectivity, raised to the infinite power.

No one person can adequately approximate the stance of this one who knows. Although I have sought to research, as thoroughly as possible in the six-year gestation period of this book, each of the various perspectives that I bring together here, and although I drew on long-term interests in psychology, history, theology, and literature, I began with an interest in Herbert and a desire to discover how formalist ideas regarding the meaning and function of poetic prosody could be revised to encompass contexts beyond the text itself.

In the fall of 1991, I began without a theory, only a sense that the dynamics of Herbert's prosody veered far closer to the domain of lived human experience than conventional formalist theory might suggest. I was simultaneously fascinated by William Pahlka's discussion of Augustinian poetics in relation to Herbert's meter, and disappointed with the abstract, disembodied notion of Divine unity, reason, and order as the source and end of verse, which Pahlka found in Augustine and attributed to Herbert.[1] In the back of my mind, an idea I later found developed by Richard Hughes and Heather Asals was formulating itself in connection with a remembered Bible verse: "And the Word was made flesh, and dwelt among us" (John 1:14 AV).[2] Herbert's form, it seemed, made words flesh.

Opening my book, I saw not flesh but the long blockish stanzas of "The Church-porch," words shaping an altar, wings. Still in poems like "Deniall" I sensed a drive toward wholeness that seemed far more affective and personal than the transcendent unity of an ethereal and remote creator or the aesthetic unity of an isolated artifact. Had Eliot referred to the unity of sensibility among the metaphysical poets or to its unification?[3] And was it the unification merely of sensibility I was perceiving in Herbertian form-content interactions—or of a whole bodily, affective, and spiritual self in relation to God?

At first I had a vague sense of having stumbled upon the Lacanian imaginary self, and perhaps from a Lacanian perspective that diagnosis was right. I read books by and about Lacan for a year thereafter. It occurred to me how telling it was that the whole self represented by Herbert's form should be from a post-modern psychoanalytic perspective "imaginary," yet in Reformation terms must be a self "in the image of God" (Genesis 1:27 AV). I had a sense of having fallen through a historical looking glass—everything backwards, nothing landing "right side up." A friend in psychology suggested I look at D. W. Winnicott's work. Through a Winnicottian lens, Herbert began to look again like the Herbert of my understanding—a poet embedded in a seventeenth-century context, yet one who could be mirrored in empathic twentieth-century terms.

I introduce my work this way because, having recently read Frederick Crews' polemics against (especially Freudian) psychoanalysis—and against "theoreticism" in general—I want to make clear what I do and do not assume.[4] I am not one to reach randomly into a bag of theories, pull out the first one that comes loose and apply it, only to discover an inevitable Eureka effect.[5] Literature and the historical context of it can and probably should shape our theoretical choices, but they can do so without closing off the possibility of creating dialogues between or among distant cultures, varying disciplines, and differing texts. While Lacanian theory negates meanings available to people in a seventeenth-century religious context, Winnicottian theory illuminates seventeenth-century meanings in often analogical twentieth-century terms.

Crews' primary agenda is to demand empirical proof for the validity of psychoanalytic models; moreover, he desires such proof to determine the priority of one model over all others. Venting frustration over the proliferation of literary theories and the pluralism of competing psychoanalytic models alike, Crews never seems to consider the possibility that some degree of relativism in regard to how we understand selves and stories may arise from the "empirical fact" of individual and/or cultural human diversity.[6] Proverbial wisdom seems a step ahead of him in this regard. Surely if "there's more than one way to skin a cat," there are more than two or three ways to understand the subjectivity of billions.

From a purely pragmatic critical perspective, I contend that one psychoanalytic model may be more useful than others in regard to specific texts and historical contexts. I might further illustrate the point by making reference to William Empson's infamous Freudian reading of a line from "The Sacrifice": "Man stole the fruit, but I must climb the tree" (202). As Empson reads the line, Christ must climb the tree to replace the fruit man stole, but he must also climb it to steal the fruit for man; he must become the thief. Empson reasons furthermore that since Christ must *climb* to attain fruit, he is not as tall as Eve, who plucks the fruit while standing on the ground; so Eve is a grown woman, Christ an "adventurous boy" climbing in his Father's orchard. Since fruit stands for female sexual organs, Christ's stealing it suggests a boy's desire to sleep with his mother; since the tree is a phallic symbol, Christ's climbing it suggests aggression against the Father; plucking fruit from the tree also bespeaks castration anxiety which accompanies Oedipal conflict. According to Empson, then, the line reveals the complicity of Herbert's Christ with Freudian "man."[7]

In a well-known debate, Rosemond Tuve takes Empson to task for this psychoanalysis and also for his New Critical assumption that "The Sacrifice" can be understood apart from its historical context. Tuve argues that the key to this and other Herbert texts lies in the medieval liturgical and lyric traditions out of which the poems arose. Although imposing modern ideas on a seventeenth-century text may validate modern systems of thought, this mode of interpretation cannot illuminate "the text" as written by a seventeenth-century author and understood by seventeenth-century readers.[8]

Subsequent Herbert criticism proves how utterly Tuve prevailed over Empson in this debate. Although these days, critics typically contextualize *The Temple* in terms of Herbert's Reformation present rather than his medieval past, historicism continues to dominate Herbert studies.[9]

I have no intention of seeking to displace historically informed Herbert scholarship with psychoanalytic readings; rather, I contend that, given post-Freudian developments in the field of psychoanalysis, rigid opposition between the historicist and the psychoanalytic camps in literary studies presents us with a false dichotomy. Winnicott's model is more commensurate with history, historicism and Herbert than Freud's. By raising historical mothers to the same power that Freud raises the libido, Winnicott accounts for the impact of history on self-experience. Furthermore, Winnicott talks more about lived experience—or in some cases, a paucity of lived experience—than Freud, who focuses on psychic structures and unconscious conflict. This theoretical difference translates into a significant critical difference. While Empson gleans from "The Sacrifice" a latent message about incest—a meaning far removed from any available to the Renaissance—I read *The Temple* to mean something about the empathic (gracious, self-sacrificing) nature of Herbert's Christ, about the centrality of the believer's relationship to him, and about the personal transformation that occurs through that relationship—issues central to Reformation Christianity.

I posit three connections between Winnicott's ideas and Herbert's text and historical context:

1. I assume throughout, and will argue especially in chapter 2 for, a connection by analogy. Specifically, the gracious, self-sacrificing nature of Herbert's Christ in relation to the human believer is analogous to Winnicott's idea of the mother-child relationship.

2. I assume a connection by virtue of a hermeneutic circle. Brooke Hopkins recognizes a probable connection between the Winnicottian idea that a toddler needs simultaneously (in a psychological sense) to annihilate the mother and to have her survive, and the Christian belief that the Christ has to die and be resurrected in order to redeem humankind. Accordingly, Hopkins notes that "Winnicott's own work does not stand wholly outside the circle of cultural influence," a point which suggests that Winnicott, whose modern British culture emerged out of Herbert's early modern British culture, may be influenced by the same ways of thinking that shape Herbert.[10] Furthermore, we may make a more specific connection between Winnicott and the metaphysical poets, since Winnicott mentions them in his introduction to *Playing and Reality;* it seems plausible, then, to assume that metaphysical poetry has contributed to the insights which I will use to explicate Herbert.[11]

3. I will argue, especially in chapter 4, for a connection based on a qualified sense of universal humanity: specifically, a univer-

sality of infantile human needs and desires. As Peter Rudnytsky discusses, in Winnicottian theory the nature of an infant is determined in part by biological predispositions which make every infant both individual and human. One need not universalize the needs, desires, goals, values, mores, self-organization, or relational capacities of adult personalities transculturally or transhistorically in order to entertain the hypothesis that *primary* experience (that of infants and young toddlers), if based in the body, may be as individual and at the same time as universal as a human body, while *secondary* experience (that of a child after socialization, education, religious or political indoctrination, and so on) may be culturally contingent.[12] Looking at the interplay between the primary and secondary dimensions of experience in Herbert's poetry, I posit a culturally scripted relationship between what is primary in Herbert's text (the need for relationship to an empathic, caring Other, for example) and what is culturally specific (the speaker's ways of engaging in, and his expectations regarding, the self-Other relationship, for example). In so doing, I hypothesize that Winnicott's model can successfully explicate primary experience (basic human needs, desires, and so on as manifested from infancy forward) as a transhistorical phenomenon. Furthermore, Winnicott's theory may account for the *relationship* between primary and secondary experience to the extent that historical research (on Renaissance child rearing practices, modes of education, social relations, and so on, as well as on Reformation theology and religious practices) becomes one important evidential basis for psychoanalysis of self-organization and object relations in Herbert's text.

The book begins with close attention to poetics in *The Temple*. In chapter 1, I argue that prosodic signification in *The Temple* sometimes exists in tension with discursive meaning; thus we may sometimes construe form as a second Herbertian persona, a "prosodic subject." The Reformation idea of the "new man" at odds with the "old man" offers a way to understand this recurrent form-content disparity. Like the "new man," the "prosodic subject" is a whole self, body and soul, in contrast to a speaker who represents himself as a loosely assembled collection of parts or as inert matter, a body devoid of soul. I also argue that two Herbertian poetics, a poetics of mortification and a poetics of quickening, represent decay of the old man and unification of the new man respectively. Throughout the chapter, I equate the new man represented by Herbert's form with the heart, where, according to Reformation belief, Christ dwells in and with the speaker; I show that *The Temple*'s poems often set up analogies between prosody and the heart, which Herbert's speaker sometimes addresses as a second self.

In chapter 2, I claim that if "father" is what the God of *The Temple* is, mothering is what he does best, a fact especially evident in *The Temple*'s form. Examining Renaissance conceptions of gender as they relate to representations of Christ, I distinguish between two versions of the feminine, the eroticized Other and the holding mother, and argue that Herbert often represents Christ in maternal rather than erotic terms—but distinctly feminine terms nonetheless. I discuss Winnicott's theory of holding as it relates to Renaissance images of mother and child, and show how this theory makes sense of Herbert's form. As a spatial construct, Herbert's prosody represents a relational space analogous to the one-body relationship between mother and infant and to the interpersonal space that develops between them as the child becomes a separate person. Within the relational spaces demarcated by form, Christ "holds" the prosodic subject, helping this persona cohere as a bodily and psychic self.

In chapter 3, I analyze the dynamics of interpersonal space and boundaries in *The Temple,* and draw on Winnicott's concepts of potential space and transitional objects to discuss *The Temple*'s place in Reformation history. Originating in the infant-mother unit, potential space is a relational space that the toddler plays out with a transitional object, such as a blanket. Potential space contributes to a child's formation of boundaries and to later capacities for autonomy, intimacy, play, and the enjoyment of culture. It is also the space of the sacraments. Despite Reformation assaults on the potential spaces of the established "mother church," even Calvinists of Herbert's day had a transitional object: the Bible. In *The Temple* transitional objects include the Scriptures, sacraments, sacramentals, and verse. These further the speaker's growth in relation to God.

In chapter 4, I contend that Herbert's speaker often shows signs of being a false (reactive) self scripted by authoritarian child rearing, restrictive education, and absolutist politics. In contrast, the prosodic subject represents an emerging true (core) self. Analyzing resistance to true selves in Renaissance texts and history, I argue that normative Renaissance family and social arrangements made false-self organization likely for the majority in Herbert's day, yet some tenets of Reformation theology made the emergence of the true self possible. Whereas Herbert's speaker defines himself in terms of a number of culturally available roles, the prosodic subject is a self left over. To the extent that Herbert's form registers aspects of self that Renaissance social structures disallowed, we may understand form as representing not merely a unique "Herbert" but, from the standpoint of broader, cultural significance, a negative of the Renaissance social contract. Within *The Temple*'s form, aspects of self not fully expressible within the matrices of Renaissance society are integrated into the Body of Christ.

In chapter 5, I contrast Winnicott's ideas to Freud's and Lacan's, arguing that Winnicott's model explains the dynamics of redemption in Herbert better than these other theories do. First, although Herbert's speaker often views fallen human beings as driven by desire for pleasure or narcissistic sustenance, the need for relatedness characterizes prelapsarian humankind and becomes the major motivator of the new Adam. Second, Herbert's poems do not always represent the self as a unit the way Freud does, but neither do they represent the self as irreparably divided the way Lacan does. Third, as Christ re-forms the human subject, illusion precedes disillusionment, deepening the self's capacity to love and cope in an imperfect world. Fourth, the determination of self by Other in *The Temple* is not always, as in Freud, a conflictual process, nor is it, as in Lacan, self-alienating. Rather, Christ establishes the new Adam on the foundation of his potential. Christ's nurturing of the core self in Herbert solidifies the foundation of a personality capable of creative living, and of harmony with God, the self, and others.

The Pulse of Praise

1

Notes Toward Another Music: Prosody as Self, Body, and Heart in *The Temple*

I

IN THE PAGES THAT FOLLOW, I WILL ARGUE THAT PROSODIC SIGNIFICA-tion in George Herbert's *Temple* sometimes exists in tension with discursive meaning; thus, we may sometimes understand form as a second Herbertian persona, a "prosodic subject." The Reformation idea of the "new man" at odds with the "old man" provides a way of understanding the recurrent form-content disparity in *The Temple*. Like the "new man," the prosodic subject is a unified self, body and soul, in contrast to a speaker who represents himself as a dispirited, unwieldy set of parts.

I will also argue that two poetics are at work in *The Temple*: a poetics of mortification, which represents the old man's body and self as broken, decaying, thing-like, and a poetics of quickening, which represents the new man's body and self as whole and alive in relation to God.

Throughout these arguments, I will rely on the fact that *The Temple*'s poems often set up analogies between prosody and the heart, which Herbert's speaker sometimes addresses as a second self. According to beliefs current in Herbert's day, the heart is the bodily and spiritual site where self meets Other, the matrix out of which the new man arises.

Since the approach I have outlined will enable us to under-stand the meaning of *The Temple*'s form-content relation in terms historically available to Herbert, in this first chapter I will develop it at length. But because I believe that for Herbert and others of his day, spiritual life was as much a complex of felt experiences as a set of theological concepts, at the end of the chapter I will gesture toward, and in subsequent chapters de-velop, a psychoanalytic account of personal transformation through self-Other relation in *The Temple*.

21

My grounds for taking this tack are simple. From a psychoanalytic standpoint, whatever is experienced as real *is* real and has
consequences in the personal and interpersonal domains. I seek
to account not only for what Herbert's prosody *represents,* ideologically speaking, but also for what it *enacts:* a relational praxis
leading to genuine intrapsychic and interpersonal change—a
praxis founded as much on faith as on actual experience of
others in the world.

II

Whereas formalist critics over the years have valued poetic
prosody for what it contributes to the artistic value of a poem as
a whole, critics interested in history, psychology, religion, gender
relations, and other social concerns, past and present, have
tended to ignore prosody altogether. To a large degree, Herbert's
critics have been an exception. As even the most perfunctory
survey of twentieth-century criticism on *The Temple* will reveal,
almost everyone who deals with Herbert makes at least occasional reference to rhyme and metrics, the shape and motion of
words on the page. Furthermore, *The Temple*'s prosody rewards
explicit attention from multiple angles, as we may infer from a
list of several typical ways that Herbert's prosody has engaged
critics in recent years. Some studies have treated Herbert's form
as a musical phenomenon.[1] Others have approached it as a visual
construct.[2] Some critics have read the prosody for what it has
to say about philosophical and theological ideas prevalent in the
Renaissance.[3] Still others have concerned themselves with the
workings of Herbert's poetic form within the boundaries of "the
text itself."[4] From Joseph Summers' seminal discussion of Herbert's hieroglyphic form to Stanley Fish's more recent considera-
tions of Herbert's artifacts as they entice and instruct Herbert's
readers, Herbert's twentieth-century critics, regardless of theoretical orientation, have perceived and responded to the workings of prosody in *The Temple.*[5] They have done so, I think, for
one very simple reason: form matters in *The Temple; it matters*
in both senses of the word.[6]

Beginning with Summers, critics have accounted for the role
of material form in *The Temple* in varying ways. Both Summers
and William Pahlka claim that Herbert's material form has primarily spiritual meaning and importance—that prosody signifies divine unity, reason, measure, or order—and both cite

Augustine as a historical source for this conception. While Summers claims that for Augustine and Herbert, prosody's capacity to "[reflect] the divine pattern" sanctions materiality, Pahlka contends that for Augustine and Herbert, form's appeal to the senses is sinful even though form serves as a vehicle for the Divine Logos.[7] Heather Asals also views Herbert's poetics as Augustinian, but she emphasizes that form, the textual equivalent of the flesh, is not opposite to the spirit but contains and is contained by it in Herbert's poems, which ultimately concern the reunion of flesh and spirit.[8] In this regard, Asals follows Richard E. Hughes, who relies on the Christian equation between the incarnate Christ and Logos to argue that each of Herbert's poems in "subject . . . form, technique and meaning" is "a miniature version of the Incarnation" and enacts the "triumph of order over chaos" by making the Word—and words—flesh.[9]

In what follows, my position will be close to that of Asals and Hughes. However, I will pursue further than Asals the implications of corporeal form for "the reconciliation of spirit and flesh as healed and *whole*" in *The Temple*.[10] Specifically, I will argue that Herbert's prosody configures a matrix out of which a "healed and whole" self arises. In poem after poem, Herbert's form supports the speaker's claims of hard-heartedness, dullness, brokenness, ego disintegration, and bodily and spiritual mortification. But in some of the same poems, prosody simultaneously points us beyond the speaker's awareness, enacting a suppling, a quickening, a reunification, a reintegration, a resurrection. Coburn Freer notes the "disparity" in some Herbert poems between "prose sense" and poetic form.[11] I mean to argue that in such poems, form becomes a "prosodic subject," a bodily and spiritual self emerging in and through the Divine Other of *The Temple*.

Herbert's form, I believe, frequently gestures toward, and occasionally enacts, a subjectivity opposed to the speaker's. The contrast between discursive statement and prosodic signification is often minimal, but even in these instances suggestive. In the second stanza of "The Church-porch," for example, as Herbert's speaker warns about on the dangers of lust, the Venus and Adonis stanza quietly alludes to a Renaissance tradition of erotic narratives:

> Beware of lust: it doth pollute and foul
> Whom God in Baptisme washt with his own blood.
> It blots thy lesson written in thy soul;

The holy lines cannot be understood.
How dare those eyes upon a Bible look,
Much lesse towards God, whose lust is all their book?

                                                    (7–12)

Readers may account for the disparity in either of two ways: we may view this choice of form as an instance of sacred parody and argue that the speaker-poet transforms the verse by using it to moral ends; or we may view this choice as an instance of irony and argue that the form playfully undercuts the speaker's letter-of-the-law agenda. While the preacher is preoccupied with the task of reforming sinners, a prosodic subject hums a bawdy tune.[12] In the latter reading, we have afforded Herbert's prosody a small measure of authority and/or agency.[13]

A similar disparity between form and content in "Redemption" suggests a wider gap between the two Herbertian selves. A naive speaker seeks to arrange a new contract with his landlord in pragmatic, impersonal terms. He reports just the facts—why he needs to renegotiate his lease, where he seeks his Lord, and where he finds Him. In the end, when the speaker confronts the scene of the Passion, he seems unable to process the connection between the Lord's statement, "Your suit is granted," and the Lord's death, which seals the utterance (line 14). The poem's sonnet form accurately suggests that the relationship between self and Other is far more personal than the speaker knows. Here form manifests not merely an attitude in contrast to the speaker's, but a relational intelligence that the speaker lacks.

Most significantly, in some poems the discursive and formal Herberts differ in how they are organized as selves. The speaker of "Deniall," and "Longing," to name two of many examples, is a composite of loosely assembled parts, a man at odds with himself. Disintegrating, he experiences the self as both divided and multiplied: the speaker's thoughts "flie asunder" and become persons, each with a "way" of "his" own; the speaker becomes a "pile of dust, wherein each crumme / Sayes, Come"; his heart breaks, and it seems to him "that ev'ry part / Hath got a tongue!" ("Deniall," 8–9; "Longing," 41–42, 75–76). The raving persona of "The Collar" becomes so dissociated by rage that he addresses his heart as a "thou" whom he imagines as having hands (17–18).

In these poems, prosody enacts a double motion. On one level, form mimetically supports the speaker's sense of dissolution. In "Deniall," irregular line lengths, accents which fall unpredictably within lines, and an unrhymed last line in all but the last stanza echo the speaker's claim that his heart and verse are "broken." In "Longing" we sense fragmentation and the anxiety it entails in multiple fast-paced short lines, of which some are syntactically fragmentary. In "The Collar," line lengths vary in random sequence and rhymes come in no set pattern. Yet on another level, form in these poems comes behind the speaker, putting the pieces in order. The verses of "Deniall" remain roughly four duple feet in the first line, two in the second, five in the third, three in the fourth, and two in the fifth in each stanza. Unrhymed lines always come at the end of stanzas, and the closing rhyme which contrasts the unrhymed endings of previous stanzas dramatizes the grace which mends verse and heart. In "Longing," although seemingly arbitrary line lengths (counting feet, 342241) are unsettling at the local level of each stanza, from the God's-eye-view of the whole poem the stanza form begins to seem coherent through being repeated; formal units come together, though the speaker remains in pieces.[14] Finally in "The Collar," lines range always between two and five feet, and all the lines rhyme; the last four lines reiterate all the line lengths which have contained the speaker's words and bring the poem to rest on a familiar pattern: a quatrain with alternating rhymes.[15]

In poems like "Deniall," "Longing," and "The Collar," prosodic order, at first subtle, gradually overshadows the speaker's chaotic sense of self. The speaker is a self in process, the process disintegrative. Prosody is the core (or heart) which precedes and the self who emerges from the fragments. Furthermore, the speaker is a non-relational self. In the first two examples, he is abjectly dependent and abandoned: "O that thou shouldst give dust a tongue / To crie to thee, / and then not heare it crying!" he complains ("Deniall," 16–18). "Thou tarriest while I die, / And fall to nothing" ("Longing," 55–56). In the third, at least until the end of the poem, he is falsely independent: "My lines and life are free; free as the rode, / Loose as the winde, as large as store. / Shall I be still in suit?" (4–6). In contrast, the prosodic subject of these poems is a relational self rooted in the Other whose grace is manifested in the hidden order of form.

The prosodic subject then is a re-formed self whose presence in *The Temple* is intimated by prosodic signs.[16] We may imagine this second persona as situated in the heart, which Herbert's prosody often figures and which Herbert's speaker sometimes addresses as a second self. As I will argue, the heart in *The*

Temple is a bodily and spiritual place where the Christian is inspired by an indwelling Other, the Holy Spirit; thus, it is the site of personal transformation, the matrix out of which the "new man" arises.

By Luther's definition, "the term 'old man' describes what kind of person is born of Adam, not according to his nature but according to the defect of his nature."[17] Like Herbert's speaker in some poems, he is the postlapsarian self—rebellious, broken, dying. The "new man" is born of the Spirit. Although the death of the old man within the believer is an ongoing process—which entails, in Melanchthon's words, "Patience in suffering or affliction or earnest terror in the face of the wrath of God against sin"—the new man enjoys spiritual aliveness and anticipates bodily resurrection.[18] While in the old man "the whole man is entirely flesh," "only outward," and essentially dead, the new man is also spiritual and inward; thus, the believer is "at the same time both dead and set free" (Luther, *Works,* Vol. 25, #332–34).

According to Luther, the new or spiritual man is often at odds with the flesh: "although he is present in all things with his senses, yet in his heart he is entirely withdrawn from these things" and even "glories in the fact that he is like a dead body" (#312). Nevertheless, inasmuch as his spirit and flesh constitute a single whole, "the flesh itself no longer serves the Law or sins, but it is freed because of the fact that the inner man has been set free, with whom it makes up one man, whose wife it is and was" (#333).

In Luther's *Lectures on Romans,* the mathematics of Christian subjectivity is tricky. On the one hand, the Christian self is divided into two parts: flesh and spirit, which "are intimately bound together into one, although they completely disagree with each other" and which will be reconciled at the time of the general resurrection (#333, 309–10). Since the Christian life in time involves ongoing warfare between the flesh, which inclines toward sin, and the spirit, which desires not to sin, the believer cannot fulfill "the perfection of righteousness . . . in [the] corruptible flesh" (#342). On the other hand, the Christian is divided into two selves: the old man (a self of flesh without spirit) and the new man (a self of the Spirit—whose flesh and spirit both have been redeemed). As "the beginning of God's creature," the believer is like "a house which has fallen into disrepair" and "is in the process of reconstruction" (#341). The old man, subject to sin and the demands of the fallen flesh, is falling apart;

the new man, subject to grace and the guidance of the Holy Spirit, is coming together; during the ongoing process of conversion, these modes of being coexist in one body: "for it is the same body which seeks health and yet is compelled to do these things which belong to its weakness" (#341). Yet the old man of the past and the new man of the future have very different bodies: one analogous to a shambles, the other to a "spiritual house" which "grows into a holy temple in the Lord" (#340–41).

In his later writings, Luther equates the negative Pauline term *flesh* not with the body *per se* but rather with the desires, intentions, and acts of the old Adam; these are opposed to the desires, intentions, and acts of the new man, who is actualized in moments when the Spirit of God motivates the believer in soul *and* body (vol. 37, #99).[19] This later Lutheran definition of *flesh* seems more commensurate with Romans, where Paul implies that to the extent Christians accede to the death of the "old man," they are freed from sin's reign "in [the] mortal body" and, entering into Christ's resurrection, may "yield . . . [their] members as instruments of righteousness unto God" (Romans 6:6, 12–13 AV). Thus as Herbert may have gleaned from Paul or Luther, the believer's experience of the body entails not only the mortification of the old man but also, in moments of grace, the corporeal freedom of the new man to act according to God's will. While the old man remains "lost in flesh," without access to "minde," "all earth," God gives the new man "quicknesse"; his body is *inspired*—animated by a spirit which proceeds from the Spirit of God (Herbert, "Dulnesse," 21, 23, 2, 3; cf. Romans 8:11 AV).

In equating the speaker of many Herbert poems with the old man of Pauline theology, I do not mean to imply that the speaker is typically non-Christian. Whereas the speaker of "Redemption" does not yet understand the New Covenant, the speaker of "The Collar" is an English priest, who, having previously enjoyed the fruits of "the board," precipitously rebels against God and the life of self-denial his calling entails (1). As he voices the demands of the old man within him, subtle formal order suggests that the "heart" cannot "forsake [its] cage" ("The Collar," 17, 21). In "Deniall," the speaker is a believer who feels cut off from God's presence and grace. While he suffers with great reluctance the death of the old man within him, the prosodic subject adds to his discourse signs of personal transformation in and through Christ.

Like the old man and the new within a single believer, Herbert's speaker and prosodic subject are two selves and also two different ways to be a self. If not literally two subjects, they seem very nearly so at times, and we may gain insight into the devices of self-representation, the dynamics of self-Other relation, and the depths of self-transformation in *The Temple* by treating them provisionally as such.

III

My thesis is that Herbert's prosody is a mode of self-representation, and furthermore that the self represented by form is not always merely an extension of the speaking "I" of *The Temple* but often a self or aspect of self from whom the speaker is divided. Their difference is most apparent in poems where prosody seems flatly contradictory to the speaker's meaning or tone, but it exists in some other poems as well. "Easter-wings," for instance, is a classic example of mimetic form because its prosody visibly and audibly supports what the speaker says. Nevertheless, I will contend that there are good reasons to construe the poem's form and content as two Herberts.[20] First, form in "Easter wings" anamorphically emblematizes the body, juxtaposing an emblem of the mortal body with an emblem of the resurrected body. Second, form conveys a global awareness that the I-speaker does not appear to possess. In representing both soma and psyche, form figures a human subject; in representing a body and awareness which are not the speaker's, form may be construed as a second self in the text.

Robert W. Halli Jr. discusses the visual pun in "Easter-wings"—how the poem's shape signifies wings when the poem is approached sideways, but changes to an image of two hourglasses when the page is turned so the words become readable. Halli points out that hourglasses and wings were often used together in the Renaissance to emblematize the ideas of mortality and immortality; furthermore, the equation between the fallen body and an hourglass exists elsewhere in *The Temple*: "flesh is but the glasse, which holds the dust / That measures all our time" ("Church-monuments," 20–21).[21]

Halli does not explicitly address whether we should understand the double emblem in "Easter-wings" as signifying a dualism between the mortal body (hourglass) and immortal soul (wings), or construe it rather as signifying another contrast: between the postlapsarian body/self in time (hourglass) and the resurrected body/self rising toward eternity (wings). Each of these understandings is implicit in some of his arguments, and both understandings will inform my own interpretation. But since my reading will hinge on the way these somewhat disjunctive meanings come together in "Easter-wings," I would like to develop the issue before looking more closely at the text.

In the context of other Herbert poems, the notion that the wings signify a disembodied soul is entirely plausible. Herbert frequently uses flight imagery in *The Temple* to represent the soul's rising toward God in worship or prayer.[22] In "Church-musick," the speaker feels himself to be "without a bodie . . . / Rising and falling with [the] wings" of church-music (5–6). Likewise in "Prayer" (I), Herbert's speaker figures prayer as "The soul in paraphrase, heart in pilgrimage," and figures the movement of heart and soul in prayer as an upward journey (3). Among other things, prayer is "The milkie way, the bird of Paradise" and "Church-bels beyond the starres heard" (12, 13). The idea that the soul can rise to the exclusion of the body appears also in "Mans medley," when the speaker summarizes man's double nature: "In soul he mounts and flies / In flesh he dies" (13–14). It appears again when the speaker of "Home" begs God to unmake the uncomfortable marriage between his soul and body:

> Oh loose this frame, this knot of man untie!
> That my free soul may use her wing,
> Which now is pinion'd with mortalitie,
> As an intangled, hamper'd thing.
>
> (61–64)

The first line of this passage echoes Donne's "Holy Sonnet XIV" in which Donne's speaker beseeches God to "divorce" him from God's "enemie" to whom he is "betroth'd," or more pertinently to "untie, or breake [the] knot" which couples them (9–10).[23] The enemy of Donne's poem may be Satan or the flesh; the enemy of Herbert's stanza is unambiguously the mortal body.

But the opposite of the mortal body is not always the "free soul" in *The Temple*. Herbert also writes about the *immortal* body—the body of Christ on Easter, the body of the believer on the day of general resurrection. In spite of his frequent experimentation with Neo-Platonic and Neo-Pythagorean imagery and ideas, Herbert's dualism is not that of a gnostic who believes that the soul will finally be free of the flesh; rather it is that of a Christian who believes (after Augustine) that flesh and spirit, at odds with each other in time, will ultimately be reunified:

What though my bodie runne to dust?
Faith cleaves unto it, counting evr'y grain
With an exact and most particular trust,
Reserving all for flesh again.

("Faith," 41–44)

In this stanza, faith functions much like the "subtile wreath of haire, which crowns [the] arme" of Donne's persona in "The Funerall" (3). Donne's speaker imagines that a relic which preserves his bond with a female other (a bracelet made of her hair) will go with him to the grave. Replacing "the sinewie thread [his] braine lets fall / Through every part," to "tye those parts, and make [him] one of all," it will "keep [his] limbes, her Provinces, from dissolution" (9–10, 11, 8). Herbert's speaker imagines that the faith which constitutes his relationship with the Divine Other will ensure not bodily integrity within the grave but body/ soul unity beyond the grave. Faith, a spiritual condition, will effect reintegration of the body *after* its dissolution. In essence, present faith is the spine of a future body/self. Dust particles will cohere because they are matched by a trust as "particular" as the grains.

Again in "Dooms-day" what God will "summon . . . to rise" is not a disembodied soul (3). Souls will be reunified with "all the dust" of human corpses "Parcel'd out to all the world" (3, 28). Herbert's emphasis on the physical nature of the resurrection is even more intriguing in "Death," a poem in which the speaker addresses a not-so-grim reaper. Although Death was "once an uncouth hideous thing, / Nothing but bones," Christ's death has "put some bloud / Into [his] face" (1–2, 13–14). Here both terms of the speaker's contrast, the emaciated corpse and the healthy body, are corporeal; the speaker thus registers his faith that the flesh itself will be redeemed. He underscores that faith by extending the possibility of resurrection to the utterly carnal figure, Death, whom Donne, in contrast, figures as the only truly mortal being in the universe: "One short sleepe past, wee wake eternally, / And death shall be no more, death, thou shalt die" ("Holy Sonnet X," 13–14).

Flight imagery appears in Herbert's "Death" as well and pertains to the body as well as to the soul. The speaker figures human corpses as "The shells of fledge souls left behinde," and imagines the day when "souls shall wear their new aray" (11, 19). Since the conceit equates death with the hatching of young birds (souls), it follows that resurrection marks the time when these birds will take flight, their "new aray" being mature, winged bodies rather than eggshells.

If we contextualize "Easter-wings" by other Herbert poems, we come to no definitive conclusion about what the wings symbolize. They may represent either the disembodied soul or the resurrected body; or given Herbert's apparent belief that dualism exists in time but that the resurrection will restore body-soul unity, they may represent both. If we add to this contextualization due attention to the poem's occasion, we may arrive at a stronger conclusion. Since "Easter-wings" celebrates Christ's rising from the dead and his bodily ascension, it seems virtually inescapable that the wings represent not merely (or not only) spiritual ascension and the soul's immortality, but physical resurrection, the reunion of flesh and spirit, the immortality of the embodied self.

As I read "Easter-wings," the poem is doubly anamorphic: the reader may see not once (wings) but twice (wings/hourglasses) and interpret the double emblem not once (to mean either body versus soul or the mortal body versus the resurrected body) but twice (to mean body-soul tension in time *and* the transcendence of that divided condition in the resurrection). And if we look again, we may perceive yet a third image embedded in the form. Rather than hourglasses, we may glimpse two capital I's—two selves who come together in the global wings image:

LOrd, who createdst man in wealth and store,
    Though foolishly he lost the same,
        Decaying more and more,
            Till he became
                Most poore:
                With   thee
            O let me rise
        As larks, harmoniously,
    And sing this day thy victoires:
Then shall the fall further the flight in me.

    My tender age in sorrow did beginne:
        And still with sicknesses and shame
            Thou didst so punish sinne,
                That I became
                    Most thinne.
                    With   thee
                Let me combine
            And feel this day thy victorie:
        For, if I imp my wing on thine,
    Affliction shall advance the flight in me.

At this point, we may coordinate visual perception with interpretation thus: the body ages, dies, and disintegrates in time (hourglasses), but even in time the soul may rise toward God (wings); furthermore, the resurrected self transcends time and decay, though not embodiment per se (wings as immortal body); finally, in order to attain resurrection, the mortal self must combine with Christ (two I's coming together in a single pair of wings).

Prosody keeps the synchronic picture in focus; it also mimetically follows the speaker, who pieces the picture together diachronically. Visually, both stanzas image mortality and resurrection through diminishing and increasing line lengths. In stanza one, contracting lines show man's loss, his decay, and his becoming "Most poore"; expanding lines signify the improvement of man's condition when Christ enters the second half of the stanza; likewise in stanza two, shrinking prosody images the speaker's diminution through disease till he becomes "Most thinne"; fattening lines signal a reversal as the speaker prays to combine with Christ.

Aurally, prosody supports the speaker's words as well. In line ten, for example, the rhythm mimetically flutters: "Then shall the fall further the flight in me." And again, even as the lines "Most poore" and "Most thinne" lose visual substance, form adds weight to them; as spondees they gain accentual and affective heaviness, emphasizing the gravity of the human condition in a fallen world.

Halli argues that if these stanzas ended halfway through, they would emblematize a triangle, its apex pointing downward toward "death, hell, and oblivion"; the second half of each stanza, focusing on Christ, figures another triangle, its apex pointing upward "to God, heaven, and eternal life."[24] While the arrow sign may suggest that resurrection is deferred (not here, not now), the visual growth and musical crescendo of lines in each stanza's second half suggest that the believer may "sing" and "feel" Christ's "victorie" "this day."

John Donne provides a multifaceted definition of *resurrection* which supports our present conception of form's multiple meanings in "Easter-wings." Donne emphasizes that *resurrection* pertains not only to Christ on Easter but also to the believer, who may experience resurrection at several levels:

First, a Resurrection from dejections and calamities in this world, a Temporary Resurrection; Secondly a Resurrection from sin, a Spirituall Resurrection; and then a Resurrection from the grave, a finall Resurrection.[25]

All three senses of *resurrection* apply to "Easter-wings." Stanza one focuses on original sin—the foolish loss of "wealth and store" and the subsequent decay of humankind. Although "dejections and calamities" are part of the picture, the stanza's primary emphasis is on man's willful self-impoverishment and need for a "Spirituall Resurrection." The speaker's flight will transcend the fall and render it fortunate. Stanza two explicitly mentions "sinne" but emphasizes the speaker's need for a "Temporary resurrection." The speaker prays to combine with Christ, hoping to gain a reprieve from sin's consequences: "sorrow . . . sicknesses and shame." Resurrection in this stanza opposes— yet is advanced by—"affliction." Either stanza might be read to represent one pair of wings and to signify Donne's third idea, "a finall Resurrection." But as printed in most editions, the stanzas stand together—two pairs of wings or a pair of hourglasses (or I's) which merge to form a fuller body with two wings.[26] The prosodic merging of bodies parallels the speaker's request to combine with Christ (like sand) and to imp—that is, graft—his wings onto Christ's. But the prosodic subject actually experiences bodily resurrection in Christ while the speaker merely desires it.

The hourglasses also signify two different time scales in the poem, both of them opposed to the wings as emblems of eternity. The first is Christian history, which the speaker addresses in stanza one; it begins with the creation and the fall of humankind through Adam. The speaker of stanza one is an Everyman figure, who needs to rise with Christ because of original sin. The second time scale is the speaker's lifetime, which he discusses in stanza two; here the speaker speaks as an individual, who needs to combine with Christ because of his personal sin.[27] Just as the hourglasses represent both collective and individual history, the wings represent both individual bodies (Christ's body rising on Easter and the believer's body transcending time in its individual resurrection) and a collective body, the transcendent Body of Christ, which incorporates all the members of the Church Triumphant.

Form indeed reinforces content in this poem, but it does not merely reiterate what the speaker says. Rather, form supports content as a prosodic subject who operates from a synchronic, multi-perspective which the speaker does not fully share. While the speaker discusses resurrection in the future tense ("Then *shall* the fall further the flight in me" and "Affliction *shall* advance the flight in me"), the prosodic subject flies. Prosody communicates multiple perspectives through physical gestures anamorphically orchestrated to spell, by a single shape, two dimensions of the Christian's experience in time (decaying flesh; rising spirit), two soul-body relationships (division in time; a unified self in eternity), three temporal dimensions (historical time, the speaker's lifetime, and eternity) and multiple bodies (the mortal body of Everyman versus the resurrected body of Everyman; the mortal body of the speaker versus the resurrected body of the speaker; the resurrected body of Jesus, himself both Everyman or the second Adam and a historical individual, both human and God; the merging of Christ and the Christian self in the transcendent Body of Christ). This multidirectional signification is too complex to be attributed to a speaker, who, subject to time and decay, can at best "see through a glass, darkly" (1 Cor. 13:12 AV).

In "Easter-wings," prosody communicates meanings that lie beyond the speaker's present experience and awareness. Form makes the poem equal more than one meaning. Furthermore, since prosody shapes various bodies—mortal and immortal, Everyman's, the speaker's and Christ's—its movements may be understood as the textual equivalent of body language. The poem's form is subjectified and becomes an imaginary locus of human, perhaps even of divine consciousness.

IV

Once we understand Herbert's form as self-representation, we must deal with the hieroglyphs of *The Temple* from a new perspective. What does it mean when prosody, representing the body and a subjective consciousness signified through body language, stiffens into a quasi-inorganic state in Herbert's poetry? To return to a now familiar example, in "Easter wings" prosody shapes two hourglasses (objects) of which the physical properties are suggestive of death. An hourglass is hard, brittle, rigid, and fragile (glass), and also disintegrated (dust). These properties refer to the mortal body and to the spiritual state of a human being without Christ. They are formally figured and discursively explicated in many Herbert poems, and, as I will argue, they suggest a negative Herbertian sense of self and the body-as-thing.

This negative sense of body, self, and form is typically opposed in *The Temple* not by a prosody which stands for the free soul but rather, as the other emblems in "Easter-wings" suggest, by a positive Herbertian body/self-image which also appears throughout *The Temple*.

In "Church-monuments," the speaker "intombe[s]" his "flesh" not only in the scene of the dramatic situation (he is examining tombs) but also in the lines that he is writing, which parallel the "dustie heraldrie and lines" of the monuments' inscriptions (2, 9). The speaker means to send his "bodie" to the "school" of the graveyard so "that it may learn" to write itself as a text; at first neuter, the body is rendered as masculine once personified as a school-aged child who can learn "To spell his elements" (6, 8). Thus, the body becomes a self in the text, in this case a "he" split not only from the speaking "I" but also from the soul which "repairs to her devotion" (1). Furthermore the poem's prosody comes to stand for the body which ostensibly authors it, the flesh's deterioration suggested by multiple run-on lines and by phrases and subordinate clauses tacked loosely onto seemingly finished sentences to produce an effect of disjointedness or fragmentation. No stanza ends on a period, and in fact, in early editions, the poem has no stanzas, its one strophe constituting a single body whose parts (textually manifested as syntactic units) are loosely associated. The speaker's flesh is not merely entombed in the artifact; here the artifact *is* the flesh, itself both a second self and a tomb.

Prosody stands for the mortal body in "Mortification" as well, but whereas in "Church-monuments" death has "incessantmotion," in "Mortification" death ends motion ("Churchmonuments," 4). Here *every* stanza ends on a period—after the word "death." In the midst of each stanza, we nevertheless perceive life's motions as frequent enjambments wind lines down each strophe to a strong termination. Stanza one will illustrate:

> How soon doth man decay!
> When clothes are taken from a chest of sweets
> To swaddle infants, whose young breath
> Scarce knows the way;
> Those clouts are little winding sheets,
> Which do consigne and send them unto death. (1–6)

Here strong enjambments at the end of lines two and three suggest a twisting movement, and enjambments weakened by a

semicolon in line four and a comma in line five suggest re-
stricted movement; in this discursive context, winding form
means the swaddling of infants, the ebb and flow of a baby's
breath, decay, and the shrouding of a corpse. In the poem as a
whole, similar prosodic signs of motion accrue other meanings
as the speaker attributes differing sensory-motor experiences to
different age groups: while boys sleep, their breath "Makes them
not dead," yet "Successive nights, like rolling waves, / Convey
them quickly, who are bound for death" (*quickly* here meaning
in their very aliveness as well as with speed); the "veins" of
mirthful youth "swell"; the mature man moves "Within the circle
of his breath"; and the aged man "thaw[s] ev'ry yeare, / Till all
do melt" (10–12, 14, 21, 27).

The rhyme scheme throughout "Mortification" is *abcabc*. The
sense of enclosure that the rhyme scheme produces corresponds
to various checks on bodily movement which the speaker discusses: swaddling clothes inhibit infants' movements; "sleep
bindes" boys "fast"; "musick," which simultaneously celebrates
"mirth" and reminds youth of the "knell," limits the very pleasure it arouses; a mature man's home is a "dumbe inclosure"
which "maketh love / Unto the coffin"; the "chair or litter" which
enables an old man to get around also confines him (9, 14, 15,
17, 23–24, 29). Hence, in "Mortification" as in "Church-
monuments," prosody stands simultaneously for the body and
the things which limit the body; moreover, the conflation suggests that the body is itself a confinement and a thing.

The title "Mortification" provides a vivid commentary on a
poem about death and also offers a fitting term for Herbert's
poetics in the sort of poem we are examining. Deriving from the
Latin *mors* and *facere,* to *mortify* means in a literal, etymological sense "to make dead," as Herbert would have known. He
would also have been familiar with Sidney's parallel between
the poet as maker and God as Maker.[28] Arguably, while form in
"Mortification" implicitly emphasizes man's (hence, the poet's)
role as maker of death, the end of the poem, where the speaker
asks God to "instruct us so to die, / That all these dyings may be
life in death" underscores God's role as Maker of life (35–36).
The contrast subverts Sidney's analogical claim that the poet/
maker is to the poem, a copy of the world, as the Divine Maker
is to the world itself.[29] Unlike Sidney's poet who can "deliver a
golden" world while Nature's "world is brazen," Herbert's poet is
a man whose fallen nature renders all his ages brazen.[30] Whereas

Sidney's poet, through imagination, recuperates humankind's Edenic state (Eden being what many Renaissance Humanists believed Ovid's Golden Age represented) Herbert's speaker relies not on his own poetic vision but on God to redeem mortal experience.[31]

In Herbert, "the famous stone / That turneth all to gold" (the legendary elixir which some in the Renaissance understood as efficacious not merely in turning base metals to gold but in restoring the Golden Age) is not autonomous creative capacity but rather the ability "to make [God] prepossest," the one "for [whose] sake" all deeds are performed ("The Elixir," 21–22, 7, 15). God's art rather than the poet's recreates human beings in the image of God. The speaker of "Aaron" makes the point explicitly. While "true Aarons" ring "Harmonious bells . . . raising the dead," the speaker as "poore priest" suffers "A noise of passions ringing [him] for dead" (5, 3, 10, 8). But being poor, he is enriched because he also has Christ, who offers "Another musick, *making live not dead,*" (13, italics mine). As priest, as poet, as man, "Herbert" is only a maker of death. Herbert's Christ, on the other hand, is a Maker of life.

Prosody in *The Temple* repeatedly figures the poet's capacity to make death, but it also as often figures God's capacity to make life—and I do mean bodily as well as affective and spiritual life. We may oppose to Herbert's poetics of mortification a poetics of quickening in *The Temple*.[32] Although, as we learn in "The Forerunners," "dulnesse" can "turn" both poet and verse "to a clod," the poet's "sweet phrases" and "lovely metaphors" can also be "wash[ed] . . . with . . . tears, and more, / Brought . . . to Church well drest and clad" in the "broider'd coat" which (judging from the story of Jacob's coat to which the image alludes) the Father provides (5, 13, 16–17, 23). As in "Aaron," so here we may assume that the speaker and his verses are "well drest" only when they wear their other "head . . . heart and breast," the body of Christ ("Aaron," 15, 11–12). The speaker of "Aaron" makes his purpose for the change of wardrobe (from his own mortal flesh to the body of Christ) quite clear: "That to the old man I may rest, / And be in him new drest" (19–20).

Form in Herbert typically figures either or both of two bodies: the fallen body of "the old man" and the redeemed body of the "new man" dressed in Christ. In "Longing" the speaker implicitly suggests that his verse is a body (representing the new man) which comprises the two bodies of self and Other. The speaker claims that his "heart / Lies all the yeare," at the Lord's "feet" (80–81). The incarnate Lord has feet at which the speaker's heart lies when the speaker beholds the crucifixion (in meditation or literally in the dramatic situation), but also the poem has metric "feet" which echo the rhythms of the speaker's heart; these belong to the Lord because the speaker-poet means them for Him. So the verse units of the poem (its feet) constitute a prosodic body which is produced by the speaker for Christ and which simultaneously includes the speaker's body (his heart) and the Lord's body (his feet). The poem figures prosody as "the new man" (Herbert) so closely identified with the second Adam (Christ) that they together constitute a single body.

In *The Temple,* whether form stands for the fallen body or for the redeemed body is determined by the quality of the self-Other relationship. When the speaker is "in" Christ "Redemption measures all [his] time" ("H. Baptisme I," 10). He is able to invoke Christ's "blessed Spirit" and to "measure out [Christ's] bloud," the pun on *measure* underscoring that form is the textual locus for Christ's body ("Easter," 17; "Good Friday," 2). On the other hand, the speaker-poet sometimes fails in these aims, as in "Dulnesse." The speaker opens this poem asking, "Why do I languish thus, drooping and dull, / As if I were all earth?" (1–2). The first line itself seems languid, off to a slow start with a falling rhythm (a trochee) followed by a rise (two iambs) then another falling rhythm (a trochee which makes the line droop on "drooping") and a final reversal (iamb). If the whole line were trochaic, the falling rhythm would speed the line, but the backward and forward rhythmic shifts retard the pace. The second line, composed of mostly accentable syllables, also seems heavy, its prosody representing the dull, uninspired "I" who feels himself to be nothing but a body, "all earth." Here again—even in the minute detail of single lines—is Herbert's poetics of mortification.

Later in "Dulnesse" the speaker makes the equation I am pursuing between poem and body more explicit when he claims that the "wanton lover" writing poems to "his fairest fair" can "with quaint metaphors her curled hair / Curl o're again" (5, 6, 7–8). In this image, the lover's rhetoric mimes the curling of a hair, a body part, just as Herbert's inverted syntax and enjambment mime the curling rhetoric. An equation between form per se and the body emerges from the image. In subsequent stanzas, the speaker shifts his focus from female "lovelinesse" to Christ's, claiming that "all perfections" can "appeare" "as but one," which is the Lord's "form" (here meaning bodily form) (9, 13–14). And when that happens, "The very dust" where the Lord walks "Makes beauties here" (15–16). If the Lord, who is his "Muse," can make a beauty of dust, then why not of the speaker (again, "all earth") and of his "lines"? (16–17). In "Dulnesse," the speaker's uninspired lines derive from uninspired "flesh" in which he feels "lost" (21). Only the Lord's form can "give . . . quicknesse" to the poet, who can then let this quickness overflow into the poem. The poet's divinely inspired body will be a cup whose spirits run over into the textual body: "that I may with mirth / Praise thee brim-full!" (3–4).

The salient difference between the two poetics I have outlined is not that one is corporeal while the other is not; it is that Herbert's poetics of mortification uses form to signify the mortal body, alienated from the soul, while his poetics of quickening uses form to signify the unification of soul and body in the body of Christ. As "Easter-wings" suggests, both poetics may be present in a single poem. But while one marks the poet's signature, the other copies Christ's "fair and bloodie hand" ("The Thanksgiving," 16).

V

"The Altar" further exemplifies the poetics of mortification and quickening in *The Temple,* as careful attention to its prosody will reveal. To deepen our understanding of the felt experience that these poetics convey, I want not only to bring our Reformation context for understanding Herbertian self-transformation back into focus, but also to gesture toward a psychoanalytic account of self-image and self-Other dynamics in "The Altar," a way of interpreting Herbert (both formally and discursively) which I will develop further in chapters to come. Finally, "The Altar" will serve as a starting point for further discussion of how prosody, representing the heart, constitutes a site of self-transformation in Herbert's poems.

At first glance, prosody in "The Altar" bodies forth both an altar and a capital "I." The conflation becomes meaningful as the reader moves from apprehending the picture to reading the poem, which brings altar and heart together in the first couplet and builds on the conceit in subsequent lines:

A broken A L T A R, Lord, thy servant reares,
Made of a heart, and cemented with teares:
Whose parts are as thy hand did frame;
No workmans tool hath touch'd the same.
A H E A R T alone
Is such a stone,
As nothing but
Thy pow'r doth cut.
Wherefore each part
Of my hard heart
Meets in this frame,
To praise thy Name:
That, if I chance to hold my peace,
These stones to praise thee may not cease.
O let thy blessed S A C R I F I C E be mine,
And sanctifie this A L T A R to be thine.[33]

The idea that the poem represents a thing rather than a person dominates the reader's mind because of the altar shape. Furthermore, a sense of a hard and broken thing being reared emerges from prosodic details as early as line two, which begins with a trochaic reversal on the words *Made of*. Susanne Woods writes that in seventeenth-century prosody, "Initial trochees . . . are so common as to be hardly noticeable," but she also notes that "Herbert is sparing of them."[34] Here the stress on *made* compels attention because it underscores a central textual opposition between the poet as maker and God as Maker. That the line starts off on the wrong foot becomes even more noticeable as the line gropes clumsily back to its iambic pentameter base measure. A stress mark in some editions of *The Temple* suggests that the first syllable of "cemented" should be accented. In Renaissance as in modern pronunciation, this scansion strains the word; although the first syllable of the noun *cement* received speech stress in Herbert's day, the first syllable of the verb *cement* did not.[35] To make the same pronunciation graceful, Donne places the word in the context of a strongly rising duple measure: "Our hands were firmely cimented" ("The Extasie," 5).[36] In contrast, line two of "The Altar" gets bent if not "broken" by an initial reversal, and if it avoids becoming a four foot line where a five foot line is expected, it does so by not so "firmely" retrieving its duple measure with a rise contrary to speech stress.[37]

Not only does the line seem clumsy in itself; also the initial substitution intensifies the break between lines one and two, making them feel more like separated "parts." Ambiguous stress in the third line adds to the poem's awkwardness: should *as,* which falls in a stress position, receive more stress than *thy,* which falls in a non-stress position? The dimeter couplets in the middle of the poem add to the stop-and-start feel of the rhythm. James Boyd White hears these lines as having a "staccato" pace, and indeed the reader must move through them briskly to derive the sense.[38] But the rhyming of short lines competes with the impetus of syntactically warranted enjambment. A mere four syllables apart, perfect rhymes undermine our capacity to move from lines to sentences undistracted, instead calling our attention to each line as a "part" being "cemented" to another "part." Ambiguous stress makes the middle lines strain metrically as well. Rhythmic unwieldiness is not completely overridden until the final couplet.

A preponderance of monosyllabic words in lines three through twelve produces some of these effects and furthermore means that the poem comprises bits and pieces at the level of diction as well as meter. Analogous effects occur at the level of syntax. Multiple inversions in line one, a dangling participial phrase in line two (modifying *altar* but also *servant*) and a dangling adjective clause in line three (again modifying both *altar* and *servant*) make us aware of syntactic units as parts we must piece together. The fragmentation of syntax in the middle lines ("As nothing but / Thy pow'r doth cut" and "Wherefore each part / Of my hard heart") visually signifies God's cutting of the stone and adds to the mimetic effects. Finally, at the level of rhetoric, as White points out, "The poem is broken . . . right at the center: it logically depends on the force of 'wherefore' but what is concluded thereafter—especially the 'praise'—does not in fact follow from what precedes it."[39] Arguably then, the accidents of meter which produce effects of clumsiness and fragmentation are far from accidental; added together, they play a substantial role in the poem's overall mimetic plan. They allow us to see and hear a broken altar being "rear[ed]"—a verb which suggests graceless labor—out of rough parts or unhewn stones.

When a reader approaches the poem as representing an altar under construction, the unwieldy feel of the music makes sense. But this reading ignores the fact that "The Altar" more centrally concerns a person. Joseph Summers explains that people of Herbert's day understood the Old Testament altar of unhewn stones as a type of the human heart; although the shape of Herbert's altar is classical rather than Hebraic or Christian, the speaker Christianizes the altar by scripting it as the heart.[40] We may understand the brokenness of the altar/heart as a sign of God's grace, which inspires the speaker's profound contrition.

Nevertheless, the depiction of the self as hard-hearted and composed of loosely assembled parts is not flattering, deriving from the way a sinful self sees himself through God's eyes. As Richard Strier and Gene Edward Veith suggest, to see oneself from a God's-eye-view is a mortifying experience for a Reformation Christian.[41] Although such a moment may eventuate in the self's conversion and redemption, the first effect of self-knowledge is complete self-repudiation.

Prosody renders the speaker's mortification more vivid with an image of flesh as stone (in the altar shape of the whole) and with images of self-fragmentation (in the poem's parts). In fact, form shapes a more negative self-image than the speaker articulates. Although the speaker believes that the stones are human enough to praise God, their music is discordant until the final couplet, where the "sacrifice" is completed only as the words "mine" and "thine" merge in rhyme.[42] So long as the speaker remains separate from God, his "parts" seem poorly coordinated; his self is fixed as a broken object in the eyes of another. As the speaker relinquishes both his words and the self they signify, the prosodic subject sings a harmonious note for the first time.

Stanley Fish argues that it is only when the speaker abandons himself to God that "The Altar" becomes whole, more God's than the speaker's in the final line. He also points out that when a reader recognizes the sacrifice that has been accomplished—that of the speaker's self and perhaps the reader's as well—the shape of the poem may look as much like a cross as an altar.[43] My point is that the self being sacrificed becomes so identified with the altar or cross that he becomes indistinguishable from a thing and its parts; the self is depersonalized. As Barbara Leah Harman puts it, the poem "transforms person into icon."[44] The speaker is tied to the altar, nailed to the cross, or constricted, to borrow from Eliot, by "eyes that fix [him] in a formulated phrase" ("Love Song of J. Alfred Prufrock," 56).[45] The sense of an Other's gaze transfixing the speaker is made available to the reader through the poem's form.

As Jacques Lacan explains the Sartrean notion, "the gaze," entails an apprehension of someone else's watching, the precognition of one's own objectification in the eyes of another:

> This window, if it gets a bit dark, and if I have reasons for thinking that there is someone behind it, is straightaway a gaze. From the moment this gaze exists, I am already something other, in that I feel myself becoming an object for the gaze of others.[46]

To sense oneself being seen is to know oneself as another's object; furthermore to see oneself through an Other's eyes is to become other to oneself. Thus, as White astutely perceives, there are at least two Herberts in "The Altar":

> The speaker in "The Altar" presents himself not as a unit or integer, but as divided at least into two: the "I" (or "the servant") who acts and speaks, and the "heart," upon which both God and that servant act . . . . Here and elsewhere the speaker is conceived of as a voice and being that has a heart, with which it has a relation—the heart is where it suffers; but it can speak to the heart too, and in this poem at least, even arrange its pieces in order.[47]

As White suggests, in representing the speaker's heart, form in "The Altar" represents a second Herbertian self, who registers both the speaker's agency and God's. Prosody stands for the speaker's body in that it physically manifests his mortal status as a broken thing. As reflection of the speaker and register of his agency, prosody makes inadequacy visible and in so doing communicates a mortified sense of the Other's gaze. But although at first form seems to be a *mere* image produced as the self assumes the site (and sight) of the Other to scrutinize himself, gradually, the Other's agency perfects the form; the prosodic subject emerges as a second "I."

Simultaneously a reflection and a transformation of self, prosody represents a new self emerging through the Divine Other's mirroring in D. W. Winnicott's sense of the word. In Winnicott's model, as a baby separates from his or her mother (or other primary caretaker), the "good-enough mother" performs a mirroring function when she offers visual, tonal, or verbal cues that she recognizes, and takes pleasure in her child's emerging self.

A gleam in her eye, warmth in her voice, or specific words of praise create in the child a capacity to view and experience the self positively.[48] By communicating her sense that the child *is* whole and adequate, a mother *makes* her child whole and adequate.[49]

An adult's experience of another's gaze can evoke a self-image originating in a childhood sense of what the mother sees because each child preserves a sense of the mother's gaze within the self. From a Winnicottian perspective, an internalized Other may be more or less conducive to a sense of personal wholeness rather than self-division depending on the actual mother's empathy or lack thereof in early childhood. Considerably more negative than Winnicott's "good-enough mother," form throughout most of "The Altar" objectifies the I-speaker instead of reflecting him as a capable agent. Rather than wholeness, prosody conveys a horrifying apparition of the Lacanian "Real"—the speaker in pieces, broken, flailing, separated but not adequate.[50] So does form register a self-alienation born in the speaker's past, or does it accurately represent what the Divine Other sees? After all, no human other is objectively discernible in the world of the poem; God is, and when the speaker surrenders himself to God and relinquishes his separateness, the fragmentation of the poem in process is healed in the poem's closure.

Most readers recognize that Herbert's God is real to the speaker within the poems and alive to the Reformation consciousness that the poems bespeak; at the same time, many juggle this understanding and the approach it entails with a critical perspective on Herbert's God as a textual manifestation of Renaissance ideology or social arrangements. For them, the text has an inside where "God" in-forms the heart/altar, but it also has an outside where a historical person crafted and contemporary readers perceive the poem as an artifact. So yes, form represents what the God in "The Altar" sees; and yes, form registers traces of a historical subject's human mirror.

Here, I will focus on psychodynamics inside the text. Drawing on Reformation theology, we may safely assume that prosody in "The Altar" accurately conveys what the Other sees not only because form's negative image matches Reformation understandings of the sinful self, but also because the poem is "made of a heart," so form emerges from or embodies the part of the self informed by the Holy Spirit's indwelling presence. The heart's way of knowing is more akin to *gnosis* (intuitive knowledge), than to *scientia* (learned or empirical knowledge), except that it arises from the Other within the self rather than from the self. Thus, prosody is a subject inspired to know in and through the Other, and we may conclude once more that the prosodic subject represents a merger between Other and self in Herbert; in this case, we are focusing not on the bodily but on the epistemological merging of self and Other in Herbert's form.

Until "The Altar" closes, prosody confirms the speaker's sense of self as a broken thing before God. Only when the speaker "chance[s] to hold [his] peace"—merging with the Other, relinquishing himself—only when speaking stops can the self find affirmation. Nevertheless, as M. Thomas Hester observes, "The Altar" "is as much self-creating as self-consuming."[51] While the fallen self (the speaker) is forced to surrender, in essence erasing himself, the redeemed self (the prosodic subject) enjoys communion with God and may even be said to displace the speaker at the poem's close, as evidenced by the emergence of the prosodic "I."[52] Thus form suggests God's positive mirror role. At the same time that the Divine Other sees the speaker as a broken thing, the Divine Mirror sees the heart as whole and, seeing, creates an "I" rather than an object.

The psychoanalytic idea of the mother as her child's mirror fits the dynamic between God and the self in Herbert's "Altar" because the idea closely parallels Christian belief regarding Christ's relation to the human believer. For the Reformation believer, to encounter God means, first, to see how far short the postlapsarian self falls of original human potential as image (or mirror) of God. But it means, second, to enter into a relationship with a Christ who condescends to mirror (to become the image of, by taking on the corporeal form of) the human believer. Christ becomes human in order to bring humans back to what they can be, just as a mother enters into her child's perspective in order to help the child realize full potential.

In "The Altar," Christ's mirroring of the believer is realized most fully in the prosodic rather than the discursive dimension, the heart rather than the mind. While the speaking "I" begins as a fragmentary surface and ends in silence, the prosodic "I" emerges as a whole, core self in relation to God.[53]

My reading of material form in "The Altar" as enacting the emergence of a core psychosomatic self reverses Richard Strier's argument. Strier contends that a reader must separate the altar from the heart in this poem, realizing that the phrase "this altar" in the last line points not to the artifact but to the speaker's heart, meaning his interior state. Rejecting the icon he has written, the speaker-poet turns inward in the end, recognizing, in accordance with radical Protestant theology, that real life is insensible and internal: "The final line puts human art in its place by decisively turning away from it just as it attains its perfection."[54]

But what is at stake in "The Altar" and other Herbert poems is not a choice between the material and the spiritual, the flesh and the spirit in a strictly dualist sense, but rather a choice between the old man and the new, the flesh and the spirit by one of Luther's definitions. Strier argues that while Herbert and Luther share the doctrine of justification by faith alone, they differ in their attitudes toward the body and the physical world.[55] Yet Luther's ideas clarify why a physical "I" remains at the end of "The Altar" as the speaker's voice dies:

> We do not call "flesh" that which can be seen by the eyes or touched by the fingers . . . but . . . all is spirit, spiritual, and an object of the Spirit . . . which comes from the Holy Spirit, be it as physical or material, outward or visible as it may; on the other hand, all is flesh and fleshly which comes from the natural power of the flesh, without spirit, be it as inward and invisible as it may.[56]

In "The Altar" and other Herbert poems, what is sacrificed is not bodily life per se but the fallen nature of the speaker. The *artifacts* are not self-consuming; the speaker is. The prosodic subject is the survivor. The Old Adam is supplanted by the emergence of the prosodic "I," a new self refashioned in the image and by the mirroring of the speaker's God.

Strier's iconoclastic reading of "The Altar" and of *The Temple* as a whole hinges to some extent on his definition of the word *heart* as signifying an emotional or spiritual realm rather than a physical organ. Strier claims, "Herbert's ultimate commitment was to the Spirit and to 'feeling.'"[57] But in Herbert's day the heart was understood to encompass both the physical and the psychological dimensions I perceive in Herbert's form. Indeed, according to Donald R. Dickson, the heart was understood to be a site where body and soul interact through the mediation of "spirits."[58]

For a Renaissance thinker whose mind worked along emblematic lines, the heart was simultaneously a physical organ—which could bleed and produce a pulse—and a metaphysical place, the seat of personality and the locus of divine encounter. Thus in "Mattens" the speaker muses:

> My God, what is a heart?
> Silver, or gold, or precious stone,
> Or starre, or rainbow, or a part
> Of all these things, or all of them in one?
>
> My God, what is a heart,
> That thou shouldst it so eye, and wooe,
> Powring upon it all thy art,
> As if that thou hadst nothing els to do?
>
> (5–12)

The heart is here a *thing,* perhaps a part of other things, permeating individual boundaries to participate in nature or perhaps a microcosm which includes all of the better things in creation. But it is also a focal point for divine art—an "it" which God "eye[s], and wooe[s]"; hence it is the place where God and individual meet.

Likewise in "Easter" the speaker addresses his heart as the locus of personality, but makes clear at the end of the first stanza that the heart is physical and can be "calcined . . . to dust" at the same time that it is spiritual and can be alchemically transformed through Christ's resurrection to gold (5). In "Nature" the speaker refers to his heart as God's workmanship which has grown "rugged" and "saplesse," yet which even as stone remains a place where God may "Engrave [his] rev'rend Law and fear" (13, 16, 14). Though the tenor of the heart emblem in "Nature" is spiritual, the vehicle is matter; and the speaker emphasizes the physical nature of the heart and the person it metonymically represents when he claims that his heart is "a much fitter stone / To hide [his] dust" than "to hold" his God (17–18). Even if the heart emblematically refers to the soul, the dust emblematically underscores the materiality of the mortal heart. So the heart, like Herbert's prosody, is first of all a thing.

The human heart is a living thing, however—part of a living body—and Herbert's speaker sometimes approaches the physicality of the heart by exploiting the heart's anatomical processes. In some poems, the speaker develops the analogy I am suggesting between the physicality of the heart and the materiality of poetic form. For example, in a subtle gesture in "Gratefulnesse," the prosodic subject echoes the speaker's desire for "such a heart, whose pulse may be / Thy praise" with a pronounced systole/diastole iambic beat (31–32).

A more extended example of the correlation between material form and the physical heart occurs in "Obedience." In stanza one, the speaker works out a conceit between legal contracts or writings and the poem written on "this poore paper," which "convey[s]" to his God "a Lordship"—that is, a legal title to the speaker's person—just as deeds may convey a title "whither the buyer and the seller please" (5, 2–3). In stanza two, he continues:

> On it my heart doth bleed
> As many lines, as there doth need
> To passe it self and all it hath to thee.
> To which I do agree,
> And here present it as my speciall Deed.
>
> (6–10)

Herbert's speaker conveys not merely his emotions or spirit, but his very body, blood and flesh, "by way of purchase" to God (35). Thus in stanza eight, he claims to have "passe[d] his land"— the very dust out of which he is made—to his Lord (36). The physiology of the heart is not simply a metaphor in this context; the heart's bleeding is an image which serves metonymically to convey the whole "self." Through willing his very person into the written lines, the speaker establishes a kind of consubstantial contract, which, through the body of Christ referred to in the middle stanzas, may include a hypothetical reader's person, body and soul, as well:

> How happie were my part,
> If some kinde man would thrust his heart
> Into these lines; till in heav'ns Court of Rolls
> They were by winged souls
> Entred for both, farre above their desert!
>
> (41–45)

In the final stanza, the poem as legal contract—as the speaker's reciprocation to the New Covenant offered through the "death and bloud," the "strange love" of Christ—transcends "this poore paper" to be reinscribed by the angels "in heav'ns Court of Rolls" (26, 27, 5, 43). As in "The Altar," the poem's form represents (and in this poem's terms metaphysically embodies) the speaker's heart. The poem's ink or print is the heart's blood; its measure is the pulse. But whereas the heart remains thing-like through most of "The Altar," in "Obedience" it comes alive, com-

municating the body and soul of the speaker and his hypothetical reader to the Body of Christ.

In "Obedience," Herbert's speaker and prosodic subject work
in harmony from the beginning. Nevertheless there is a distinction between them: the heart literally bleeds lines onto the page,
thus "pass[ing] it self and all it hath" to God; the "I" "agree[s]"
to this action but is not the agent performing it (8–9). So the
speaker's heart, embodied in form, is an agent who *does* in deed
what the speaker *deeds* in words.

Although the idea of a prosodic subject does not apply to every
Herbert poem, it works well with some and allows us to keep in
mind several ideas about form's role in *The Temple.* First, Herbert's form is not a device superimposed on self-representations
to render them art objects; it is a mode of self-representation.
Second, Herbert's form does more than mimetically reinforce
the speaker's ideas of self and Other; form is the heart of Herbert's text, the site where self meets Other, the matrix out of
which a re-formed self arises. Third, the disparity between the
broken speaker of some poems and the prosodic self who
emerges whole makes good sense of the old joke, "You can't get
there from here"; in these poems, the self figured by form is
characterologically different from the speaker in the way that
the self feels, thinks, knows, relates, and organizes parts.

VI

My purpose in this chapter has been to illustrate through
close attention to a number of Herbert's poems the way they
may be re-read as representations of intrapsychic conflict or of
a relationship between two Herbertian selves. I have argued that
Herbert's form is both a material construct—which signifies the
human body or an image of it—and the locus of a subjective
consciousness somewhat separate from the I-speaker's. In the
pages that follow, I will continue reading the materiality and
subjectivity of Herbert's form through the lens of object relations psychoanalytic theory to question more specifically what
Herbert's prosody, reconceived as a subject, has to say about
what it means to be a human being in the world, constrained
both by the limits of bodily life and by the evaluations, expectations, and demands of others.

At first glance, my revision of traditional formalist strategies
may seem relatively minor. So far, for instance, I have kept my

eye rather closely on "the text itself," transforming it only slightly in my reconception of it. What difference does it make that Herbert's form can be personified or that *The Temple* seems to yield readily to such an approach? And for that matter, given that the notion of "organic form" now seems old-fashioned, extending at least as far back as Coleridge in the nineteenth century, what is to be gained by pursuing the notion further?

In simplest terms, in locating traces of the body or its image in Herbert's prosody, we may open up a route to a consideration of form from a psychoanalytic angle. Whatever the metaphysics of Herbert's poetic form may be—an issue I will touch on again in the next chapter—Herbert's form can be more meaningful to contemporary readers if we understand how much it has to say about subjectivity and relatedness in a material world. As Ellie Ragland-Sullivan puts it, "imaginary and real material infers a materiality into language that will give it density, weight, and richness at the levels of effect and affect, where body and language are joined by the 'letter' of *l'etre*."[59]

As a bodily self, Herbert's prosodic subject stands as evidence of Herbert's concern with tangible realities. Rather than escaping the material world by focusing on an ethereal otherworld, Herbert's prosody revises material reality, asserting not a medieval *contemptus mundi* attitude but a realization of the words, "The kingdom of heaven is at hand" (Matt. 3:2 AV). Even when Herbert's form signifies the transcendent Body of Christ, its utopian vision of community constitutes not an escape from political issues relevant to Herbert's society but a critique of certain seventeenth-century ideological extremes. The prosodic subject's emergence as a more genuine self than the speaker may be read as an implied criticism of compliance to secular authority or social demands at the expense of a divinely created true self. On the other hand, the prosodic subject's absolute dependence on divine authority may be viewed as a critique of the opposite extreme: an autonomous individualism that defies relatedness as an essential component in human personality, a component necessary to exist harmoniously with God, others, and the self.

In locating a second subjective presence in Herbert's prosody—a part of the self merged with the Other in the world of the poems—I am raising questions about *The Temple*'s scripting not only of self/Other boundaries but also of gender boundaries. The psychoanalytic Other, more often than not, is female (as indeed George Herbert's only surviving parent was by the time he was three). I will argue in chapter 2 that, to the extent prosody constitutes the locus of a union between self and Other, the prosodic subject represents a mother-infant unit as discussed by Winnicott.[60] Although form as a manifestation of God's "mirroring" of the speaker is so negative at times that it must be construed as a kind of false mirroring (appropriate, as I will argue in chapter 4, only because it reflects the fragmentary and rigid nature of a false self), God's identification with the prosodic subject places God in the role of mother/mirror to the speaker's true or core self. I have deliberately avoided, even at the risk of stylistic infelicities, assigning a pronoun and hence a gender to the prosodic subject. S/he, as I will argue, is ultimately an androgen, a mother-infant unit in which both mother and child vacillate in their respective gender roles.

One final boundary remains to be questioned—the boundary between text and reader, which to some extent at least my language has retained. I concede that the reading process is an intersubjective transaction. As Norman Holland points out, interpretation is always a cooperative effort between a reader and a text which the reader interprets or even to some extent produces. But it seems to me that there is an advantage to preserving, at least in language, the delusion of a text "out there," since such a strategy preserves a sense of the text as a communal locus—a place where readers can come together to reach what Holland calls a consensus.[61]

Certainly a poem like "Obedience" indicates that even Herbert and his poet-speaker recognize the permeability of textual boundaries and include "some kind [reader]" in the textual transaction. As Chana Bloch claims, "The dividing line between the self and the reader is not a wall but a semipermeable membrane." Bloch goes on to point out that Herbert "saw himself as belonging to a community of believers—one sense of the word *temple*—and did not doubt that what was true of himself would be true of others as well."[62] Thus, the text for the speaker and perhaps for the author of "Obedience" is not merely shared private property; it is a public place—the Body of Christ or the Christian community—where two or more may gather with differing insights or experiences, but with a shared sense of purpose. The idea is not that the text does not mean something about "Herbert"; it is that in signifying something about "Herbert," it includes us as well.

In "Miserie" the Herbert speaker as reader (albeit a reader of natural rather than literary signs) clarifies what a readerly tendency that we might label the projective fallacy is all about.[63] After railing for twelve stanzas about the folly of generic man, the speaker concludes:

> But sinne hath fool'd him. Now he is
> A lump of flesh, without a foot or wing
> To raise him to a glimpse of blisse:
> A sick toss'd vessel, dashing on each thing;
> Nay, his own shelf:
> My God, I mean my self.

2

On Herbert's Feminine Form

IN AN ARTICLE ON GEORGE HERBERT'S *MEMORIAE MATRIS SACRUM,* E. Pearlman argues that Herbert equates his mother with God and also notes the "identification in Herbert's imagination of 'mater' and 'metra.'"[1] But, with rare exceptions, *father* rather than *mother* remains the term of choice when critics discuss God's parenting in Herbert's English poems.[2] From one perspective, the choice to use conventional religious language makes perfect sense, of course. No one can dispute that Herbert's speaker refers to God with the pronoun *he.* But if "Father" is what the God of *The Temple* is, mothering is nevertheless what he does best, a fact especially evident in *The Temple*'s form.

Many critics have perceived in Herbert's form a building metaphor and have discussed the way the poems shape architectonic spaces under the auspices of the Divine Architect.[3] Even Pearlman writes, "Herbert suggests that by the building and enclosing of defined spaces (gardens, houses, temples), maternally modeled security . . . can be recaptured and expressed."[4] But "the *Architect* Whose Art / Can build so strong in a weak heart" is not merely a constructor of places or things ("The Church-floore," 19–20). He is a builder of persons.[5] What God is overseeing is not so much the erection of an edifice as the emergence of a redeemed self, whose very body serves as the temple of God.

As I read *The Temple,* Herbert's form bodies forth a re-formed self who may frequently, to varying degrees, be construed as a second persona in the poems. This prosodic subject sometimes plays the role of the new man in opposition to the speaker as old Adam. More often, the prosodic subject supports the speaker's words but deepens the stakes, embodying experiences that the speaker reports discursively, enacting the realization of the speaker's desire for self-transformation in relation to God.

As the body or heart of Herbert's text, prosody represents the depths of a self informed by the Other's indwelling presence; the prosodic subject, then, is as much an extension of the Other as of the speaking I. The identity of the prosodic subject as a self born of and fashioned by God places Herbert's God less in the role of architect than in the role of primary parent. Thus, as I will argue, Herbert's prosodic subtext, if viewed as a spatial construct, may be construed as representing a relational space analogous to the one body relationship between a mother and her infant and to the interpersonal space which develops between them as the child becomes a separate individual.

In Herbert's day, primary parenting of infants and young children was exclusively the province of women. If Herbert's God is maternal, then Herbert's God is feminine, or at least some aspect of him is. So to understand Herbert's God as one who mothers the prosodic subject in the prosodic subtext of Herbert's poems, we must first consider ideas about women available in Herbert's day. Also, I will examine the way in which Herbert's I-speaker sometimes figures Christ as maternal, even at the discursive level of Herbert's text.

As a general rule, while the notion of masculine dominance was fixed in the Renaissance, masculinity as an ideological construct was a very slippery category, contingent not so much on biological sex as on an individual's position in the power structure.[6] Queen Elizabeth, for example, construed herself as androgynous—biologically female yet politically a prince.[7] Androgyny sometimes extended to subordinate males in the political hierarchy, in that some courtiers self-consciously enacted their inferior social status through feminine behavior.[8] And within the Renaissance family, as Stephen Greenblatt has noted, boys were considered feminine until they were old enough to separate from their mothers.[9]

In each of these instances, the analogical thinking which equated masculinity with power ignored biological sex in the figuration of (imaginary) gender. By this line of reasoning, the phallus, signifying relative power and presence, was attributable in an absolute sense only to God the Father (paradoxically understood as a Being without a physical body). From a cosmological perspective, "mankind" was feminized in relation to this omnipotent, masculinized Providence. The church was feminized as the bride of Christ in accordance with Jesus' parable of the bridegroom and extensions of that metaphor in Paul's discussion of marriage. Even the Trinity had its relatively feminine persons. Though the bridegroom of his church, Christ was feminine—submissive in relation to the Father—a quality he demonstrated to best effect in his repeated obedience, particularly in the Garden of Gethsemane.[10]

Hence, the premise that masculinity equals power pervaded religious as well as political thought in the Renaissance. But in doing so, it ultimately reduced itself to an absurd proposition: all men are feminine. If a universal attribute, femininity can hardly be a meaningful category. While submissiveness may be a necessary precondition of Christ's femininity, it is not a sufficient one, therefore. The question remains: how was Christ feminine in a way other men were not?

Christ's self-sacrificing vulnerability (literally his capacity to be wounded) also feminized the second person of the Trinity. According to Caroline Walker Bynum, an analogy between Christ's wounds and a mother's breasts was fairly common among medieval mystics, and many speculated that Christ's flesh was particularly feminine, whether because it came from Mary (Christ having no human father) or because the human body was considered feminine in relation to the soul.[11] The assumption in medieval physiology that a mother's blood produces the mother's milk, and the Catholic emphasis on the Real Presence of Christ's blood and body in the eucharist, combined to support equations between Christ and the nursing mother.[12]

Christ's femininity, then, as understood by some in the Renaissance, rests not only on his subordinateness to God the Father, but also on his assumption of "feminine" flesh and more definitively on his self-sacrificing attitude toward and nurturing relationship to humankind. "Femininity" in this sense is a relational construct rather than a biological one, of course. But as Thomas Laqueur has demonstrated, the imaginary (the body-image as conceived of in relation to others) so pressured the way the real (the body itself) was seen in the Renaissance that the distinction between gender and sex frequently collapses in Renaissance discussion of male-female differences.[13] In the seventeenth century, to perceive a man as female-like in his social role might translate into imagining (or even seeing) him as having lactating breasts. Laqueur points out that the image of Christ as nursing mother might be related to this notion that effeminate men could actually grow breasts and produce milk. But effeminacy was generally viewed as a negative trait in men, a threat to the social order which could be caused (so it was feared) by too close association with women, among other things.[14]

Christ's femininity was necessarily more positive. It was, I believe, a sign of complete sufficiency.

A good analogue is James I. Just as Elizabeth had represented
herself as androgynous in order to diminish her subjects' anxiety about the ideological discrepancy between her femininity
and her power, so James I represented himself as androgynous,
as both father and nursing mother to his subjects.[15] Perhaps in
part James aimed to legitimate his rule by more closely iden-
tifying himself with the last of the Tudor monarchs. Though not
biologically descended from Elizabeth, James related himself to
her at the level of the represented body. But also, perhaps he
recognized at some level what patriarchal culture as a whole
attempted to deny: the site of the maternal as the psychic space
of absolute (though, as I will argue, not in fact *absolutist*) power.

At this juncture, it may be useful to distinguish between two
versions of the "feminine" available to the Renaissance: the
eroticized Other and the holding mother, two images epitomized
by the Eve/Mary polarity inherent in Christian conceptions of
woman. The first image is explicable through the myth of Eden
as related in Genesis, especially as it is re-presented by Milton
in *Paradise Lost.* Woman is created "out of man" to be his com-
panion. Derived from Adam's rib, Eve is part of Adam's body
and self. As the part of man made an object for man, woman is
eroticized, *eros* being definable as the longing for an Other to
the end of completing the self. By this definition, man's love for
woman is essentially narcissistic. But Eve's seductiveness proves
deadly when she, as an Other, allies herself with the tempter in
Eden. Her punishment for misusing a will not susceptible to
Adam's control—or to God's—is to be subordinated by God's
postlapsarian law to her husband.

The eroticized Other, then, is eroticized as an external part of
the self but subordinated as detrimentally Other and, except for
God's law (and its expression in the laws of the Renaissance
social order) potentially outside the realm of man's "self-
control." To the equation between femininity and subordinateness, one may therefore add a middle term: seductiveness,
which makes subordination necessary.

The holding mother, on the other hand, is often represented
in Renaissance art, particularly in manger scenes and scenes of
the pieta, by the mother of Jesus.[16] As virgin, Mary is the completely uneroticized, though loved [M]Other who reverses Eve's
destruction of the bond between humankind and God by serving
as the pure vessel for the child who can restore it.[17] An exception

to the rule that a woman must be one male's eroticized object in order to be another's maternal object, Mary underscores the possibility that these two versions of the feminine may be perceived as separate categories.

Though obviously in reality the two versions of the feminine are related in multiple ways, the polarization of the two underscores their differences. While Eve, the seductive Other, comes "out of man," the mother is constitutive rather than the derivative of the male body and self. Maternal contributions to the child's bodily and psychic identity were not understood in the Renaissance in precisely the same terms as they are today of course. The Aristotelian version of embryology still widely accepted in the Renaissance attempted to deny the mother's contribution to the embryo by claiming the father was the source of the child's *pneuma* (breath, life, soul) while the mother was merely the source of the raw materials shaped by the father's sperm.[18] As others have pointed out, such an account may have been to some degree a compensatory defense against the fact that maternity is concrete and irrefutable while paternity (in an age prior to genetic testing) is less verifiable. In giving paternity greater status, Aristotle legitimates a patriarchal social order. But the very need to deny the mother's importance rests to some degree on the recognition of it.[19]

Similarly in regard to the child's psychological development, people of the Renaissance had at least a deep sense of the importance, if not of their mothers per se, then of the wet nurses who played the role of primary parent in their early years. Thus, for example, literature on child rearing advised mothers to nurse their own children, or if they could not do so, it warned that the father must choose the nurse with extreme caution. Not only could the nurse's milk affect the physical health of the child; the nurse's character, it was believed, could be transmitted through the milk.[20] If writers on child rearing in the Renaissance lacked precise understanding of the way a primary parent affects human development, they nevertheless understood that primary caretakers could directly influence the child's personality.

The eroticized Other differs from the holding mother not only in being derivative from the male but also, at least in her identity as temptress, in being his destroyer. Since sexuality in the Renaissance was understood as a type of death (and the sexualized vagina as a type of hell), the holding mother distinguishes herself from the eroticized Other most significantly in the sense

that she is the origin of life rather than the bodily terminus of
the "dying" male. From a Renaissance point of view, for the male
to emerge from the female might seem less threatening than for
the male to merge (sexually) into the female, since according to
Galen's notion of the sexes, still widely believed in the Renaissance, a progression from being female to being male is the
"natural" mode of development for the male embryo (while, as
Stephen Greenblatt points out, a regression from male to female
would be unnatural).[21] To put the matter succinctly, the mother
is constructive of the male body and self, the eroticized Other
destructive.

One other difference between the eroticized Other and the
holding mother will be pertinent to the arguments which follow.
Rather than being subordinated to the male, the mother with
her child operates to some degree outside of the sociopolitical
power structure, and she does so, at least in relation to a newborn, without creating an alternative power structure. As my
next section will suggest, the best model for mother-infant interactions is a cooperative rather than a hierarchical model. The
question of Christ's maternal nature in *The Temple* is therefore
linked to questions of *authority*. As mother, Christ is author of
a new self in Herbert's poetry and therefore has immense power;
yet as maternal author, Christ is decidedly unauthoritarian.
While God the Father rules, Christ as mother "holds" the emerging subject.

The applicability of these ideas to *The Temple* rests initially
on the discursive level of Herbert's text, where the I-speaker
makes some of the distinctions I have discussed quite explicit.
Much textual evidence suggests that Herbert's speaker tends to
repudiate the seductive Other of the Renaissance love lyric, dis-
placing her with Christ. In two sonnets which the young Herbert
sent (not insignificantly) to his mother, the speaker rejects "Venus Livery" and with it "any she" for Christ and a Christian
aesthetic ("Sonnet" (I), 4, 8). His commentary on seductive female beauty is scathing: "Open the bones, and you shall nothing
find / In the best *face* but *filth*" ("Sonnet" (II), 12–13). Here
seductive femininity is equated with death. Herbert juxtaposes
with feminine decay, the eternal depth of Christ's beauty: "Lord,
in thee / the *beauty* lies in the *discovery*" (14). In seeking to
discover beauty *in* Christ, the speaker figures the relationship
in spatial terms. The idea of a movement into another may be
construed as a masculine sexual image of entering the female
body. Alternatively it may be understood as an infantile image

of being merged with a mother figure or even of returning to the womb. In either case, though the speaker rejects the seductive human Other, he does not juxtapose her to a masculinized God but to a feminized Christ.

In "Jordan" (I) the speaker again renounces the seductive human Other, abandoning "fictions onely and false hair" for the "beautie" which exists "in truth"; he rejects a version of poetry whose object is the mortal female for one whose object is "true" rather than "painted" (1–2, 5). One may argue that in "Jordan" (I) God is gendered as male in the last line, where Herbert's speaker asserts that he intends to "plainly say *My God, My King*" (15). But if applicable to James and his two bodies, the idea of an androgynous monarch could certainly be applicable to a three-personed God. And the juxtaposition between "true" and "painted" beauty in Herbert is elsewhere a contrast between two versions of the feminine. In "The British Church," while both the Anglican church and the two churches on either side of it are represented as female, the virtue of the speaker's "Mother church" is that she is neither overmade nor naked. Herbert's "deare Mother," in other words—the spouse of Christ, the *body* of Christ—is maternal rather than seductive, but distinctly feminine.

In "Home," the speaker rejects not only the fleshy feminine Other but also his own feminine flesh. Questioning the value of "this woman-kinde, which I can wink / into a blacknesse and distaste," the speaker figures the eroticized human Other as *which* rather than *whom,* as a thing (39–40). Similarly, he refers to his own flesh, "As an intangled, hamper'd thing," equating it with the feminine (64). But although the speaker's extreme *contemptus mundi* seems to include a misogynistic disdain for all he associates with eroticized femininity, sexuality rather than gender is the source of the speaker's anxieties. Hence, the speaker genders his soul as female, praying "That my free soul may use her wing, / Which now is pinion'd with mortalitie" (62–63). Furthermore, as John N. Wall argues, the speaker assigns Christ a maternal role. Christ is the one who remains at home in heaven, where the speaker longs to go because, as he claims, "my head doth burn, my heart is sick" (1).[22] Even God the Father seems rather motherly in the poem. God's "bosome" is the source of all "help" to humankind, and Christ is the manifestation of God's "pitie," the one who had to "leave that nest, / That hive of sweetnesse," to redeem humankind (16, 13, 19–20).

God is figured as maternal in other Herbert poems as well, often most explicitly so through the person of Christ. As Wall points out in such poems as "Love" (III), as well as a number of eucharistic poems, Christ is the one who "meets human needs for nurture," for feeding; also in "Love" (III) he is the one who "speaks 'sweetly' and takes [the speaker's] hand 'smiling.'"[23] Christ's maternal "sweetness" is a definitive attribute in many poems—in "Dialogue," "Longing," and "The Odour," to name only a few. The femininity of this "sweetness" is not merely implicit in Herbert's poetry. In "Affliction" (I), the Herbert speaker associates it with mother's milk:

> At first thou gav'st me milk and sweetnesses;
> I had my wish and way:
> My dayes were straw'd with flow'rs and happinesse;
> There was no moneth but May.
>
> (19–22)

Perhaps a male lover-Christ would entice a feminized believer with sweets and flowers. But the image of Christ as the nursing mother definitively places the relationship between the speaker and Christ in the realm of the maternal, also gendering Christ's sweetness as feminine.

The Temple includes not only poems in which the speaker genders God as feminine, but also poems in which he genders God as both male and female. In "Discipline," for instance, God's masculine attribute of justice is juxtaposed with his more feminine attribute of love. God is both wielder of the "rod," a God of "wrath," and one whom the speaker beseeches to "take the gentle path" (1–4). The speaker claims to "creep" to God's throne as an infant might crawl to a mother (15). The throne represents masculine power, but it is also the seat of a more feminine "grace" (16). Thus, the very tensions which characterize the Christian God sometimes translate into the terms of ambiguous gender.

The arguments which follow will not hinge on Herbert's God being maternal to the exclusion of eroticized Otherness or even feminine to the exclusion of masculinity. I mean only to contend that the speaker's occasional placement of Christ in the role of mother brings to consciousness a phenomenon that arguably goes much deeper. As I will demonstrate, Christ's mothering in *The Temple* is realized most fully at the deep level of form, often through the nonverbal communications of a prosodic subject.

Thus, Herbert's prosodic subtext may be construed as feminine, as a kind of reversed pieta, the embodiment of God as love, as mother, holding a human child.[24]

II

The "mother-infant unit" is a phrase which captures Winnicott's idea of the relationship between a mother and her baby before the child is old enough to perceive any differentiation.[25] These two act as one, the "good-enough mother" biologically and psychologically fitted to respond to the baby's natural rhythms, the baby's nature already known, intuited by the mother as the foundation of the individual who will later emerge.[26] To the infant, the two *are* one; to the mother, empathetically united with her newborn, they are very nearly so, though, unlike the baby, she can foresee their eventual separation.[27]

The mother's holding of the newborn is the quintessential expression of a relationship which comes to include a more symbolic form of holding as the child learns to walk, talk, and think of the self as separate from the Other. Psychologically speaking, the mother "holds" the child when she empathizes with and mirrors the child; she "holds" the child when she attends to her or him, mentally collecting the fragments of the child's moment to moment experiences to help the child cohere as a self before he or she is old enough to feel integrated without the mother's assistance. The "holding environment," then, is an expansion and gradual diffusion of the mother-infant unit as the child emerges from an infantile state of oneness with the mother.[28] Winnicott claims that the main function of this holding environment is "the reduction to a minimum of impingements to which the infant must react with resultant annihilation of personal being."[29] It is the first and one of the more intimate of interpersonal spaces, the space where the self is discovered and, in a healthy family, affirmed.

Margaret L. King provides evidence about family life in the Renaissance which suggests that "good-enough mothers" may have been more the ideal than the reality. King argues that the Renaissance was an age in which, "The pain of childbirth, the despair of child death, the stress of poverty, the insecurity of wealth and the ferocity of law—all engulfed mother and child." Nevertheless, "Renaissance writers grieved for the lost intimacy of childhood," and what life failed to supply, literature concocted.[30]

Thus, images of maternal holding are not uncommon in English Renaissance literature. In Robert Greene's *Menaphon,* for example, Sephestia sings her infant son a lullaby, the refrain of which underscores the notion of both physical and psychological holding: "Weepe not my wanton, smile vpon my knee, / When thou art olde, ther's grief inough for thee" (1–2).[31] Sephestia rocks the child, holding him together as an integrated body, encircling him in her arms, warding off the threat of grief and its attendant risk of psychic disintegration as well as any physical danger. As she holds him, she sings to him the story of his young life, holding him in her imagination as a person with his own identity, his own story, though one he is not yet old enough to comprehend, much less to recite:

> Mothers wagge, pretie boy.
> Fathers sorrow, fathers ioy.
> When thy father first did see
> Such a boy by him and mee,
> He was glad, I was woe:
> Fortune changde made him so,
> When he left his pretie boy,
> Last his sorowe, first his ioy.
>
> $(3–10)$[32]

The prose text framing Sephestia's lullaby likewise suggests that Winnicott's notion of maternal holding, though not articulated in the same technical theoretical terms, was an image available to Renaissance men and women:

> The poore babe was the touch-stone of his mothers passions; for when he smiled and lay laughing in hir lappe, were her heart neuer so deeply ouercharged with her present sorrowes; yet kissing the pretie infant, shee lightened out smiles from those cheekes that were furrowed with continual sources of teares; but if he cried, then sighes as smokes, and sobbes as thundercracks, foreranne those showers, that with redoubled distresse distilled from her eyes: thus with pretie inconstant passions trimming vp her babie, and at last to lull him a sleepe, she warbled out of her wofull breast this dittie.[33]

Sephestia is the mother in nature, parted from her husband, left to nurture her child in a pastoral setting. Though exiled by her father, Sephestia is really a princess disguised as a shepherd-

ess. She nurses her own child as aristocratic women rarely
would have in reality; yet mothering skills come to her naturally
as she empathetically relates to her infant, holding and mirroring him in almost symbiotic moments of connectedness.

Maternal holding is more metaphorical in "Gascoignes Lullabie." The "wag" of Sephestia's song turns "wanton" as Gascoigne's
persona attempts to lull his amorous desires:

> Sing lullabie, as women do,
> Wherewith they bring their babes to rest,
> And lullabie can I sing to
> As womanly as can the best.
> With lullabie they still the childe,
> And if I be not much beguilde,
> Full many wanton babes have I
> Which must be stilld with lullabie.
>
> (1–8)[34]

The persona's "many wanton babes" turn out to include his
"youthfull yeares," his "gazing eyes, / Which woonted were to
glaunce apace," and his "wanton will" in stanzas two through
four (9, 17–18, 25). In stanza five, the persona's autoeroticization
of maternal holding becomes explicit as the speaker addresses
his "robyn," his penis:

> Eke Lullabye my loving boye,
> My little Robyn take thy rest,
> Synce Age is colde, and nothyng coye,
> Keepe close thy coyne, for so is beste:
> With Lullabye bee thou content,
> With Lullabye thy lustes relente,
> Lette others paye whiche have mo pence,
> Thou arte to poore for suche expense.
>
> (33–40)

This passage illustrates the extent to which maternal intimacy
with a child psychologically colors all intimate relational spaces;
the persona's relationship to himself, both psychically and physically, is an extension of the infantile relationship with the
mother. Retrospectively interpreting that relationship through
an Oedipal lens, Gascoigne's speaker sexualizes the pre-erotic
space of maternal holding, but at the same time the pre-erotic
space of maternal comfort pervades the adult male's sense of
how to relate, even to himself.

As Gascoigne's poem eroticizes maternal holding by extending it to include the aging lover's relationship to his own body, Herbert's poems often spiritualize the idea by extending the experience of being held into the relational space between the believer and his God. Winnicott's notion of holding is similar to an image articulated by the I-speaker and literalized by the prosodic subject in "Paradise":

I Blesse thee, Lord, because I G R O W
  Among thy trees, which in a   R O W
To thee both fruit and order   O W.

What open force, or hidden   C H A R M
Can blast my fruit, or bring me   H A R M,
While the inclosure is thine   A R M?

Inclose me still for fear I   S T A R T.
Be to me rather sharp and   T A R T,
Then let me want thy hand &   A R T.

When thou dost greater judgements   S P A R E,
And with thy knife but prune and   P A R E,
Ev'n fruitfull trees more fruitfull   A R E.

Such sharpnes shows the sweetest   F R E N D:
Such cuttings rather heal then   R E N D:
And such beginnings touch their   E N D.

Although the garden conceit in the poem suggests the Edenic origins of the human race in Christian history, another important focus of "Paradise" is the origin, emergence, and development of the "new man" as opposed to the "old Adam." The speaker's metaphorical references to personal development and parental holding—to growth and enclosure in God's arm—are genuine experiences for the prosodic subject. For God to "pare" the human subject means for God to "spare" him by making him fruitful. Like trees which need not do anything but simply "are," the prosodic subject is free within the holding environment God provides to experience life at the level of being, without fear of impingements, of "open force . . . hidden charm" or other "harm." Like Sephestia's infant, the prosodic subject remains protected so long as s/he is circumscribed by the Other's arm.

God's holding is experienced somewhat differently by the speaker and the prosodic subject, however. On the discursive level of the poem, the imagery of enclosure or holding competes with the imagery of paring (the former suggesting union, bonding, cohesion—the maternal function—the latter suggesting rending, cutting, separation). On the prosodic level, masculine images of cutting and separation give rise to feminine images of holding and merger.

As initial letters are clipped away to form successive rhyme words in each triplet stanza, the prosodic subject enacts the pruning metaphor which the speaker makes explicit in line three, experiencing bodily what the speaker experiences spiritually. The pruning conceit is not without ominous implications. Even more than the speaker, the prosodic subject undergoes what Michael Schoenfeldt perceives as a kind of "salutary emasculation."[35] But if, as I am arguing, the prosodic subject is a preverbal persona undifferentiated from a maternal God, then what Schoenfeldt reads as a prosodically indicated castration, what the speaker dreads as "sharp and tart" though he prefers it over abandonment, may represent from the prosodic subject's point of view nothing more threatening than an infantile state of merger between the archaic self and the maternal body.

At the beginning of his life, even a male infant perceives the maternal Other as part of the self, the self as part of the Other. A baby in this stage (the prosodic subject) has no concept of gender difference. The male child's separation from the mother is the first step toward recognition of his masculinity. Maintenance of that separateness later becomes for the child (and I believe for Herbert's speaker) an important safeguard against being feminized. Indeed, theorists speculate that the male tendency toward valuing autonomy and independence rather than relatedness has its genesis in the fear of being emasculated.[36] Arguably then, while the speaker perceives God's holding *as* emasculation or paring, the source of the speaker's anxiety is the prosodic subject's paradise.

I am postulating that in "Paradise," the Herbertian self is split, his more masculine, older self verbalized by the I-speaker, his more feminine, infantile self embodied in the preverbal maneuverings of the prosodic subject. God also is both male and female. As Divine Gardener, he is predominantly male, as suggested by a passage from *The Country Parson* in which Herbert assigns to the father the task of "pruning" the family:

His family is his best care, to labour Christian soules, and raise them to their height, even to heaven; to dresse and prune them, and take as much joy in a straight-growing childe, or servant, as a Gardiner doth in a choice tree. Could men finde out this delight, they would seldome be from home; whereas now, of any place, they are least there.[37]

Yet the speaker of the poem makes clear that his emphasis is not on rending but on healing, a task assigned in *The Country Parson* to the parson's wife.[38]

As I read "Paradise," God is the father who prunes the fallen self in order to become mother to the redeemed self. As a paternal God threatens to render the speaking self effeminate, a maternal God nurtures the preverbal self, to whom gender differences mean nothing. Both the prosodic subject and God are feminized in a holding relationship which the speaker both desperately fears and deeply desires. The split between speaker and prosodic subject in this poem is determined by and at the same time constitutes the solution to the speaker's unconscionable ambivalence.

The last line of the poem—in alluding to the Biblical notion of God as Alpha and Omega, the beginning and the end—both mystifies the poem's alphabetical explorations (the search through letters for the Spirit or for the Divine principle of Logos) and reasserts the encircling, enclosing presence of God.[39] For Herbert, to be in paradise is to be held.[40]

III

In "Paradise," Herbert feminizes poetic form by equating it with an enclosure constituted by and extending from the maternal body ("the inclosure is [God's] ARM."). As represented by Herbert, especially through the prosodic subject, the idea of holding means protective space, often body to body contact—in any case intimate interpersonal relating. But if such an idea of form is "feminine," what "masculine" equivalent provides a contrast?

Theoretical equations between poetic form and masculinity are readily available in the history of ideas about form. Aristotle and Aquinas masculinize the idea of form in discussing animal and human generation. Both argue that while the mother's contribution to the embryo is matter, that which is inert, passive, and receptive, the father's contribution is form, that which gives liveliness, shape, and structure.[41] The male is the efficient cause, the "maker" of the living being, the female the material cause.[42] Furthermore, "while the body is from the female, it is the soul that is from the male."[43] Hence, the masculine, active principle "rules" the body (and, I infer, the text as body), both in the sense of shaping it and in the sense of governing it.

To answer my question from an Aristotelian or Neo-Aristotelian perspective, then, a masculine notion of form emphasizes governing rather than holding, structuring rather than protection, the Lacanian Law of the Father as opposed to Winnicott's holding environment. But Aristotle's theory also assigns to the male formal principle the capacity of quickening, a concept many twentieth-century readers would associate as readily with the holding and nurturing of a fetus inside the womb as with insemination.

This life-giving capacity, rendered masculine by Aristotle, is one Herbert's speaker does indeed assign to Christ. In "Dulnesse," for example, the speaker equates himself as uninspired poet with the principle of matter: "Why do I languish thus, drooping and dull, / As if I were all earth?" (1–2). From an Aristotelian perspective, the author-persona is himself the mother of the poem he longs to write, its material cause. Christ is the one who can give "quicknesse," inspiring the speaker to overflow with praise (3). The speaker explicitly figures Christ's "form" as the archetype of "all perfections," the form which makes "the very dust" beautiful (13–15). Though the speaker is "lost in flesh," Christ is the one who "didst put a minde there" (21, 23) Thus, Christ is the paternal source of *pneuma*. In inspiring the speaker, Christ gives the poem life, quickening the text as body. Christ fathers both the speaker and the text which the speaker holds—lifeless—inside of him.

But if Christ as transcendent Word has a seminal role in Herbert's poetry, Christ as the Word made flesh has a maternal role. The end of "Jordan" (II), at least, implies this possibility. A friend advises the author-persona to stop bustling in a frenzied effort to perform poetically for God. The poet is told to "save expense" (an insemination metaphor) by copying out that which is "in love" (17–18).[44] The poet's role is that of neither father nor mother but of midwife. Love—both the love between the speaker and Christ and Christ himself as Love—is pregnant with poetry, which is to be a kind of virgin birth.

Aristotle is not alone in offering a metaphysical account of form which renders it masculine. Augustine's Neo-Platonic or Neo-Pythagorean ideas about form resemble Aristotle's, though

certainly Aristotle and Augustine differ in many important respects.[45] Augustine's ideas of form as recorded in "De Musica"
are more abstractly masculine in equating the heard rhythms
of poetry with sensual temptation, which Augustine's contemporaries often associate with femininity. Though meter is a useful
avenue to reflections on rational number and may serve as a
means to intimations of Divine Oneness—the transcendent
unity of an ethereal God-the-Father who preexists the material—sensible "number" or "measure" constitutes a danger to
fallen human beings, who may derive from it merely sensual
pleasure, never transcending the body to edify the soul.

Though one may argue that Augustine's Neo-Pythagorean and
Neo-Platonic quest feminizes the human soul in its search for a
masculine principle fully existing only in God, it is equally true
that Augustine projects a monastic fear of the feminine onto the
materiality he perceives in poetic number. The Edenic fall into
time, perpetrated by the female, is reversed in Augustine's ratio-
nalist maneuvering away from the fleshly and temporal (psychoanalytically speaking, away from the maternal body) toward a
masculinized Spirit, one who is metaphysically prior to all derivative states of being, including both materiality and femininity. If Augustine's move is toward an Edenic state of oneness
with God, it is also toward the Eden that Adam possessed when
all his ribs were intact, the Eden of Marvell's "Garden." Properly
approached, poetic or musical measure serves as the mere vehicle for Ideal Form, which is itself transcendent rather than im-
minent, spiritual rather than material, masculine rather than
feminine; material form directs human awareness to Logos,
pointing in a straight and upward direction, pulling the soul
away from the body through the mind and beyond itself to God
rather than serving as a secure maternal enclosure, a material
space made safe for emerging subjectivity.[46]

Several recent critics argue that Herbert's poetic form and his
use of numerological symbolism show signs of Augustinian influence. They point out that Herbert probably read Augustine,
whose works are the only books specifically mentioned in Herbert's will.[47] Certainly in such poems as "Trinitie Sunday" and
"Aaron," to mention only two of many examples, Herbert very
self-consciously toys with Christian numerology, in the first constructing three three-line stanzas reminiscent of the trinity, in
the second five five-line stanzas suggestive of the priesthood.
Augustine is a likely source for such an approach. But the prob-

ability of influence need not imply Herbert's unquestioning assimilation of the principles of Augustine's aesthetic system.

Herbert's emphasis on the physical being and intimate presence of Christ colors many of Herbert's more Neo-Pythagorean poems, differentiating his idea of form from Augustinian theory in these instances.[48] In "Easter," for example, though Herbert Christianizes Pythagorean numerology, relating the trinitarian number three to musical and cosmic harmony, the source of such harmony is not a transcendent music of the spheres or an idea of order in the mind of God the Father.[49] It is the suffering body of Jesus:

> Awake, my lute, and struggle for thy part
> With all thy art.
> The crosse taught all wood to resound his name,
> Who bore the same.
> His stretched sinews taught all strings, what key
> Is best to celebrate this most high day.
>
> Consort both heart and lute, and twist a song
> Pleasant and long:
> Or, since all musick is but three parts vied
> And multiplied,
> O let thy blessed Spirit bear a part,
> And make up our defects with his sweet art.
>
> (7–18)

After the resurrection, harmony must be established through the physical means of "both heart and lute" inspired by the indwelling presence of Christ's "blessed Spirit." As the suffering body of Jesus brought concord out of discord, yoking all oppositions—God and humankind, spirit and flesh, male and female—together through passively submitting to a violent death, so the heart and lute must "twist a song," a vividly physical image, and the believer must reincarnate Christ's spirit in his or her own body. Herbert does not shy away from the physicality of incarnate form; rather, he suggests that it has an analogue in the body of Christ.

Similarly, in "Aaron," Herbert's Christ becomes not merely the speaker's "musick," the one who tunes the speaker's doctrine; Christ's body becomes the speaker's body: "Christ is my onely head, / My alone onely heart and breast" (16–17). The speaker puts on Christ, "That to the old man I may rest, / And be in him new drest" (19–20). The body of Christ thus clothes or encloses the speaker's body. Christ is not only the paternal source of *pneuma;* he is the maternal source of redeemed flesh. Furthermore, Christ is not only, in accordance with Renaissance analogical treatments of the human body, the masculinized "head"; he is the more feminine "heart" or "breast."

Of course, such poems as "Home" demonstrate that Herbert's speaker does occasionally tend, with Augustine, in a world-or flesh-rejecting direction. On the other hand, "verse," as the speaker himself represents it in this poem, is so material that it prays along with the speaker's "flesh and bones and joynts," against its own "ryme and reason" for God to come (74–76). Rather than serving as a map which directs the speaker through reason to God-the-Father, "verse" becomes a physical expression of the speaker's longing for a home which has striking affinities with a maternal holding environment—a heaven which is ultimately God's "bosome," or "nest" (16, 19). As in "Easter" and "Aaron," in "Home" Herbert's notion of "verse" seems more radically material than Augustine's, his idea of God more maternal. Even Herbert's approach to God's transcendent oneness is affective and personal, while Augustine's is rational and transpersonal. Though Augustine's ideas about verse may explain some aspects of Herbert's verse practice, to claim that Herbert appropriated Augustinian theory as a monolithic poetic dogma is to overstate the relationship.

In theories of form potentially available to Herbert, there is at least one voice for the materiality of form and the maternal nature of the form-content relation. Spenser's Garden of Adonis, over which Venus presides, is a kind of demiurge, where primal, immutable feminine substance takes on forms that are subject to decay (*Faerie Queene,* III.vi). Though Spenser writes about a transcendent rather than a temporal marriage of form and matter, Spenser, like Aristotle, equates form with the masculine principle of generation in that Venus' mortal lover Adonis is "the Father of all formes" while Venus is the mother of all things (III.vi.47.8). But while Aristotle valorizes the male term as the more active, Spenser valorizes the female as the more stable. As formal principle, Adonis is dependent on Venus. Having been wounded by a boar, Adonis can survive only in an altered state. He must be held by the garden, "Lapped in flowres and pretious spycery" (III.vi.46.5). The eternal female principle of unchangeable matter sustains the active male principle generating form. Thus Spenser represents the origin of all temporal bodies as a feminized holding environment.[50]

Spenser's theories about the dependence of form on matter as parabled in the Garden of Adonis may be juxtaposed with his own more masculinist idea of poetic form in an earlier letter to Gabriel Harvey, which treats poetic form in terms of territorial conquest and the imposition by violence of law, reason, or civility. Spenser engages with Harvey in a dialogue about the efficacy of imposing classical quantitative verse forms on English poetry:

> But it [i.e., a reformed system of verse] is to be wonne with Custome, and rough words must be subdued with Use. For, why a Gods name, may not we, as else the Greekes, haue the kingdome of oure owne Language, and measure our Accentes, by the sounde, reseruing the Quantitie to the Verse[?][51]

In this passage, Spenser draws an equation between governing a kingdom and ruling a language. The idea of form Spenser here advocates is an idea of form as a type of dominance over unruly matter, specifically the material of the "Moother tongue."

In fact, the entire Spenser-Harvey correspondence deals with poetic form in terms historically gendered as masculine. As Richard Helgerson explains, "The quantitative movement chooses for itself the language appropriate . . . to its own absolutist ambition, the language of power."[52] Harvey's response to Spenser figures the establishment of prosodic conventions in terms reminiscent of the British legal system:

> *We Beginners* haue the start, and aduauntage of our Followers, who are to frame and conforme both their Examples, and Precepts, according to that President which they haue of vs: as no doubt *Homer* or some other in *Greeke,* and *Ennius,* or I know not who else in *Latine,* did preiudice, and ouerrule those, that followed them, as well for the quantities of syllables, as number of feete, and the like: their onely Examples going for current payment, and standing in steade of Lawes, and Rules with the posteritie.[53]

Harvey's advocacy of a classical program for English prosody is less interesting for its own sake than for its implicit assumption that poetic form is an idea of order to be legislated rather than allowed to emerge. The masculinist tenor of this program is underscored by Thomas Nashe's reaction. Against Harvey's experiments with founding an English hexameter and his advocacy of classical rules for English verse, Nashe argues:

> The hexamiter verse I graunt to be a Gentleman of an auncient house (so is many an english begger); yet this Clyme of ours hee

cannot thriue in. Our speech is too craggy for him to set his plough in; hee goes twitching and hopping in our language like a man running vpon quagmiers, vp the hill in one syllable, and downe the dale in another, retaining no part of that stately smooth gate which he vaunts himselfe with amongst the Greeks and Latins.[54]

Nashe here underscores the aggressive masculinity inherent in Harvey's patriarchal approach to formal legislation. The implication is that the ground of English verse, constituted by the materials of the "mother tongue," is too unruly, too craggy, to be receptive to the plough, the imposition of order according to classical rule. The image is almost sexual, certainly violent, yet ultimately the tenor of Nashe's image is the ludicrousness of attempting to wrest artificial order by violence from a language which is by "nature" opposed to such arrangements.

In treating form as a political rather than a metaphysical construct, Spenser and Harvey provide an interesting contrast to Aristotle and Augustine. At the same time, they supply another background against which Herbert's form often stands out as comparatively feminine. By Herbert's day, of course, even though poets like Milton continued to debate the relative aesthetic merit and dignity of native rhyme as opposed to rhymeless forms like English blank verse, the question of imposing classical quantitative measure on English was largely an issue of the past.[55] But the nature of the relationship between form and matter remained (and remains still) a live issue.

As I will argue, Herbert resists a patriarchal sense of form as the governor of matter for essentially theological reasons. According to Martin Luther, the whole point of Christ's establishing the New Covenant of Love in place of the Old Covenant of the Law is that effective laws must be "written by nature into [human] hearts" rather than legislated like the laws of Moses from without.[56] Luther argues that even in civil societies, an internalized sense of justice is preferable to legal statutes:

If the ruler is wise, he will govern better by a natural sense of justice than by laws. . . . Therefore, in civil affairs more stress should be laid on putting good and wise men in office than on making laws; for such men will themselves be the very best of laws, and will judge every variety of case with a lively sense of equity. And if there is knowledge of the divine law combined with natural wisdom, then written laws will be entirely superfluous and harmful. Above all, love needs no laws whatever.[57]

Like Luther's sense of justice, Herbert's sense of form is "natural" as the term *natural* was understood by Reformation Christians. As products of God's "Architecture," the Herbertian "frame and fabrick" proceed from "within," and are born through the self's relation to the Other: "There is in love a sweetnesse readie penn'd" ("Sion," 11–12; "Jordan" (II), 17). The sweetness born of love is not merely the poem; it is a re-formed self emerging in the relational spaces constituted by the poem. Herbert's form as a means of discovering the self-embedded-in-the-Other and as a space for holding and intimacy is more maternal than patriarchal, in spite of the predominance of masculinist approaches to the theory of form in Herbert's day.

IV

The idea of Herbert's verse as a holding environment contrasts with Robert Higbie's sense of enclosure in Herbert's poetry. Higbie asserts that Herbert's (discursive and prosodic) enclosures are meant "to give us a sense of the straitness of our earthly dwelling-place, to make us feel imprisoned in it, and by doing so to make us want to transcend the earthly and seek the divine."[58] Of "The Church-porch" Higbie writes, "enclosure is the physical embodiment of 'rule.'"[59] Yet he also asserts that there is "something childlike about this desire for self-enclosure, for a home, a space within which the poet can be protected by an all-providing Father."[60] Higbie differentiates enclosures which exclude God and come to feel punitive from those which include God and feel protective.

Higbie's point that isolation from God often results in a sense of enclosure as punishment is a good one, and indeed enclosures which include God are the ideal in Herbert. I want to argue, however, that the relational space constituted by the more positive enclosures in Herbert's poetry is as much maternal as paternal or patriarchal, a function more of Christ's grace than of the Father's law. Furthermore, Herbert's emphasis is not always on transcending the human body but often on intimate relatedness, even merger, between two bodies, the body of the believer and the body of Christ, whether in time or beyond.

While the discursive level of many of the poems I will discuss makes the distinction between the "Law of the Father" and the grace of the Son as mother clear conceptually, form communicates a deep sense of separation versus holding in *The Temple*.

Form renders Herbertian self-experience more immediate—textually embodying it—whether or not a prosodic subject seems completely differentiated from the discursive speaker. Prosody conveys in material (virtually corporeal) terms two senses of self: 1) an isolate self, fragmented and depersonalized (rendered an object) in the face of God's wrath or absence; and 2) a relational self unified and subjectified (re-created as an "I") in the presence of a loving Other. I argued in chapter 1 that these competing senses of self are conveyed through Herbert's poetics of mortification and quickening respectively. Here I will contend that these self-experiences are functions of Divine holding or the lack of it.

As transcendent judge and ruler, the God of Herbert's speaker seems particularly punitive in such poems as "Sighs and Grones," a poem in which prosody suggests a deep sense of God's wrath through a painful, almost prison-like stanzaic enclosure.[61] Herbert's I-speaker relates to this aspect of God with self-deprecating fear:

> O Do not use me
> After my sinnes! look not on
> my desert,
> But on thy glorie! then thou wilt reform
> And not refuse me: for thou onely art
> The mightie God, but I a sillie worm;
> O do not bruise me!
>
> (1–6)

The speaker ascribes to God the Father all power when he claims "thou onely art / The mightie God"; prosodic enjambment suggests further that "The mightie God" alone has Being ("thou onely art") while the speaker is nothing or if anything at all "a sillie worm." Through a stanza form tying together the first and the last lines, which refer to punitive actions on God's part, prosody images something like a press, crushing the speaker between negative possibilities—that God will "use" him according to his sins, or "bruise" him. In this way, the prosody gives substance to the speaker's fears. Formal enclosure here seems anything but comforting and maternal.

Prosody only vivifies further the crushing weight of the speaker's sin and God's punishment in the next three stanzas. But in stanza four the speaker, begging God not to force him to drink "bitter wrath," reminds God that because of Christ's sacrifice, God has "other vessels full of bloud" for the speaker to

drink. The wine of the eucharist offers at least the possibility
that God need not "fill" the speaker with "bitter wrath" or "kill"
him (19–21, 24). Having seized on the justifying power of Christ,
the speaker is freed to tell God what he desires rather than what
he fears in the fifth stanza:

> But O reprieve me!
> For thou hast life and death at thy command;
> Thou art both *Judge* and *Saviour, feast* and *rod,*
> *Cordiall* and *Corrosive:* put not thy hand
> Into the bitter box; but O my God,
> My God, relieve me.
>
> (25–30)

Here the crushing weight of sin gives way as the words "reprieve
me" and "relieve me" construct a more positive enclosure at the
level of form. Interpreted with reference to the discursive content which it substantiates, the same stanza form which initially
depicted the "bitter box" of God as judge and wielder of the rod
here comes to represent the nurturing and holding capacities
of God as Savior and bodily, hence maternal, source of the feast.
Thus, with a single stanza form, prosody represents a God of
wrath's punishment and a God of love's holding, and realizes in
material terms the speaker's fear of being crushed and his desire
to be held. Self and Other are unified in a single prosodic body.

As in "Sighs and Grones," in "Even-song" the speaker focuses
on both the transcendent and the immanent qualities of God,
and prosody supports the speaker's words with an image of divine enclosure. But "Even-song" works out the dialectic in a very
different way:

> B Lest be the God of love,
>   Who gave me eyes, and light, and
>   power this day,
> Both to be busie, and to play.
> But much more blest be God above,
>   Who gave me sight alone,
> Which to himself he did denie:
> For when he sees my waies, I dy:
> But I have got his sonne, and he hath none.
>
> (1–8)

Though it is tempting to equate "the God of love" in line one
with the Son, juxtaposing this aspect of the trinity with the

"God above" mentioned in line four, the equation will not work perfectly since the God of love as giver of "eyes, and light, and power" is more creator than savior. God as creator exists in all three persons in Genesis, at least as interpreted by Augustine and Luther. The Father through the Son creates the world; the spirit broods on the abyss. Nevertheless, Herbert's speaker represents God as both the immanent "God of love" and the transcendent "God above" and claims that in his transcendent function as judge, God limits himself, not seeing the wrongs of the speaker who "[has] got his sonne." In the meantime, the immanent God of love provides the speaker all he needs "both to be busie, and to play," a line suggesting God's maternal relationship to the speaker.

Stanley Fish argues that the division between "God of love" and "God above" in the first four lines "is . . . suspect and is . . . challenged by the unifying force of the rhyme 'love-above.'" By the end of the stanza, "the two deities have become one, or, what is in effect the same thing, two coequal and coincidental members of a trinity."[62] Fish's reading suggests the possibility that, in this stanza at least, a prosodic subject more successfully comprehends the unity of God than the speaker does. But the childlike speaker's splitting of the punitive aspects of God the Father from the maternal aspects of God (whether God the three-in-one creator or God the Son) need not be read as an objective assertion equivalent to Arianism; rather it may be construed as a subjective division involving split perceptions of the one God, an infantile psychological strategy for preserving a relationship in spite of extreme conflict. The two aspects of the one God must remain separated in the mind of the child-speaker in order for the speaker to preserve one image of God he can relate to. As Nancy Chodorow explains, the infantile defense mechanism of splitting "avoids anger at the person her or himself, who can now be experienced as all good and gratifying."[63]

But despite a preserved image of God as all-loving, the speaker worries in stanza two over the apparent unproductiveness of his day in regard to making spiritual gains:

> What have I brought thee home
> For this thy love? have I discharg'd the debt,
> Which this dayes favour did beget?
> I ranne; but all I brought, was fome.
> Thy diet, care, and cost

> Do end in bubbles, balls of winde;
> Of winde to thee whom I have crost,
> But balls of wilde-fire to my troubled minde.
>
>   (9–16)

God is here both masculinized as the person to whom the speaker owes a debt and feminized as the one who waits at home for the repayment of "love" and such maternal provisions as "diet" and "care" as well as "cost." The speaker's self-assessment, "I ranne, but all I brought, was fome" is reinforced by the run-on lines of the prosodic subject, whose restlessness makes vivid not only the speaker's rushed day but also his retrospective discomfort, metaphorized as a digestive ailment.[64]

The speaker's claim that he has "crost" God is a three-level pun, meaning first that he has disregarded God's will, second that he has made God "cross" or angry, and third that through his wrongs he has put God on the cross. Prosody supports especially this third sense, when the last two words of line fourteen, "of winde," cross over to become the first two words of line fifteen, a gesture toward chiasmic form. Also the rhyme scheme changes. Stanza one brings two envelope quatrains together in an octave rhyming *abbacddc,* while stanza two begins with the envelope quatrain pattern but completes the octave with a pattern of cross rhyme: *abbacdcd.*

In fact, in some editions the poem is printed in quatrains, the first three rhyming *abba,* the fourth suddenly shifting to the cross rhyme pattern as the speaker mentions crossing his God.[65] In these editions the complexity of prosodic maneuvers is enhanced, since line lengths create two alternating quatrain shapes. If the reader counts feet or accents, the numerical pattern in quatrain editions of "Even-song" is 3544; 3445; 3544; 3445. Just as repetition sufficient to clarify this pattern is established in the fourth quatrain, the rhyme scheme changes, a shift which underscores the speaker's sense of restlessness and necessitates four more stanzas to resolve the pattern symmetrically.

A sense of form in direct contrast to this restlessness emerges in the last two octaves (or the final four quatrains) as the poem's focus moves from the speaker's day to nighttime and repose. Though the speaker has "crost" God, consigning Christ to suffering and death, Christ's last words, "It is finished," reverberate as a message of comfort to humankind (John 19:30 AV):

Yet still thou goest on,
And now with darknesse closest wearie eyes,
Saying to man, *It doth suffice:*
Henceforth repose; your work is done.
Thus in thy ebony box
Thou dost inclose us, till the day
Put our amendment in our way,
And give new wheels to our disorder'd clocks.

I muse, which shows more love,
The day or night: that is the gale, this th' harbour;
That is the walk, and this the arbour;
Or that the garden, this the grove.
My God, thou art all love.
Not one poore minute scapes thy breast,
But brings a favour from above;
And in this love, more then in bed, I rest.

(17–32)

Form in these stanzas repeats the patterns of the first half of
the poem, in the last half of stanza four repeating the cross
rhyme which constituted a departure from the form at the end
of stanza two. Thus, in collaboration with God, form "give[s] new
wheels to [the] disorder'd [clock]" the speaker's words put together and creates a protective enclosure out of disparate line
lengths and differing rhyme schemes.[66] As in other poems, what
the speaker talks about, the prosodic subject experiences. Notably closure and enclosure occur simultaneously in this poem.

Like the Egyptian night in the second stanza of "Sighs and
Grones," the ebony box in "Even-song" represents night, yet also
is suggestive of death; analogously, the day mentioned in line
twenty-six is both the morning to come for the speaker in time
and the day of the general resurrection, when the speaker's "disorder'd clock"—his fallen flesh—will finally be brought back
into synch with God's original plan.

But in "Even-song," the speaker's sense of nocturnal enclosure, whether it intimates death or not, includes the loving presence of God who holds within his "breast," his body, all of the
speaker's moments. As in "Paradise," in "Even-song" God's enclosure is a comforting space, where love rather than judgment
characterizes a relationship so intimate that the speaker conceives of even his poorest minutes as existing in God's breast
and conceives of himself as surrounded, held, nurtured "in"

God's love. As God is both transcendent and immanent, both above and within the speaker, so the believer, though subject to God as ruler of the universe, is subjectified, made human, comforted, by the surrounding presence of God as Love.

In "Even-song" God is represented as having both patriarchal and maternal qualities, though because of the speaker's relationship with Christ, God chooses to limit himself, not to see the speaker's sinfulness or to exact retribution for it but instead to hold the speaker and bring restful order out of his chaotic restlessness. The prosodic subject's gestures both affirm the speaker's self-assessment and collaborate with God to enclose the speaker in a comforting and restful maternal space.

Christ's maternal holding is not always so idealized as it is in "Even-song." From the speaker's point of view at least, Christ is sometimes the mother who fails, choosing to absent herself or not to provide the comfort the speaker desires. In fact, the prosodic subject splits off from the speaking-I to constitute an opposing point of view most often in poems in which the speaker does not feel held. Such is the case in "Longing," a poem in which the I-speaker's complaint that God has abandoned him matches point-for-point the infantile sense of being abandoned which Winnicott attributes to "gross failures of holding." These failures "produce in the baby *unthinkable* anxiety" which manifests itself in the infant's sense of "going to pieces," of "falling forever," of "complete isolation because of there being no means for communication," or of "disunion of psyche and soma."[67]

In "Longing," the speaker suffers all of these symptoms. In the first two stanzas, feeling sick, broken, and abandoned, he cries to his Lord for motherly comfort:

> With sick and famisht eyes,
>   With doubling knees and weary bones,
>   To thee my cries,
>   To thee my grones,
> To thee my sighs, my tears ascend:
>   No end?
>
>
>   My throat, my soul is hoarse;
> My heart is wither'd like a ground

>   Which thou dost curse.
>   My thoughts turn round,
>   And make me giddie; Lord, I fall,
>   Yet call.

(1–12)

In terms of any theology available to Herbert, Christ cannot fail, of course; only the speaker or the speaker's perceptions can fail. But the sole evidence of this fact in "Longing" is formal. The prosodic subject here establishes a verse form which initially seems jarring but which gradually gains smoothness, in part by remaining constant throughout fourteen iambic stanzas. Counting feet or accents, the numerical progression in each stanza is 342241. The rhyme scheme is *ababcc*. Whereas the form seems arbitrary and unsettling at the local level of each stanza, from the God's-eye-view of the whole poem the form enables the speaker to achieve and maintain coherence as a bodily and psychic self, regardless of the speaker's own sense that he is falling apart. In this way, the prosodic subject manifests an awareness separate from the speaker's that Christ is still holding his child.

But despite prosodic consistency, the speaker's feelings of pain, fragmentation, and disintegration are affirmed by the prosodic subject's twisting, contorted lines and by restless enjambments. As the speaker claims that his "thoughts turn round," the prosodic subject spins, leaving even the sensitive reader "giddie," reeling. The prosodic subject's consistently rising iambic beat contrasts with the speaker's sense that he is falling, yet this discrepancy only further adds to the disorienting speed and agitation of the spinning verses, each of which must stand, prosodically speaking, on a single, final foot.[68]

In stanzas three and four, the speaker specifically equates his God with human mothers:

>   From thee all pitie flows.
>   Mothers are kinde, because thou art,
>   And dost dispose
>   To them a part:
>   Their infants, them; and they suck thee
>   More free.

Bowels of pitie, heare!
Lord of my soul, love of my minde,
Bow down thine eare!
Let not the winde
Scatter my words, and in the same
Thy name!

(13–24)

As the source of all motherly compassion, Christ himself is maternal. Christ's pity flows like a mother's milk, linking God to humankind as a mother is linked to her child. Interestingly, in line seventeen, no verb, only a comma, separates the words "Their infants" from "them," referring to mothers. One implication is that mothers and infants are so close that they are almost identical. Though the elliptical construction finds its verb "suck" as the speaker equates the infants' sucking milk from their mothers with the mothers' sucking pity from Christ, the lack of a verb in the first clause creates a striking image of near merger, an image which clarifies what the speaker desires from Christ.

Initial trochaic substitutions in each line of stanza four except the last, and a trochaic substitution after the medial caesura in the stanza's second line (line twenty) create a swaying, falling effect which is resolved by the prosodic subject's return to rising iambic motions at the end of each phrase. Thus, as the speaker continues his appeal for mothering, a maternal presence rocks the prosodic subject "as womanly as can the best," to borrow Gascoigne's phrase. The speaker remains unsoothed. Recognizing his absolute dependence on Christ as mother, he continues to feel terrified that he has been abandoned.

Disintegration and depersonalization culminate in stanza seven:

Behold, thy dust doth stirre,
It moves, it creeps, it aims at thee:
Wilt thou deferre
To succour me,

Thy pile of dust, wherein each crumme
Sayes, Come?

(37–42)

Feeling separated from God, the speaker sees himself as an "it," as dust impelled more by willful deliberation than genuine life, which exists only in God. The prosodic subject echoes the speaker's deliberateness, his stirring, moving, creeping, aiming, with an insistent iambic beat. In typical gestures, the prosodic subject mirrors the speaker's agitation and disintegration with restless enjambments in the short lines and a sharp distinction between poetic line divisions and syntactic units, especially in the last two lines where the subject of a clause is separated by a line break from its predicate.[69]

In stanzas nine and ten, the speaker implicitly requests that God act as mother rather than ruler:

> Indeed the world's thy book,
> Where all things have their leafe assign'd:
> Yet a meek look
> Hath interlin'd.
> Thy board is full, yet humble guests
> Finde nests.

> Thou tarriest, while I die,
> And fall to nothing: thou dost reigne,
> And rule on high,
> While I remain
> In bitter grief: yet am I stil'd
> Thy childe.

(49–60)

As author of the book of nature, God "holds" all things (including the speaker as "it") and assigns identity to each. God's board, supplied with the food of Christ's body, provides for even humble guests. The speaker's nest image suggests that God's province is domestic, protective space; yet the speaker also suggests an alternative image, God as a king who rules from on high, deliberately separating himself from his child.

The poem continues grappling with the problem of the speaker's feeling separated from his sole source of comfort. The speaker argues in the next two stanzas that since "sinne is dead" God has no cause to act "hard" toward his creation. In the penul-

timate stanza the speaker pleads with "Lord JESU" to listen to
his broken heart, the parts of which have grown tongues and
become beggars. Only in the last stanza does the speaker insinu-
ate hope:

> My love, my sweetnesse, heare!
> By these thy feet, at which my heart
> Lies all the yeare,
> Pluck out thy dart,
> And heal my troubled breast which cryes,
> Which dyes.
>
> (73–84)

I argued in chapter 1 that the speaker's heart is the relational
space represented by Herbert's prosody; hence, the heart is the
holding environment in which God as mother resides. In "Longing," as the speaker invests himself "all the yeare" in the process
of versifying, he places his heart at the Lord's "feet." The "feet"
the speaker swears by are as much the feet of the poem as the
feet Mary Magdalene washed with tears. The prosodic subject is
merged with Christ, is part of the body of Christ. If God the
Father is looking down in some disinterested way on the
speaker, God as mother is nevertheless cradling the prosodic
subject and integrating rhythmic parts within the prosodic
spaces.

The next poem in *The Temple*, "The Bag" confirms the point
that God has heard the speaker's prayer. The poem begins
abruptly as if responding directly to the speaker's despair in
"Longing": "Away despair! my gracious Lord doth heare" (1). In
stanza one, the speaker equates the sighs and groans of "Longing" with a tempest through which God has steered him to
safety. Though the eyes of God the Father may have been closed,
the heart of Christ has been open to the speaker's pleas.

After stanza one, "The Bag" presents a childlike fable in which
the masculine "God of power" who wears "majestick robes of
glorie" decides to "descend" to earth, "undressing all the way"
(9–12). He sheds not only royal vestments but also weapons—
"his bow," and "his spear"—to take on "new clothes a making
here below" (14, 18). The Lord's life is told in elliptical fashion
in the fourth stanza. The last three stanzas, particularly in com-
bination with the mother imagery in "Longing," underscore the
femininity of Herbert's dying Christ:

But as he was returning, there came one
　　That ran upon him with a spear.
　　He, who came hither all alone,
　　Bringing nor man, nor arms, nor fear,
　　Receiv'd the blow upon his side,
And straight he turn'd, and to his brethren cry'd,

If ye have any thing to send or write,
　　I have no bag, but here is room:
　　Unto my Fathers hands and sight,
　　Beleeve me, it shall safely come.
　　That I shall minde, what you impart,
Look, you may put it very neare my heart.

Or if hereafter any of my friends
　　Will use me in this kinde, the doore
　　Shall still be open; what he sends
　　I will present, and somewhat more,
　　Not to his hurt. Sighs will convey
Any thing to me. Harke, Despair away.

(25–42)

Having given up his own spear, Christ passively receives the blow inflicted on him. This phallic wounding opens a metaphysical channel between God and humankind, "room" in Christ's Body "very neare [his] heart"; this "room" which takes the place of "a bag" is womb-like.[70] It is the place in Christ's body where the desires of the believer will be empathetically held, where the boundaries separating God and human beings will be dissolved. Christ's very body, vulnerable, wounded, feminized, here becomes the door through which believers may come to new life with the Father just as infants enter life through the mother's womb. Christ's body, *his* heart, constitutes the relational space between God and humankind.

Prosody in "The Bag" is far less agitated than in "Longing." Though both poems have six line stanzas rhyming *ababcc,* line lengths in "The Bag" are longer on the average and the progression is smoother by far. Syntactic integrity is more consistently maintained by the poem's longer lines as well. Since the subject matter is Christ rather than the I-speaker, the symmetrical form seems appropriate. The diminishment of line lengths in the middle four lines may be read as mirroring the poem's narrative development. Heroic pentameter lines represent Christ's glory before he descends from and after he returns to his transcendent (and perhaps absolutely masculine) state; tetrameter lines represent temporal diminishment as Christ humbles himself before humankind. Furthermore, the indentation of the middle tetrameter lines further to the left than the frame pentameter lines opens up a space at the heart of the stanzaic body which parallels the opening in Christ's side; thus form represents the wounded body of Christ.

The two-body relationship between the incarnate God and human individuals changes to a one-body relationship at the end of "The Bag," and the gap between God the Father and his creation is closed up by the opening in Christ's side. Just as maternal holding facilitates a child's capacity to relate to others, so Christ's holding enables human beings to relate to God. In "The Bag" the intimacy of Christ's relationship to the speaker is represented in terms of merger. Thus, Christ's final three words "Harke, Despair away," resonate with the speaker's opening words, two voices becoming one at the poem's close.[71]

Two final examples will further illustrate the maternity of Herbert's Christ and further clarify how form conveys the self's sense of being or not being held in *The Temple*. Like "Longing," "Deniall" and "Jesu" embody in form two psychosomatic states: one of brokenness and objectification, the other of wholeness and bodily aliveness. Although Christ's role as holding mother is in no way explicit at these poems' discursive levels, the idea of the Other as one whose absence means brokenness and depersonalization for the self and whose presence means quickening and self-unification (holding) is quite clear.

"Deniall" begins as a complaint by a speaker who believes that God has abandoned him and who feels broken as a result:

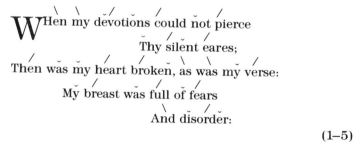

(1–5)

An equation between heart and verse is made explicit in line three, both by the speaker's comparison of one to the other and by the broken iambic pentameter. If verse is the heart, it is, as I have argued, the bodily place where self and Other merge, the matrix out of which a re-formed self arises. But if we consider this stanza in isolation, verse conveys not the Other's shaping presence, but rather the self's chaos in the Other's absence. Line lengths are so irregular as to seem almost arbitrary. The sharp edges of the verse and the fragmentation of syntax prosodically convey the speaker's brokenness and his sense of his pain as piercing, though not sharp enough to penetrate God's "silent eares."

The speaker's attribution of the silence he experiences to God's ears suggests that he is experiencing the boundary confusion which accompanies ego disintegration; his attribution of his own sense of fragmentation to God, whom he represents through an anatomical part, similarly confuses the boundaries between himself and his apparently absent Other. And even as the speaker construes the Other in terms of the self, he construes parts of himself as other. The externalization, materialization, and personification of the speaker's thoughts in the second and third stanzas underscore the idea that the speaker, separated from the divine Other, separates also from himself, dividing into warring fragments:

My bent thoughts, like a brittle bow,
Did flie asunder:
Each took his way; some would to pleasures go,
Some to the warres and thunder
Of alarms.

As good go any where, they say,
As to benumme
Both knees and heart, in crying night and day,
Come, come, my God, O come,
But no hearing.

(6–15)

In these stanzas, form continues the broken iambic beat of a broken heart and also mimics the speaker's bent and scattered thoughts in lines sprinkled haphazardly across the page. But prosody also maintains partial order amidst the chaos. As if coming behind the speaker to pick up the pieces, the prosodic subject puts the fragments together in a stanzaic pattern which maintains consistency from one broken verse to another. The verse form remains roughly four duple feet in the first line, two in the second, five in the third, three in the fourth, and two in the fifth in each stanza; although substitutions and ambiguous stresses render the pattern virtually invisible, we may assume that Herbert is extrapolating from an iambic base measure here.[72] Also, the rhyme scheme remains a constant *ababx,* the *x*'s, or rather the lack of rhyme they signify, mimetically echoing the speaker's disorder, sense of alarm, and sense of God's absence respectively.[73]

The speaker's thoughts, which seem piercing like arrows in stanza one, remain things in the beginning of stanza two but become brittle bows rather than arrows. In other words, they move closer to the mind that generates them, but then they "flie asunder" and become finally persons, each with a "way" of "his" own at the end of stanza two. The bentness of the speaker's thoughts parallels the bending of his knee, mentioned in stanzas three and four. As he shifts from awareness of his thoughts to awareness of his body, the speaker realizes his sense of abandonment in vivid somatic terms:

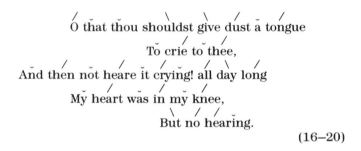

O that thou shouldst give dust a tongue
To crie to thee,
And then not heare it crying! all day long
My heart was in my knee,
But no hearing.
(16–20)

Here the speaker perceives his body from a depersonalized perspective, as a grotesque: disintegrated ("dust"); deformed ("dust" with a crying tongue, the heart dislocated to the knee); and degendered (an "it"). In contrast, the prosodic subject shows signs of quickness through a rapid pulse in these lines. The pulse is speeded not only by the speaker's excitement but also by enjambment. Even sentences run together. The word *all,* which begins a second clause just past the middle of the stanza, is not capitalized; one implication is that the speaker hardly stops for breath until the end of line four, where the comma indicates that he pauses before repeating the previous stanza's

despairing conclusion—a subjectless and fragmentary refrain.[74]
He continues:

> Therefore my soul lay out of sight,
>> Untun'd, unstrung:
> My feeble spirit, unable to look right,
>> Like a nipt blossome, hung
>>> Discontented.
>
> O cheer and tune my heartlesse breast,
>> Deferre no time;
> That so thy favours granting my request,
>> They and my minde may chime,
>>> And mend my ryme.

>>>> (21–30)

The bow of the second stanza, which represented the speaker's bent thoughts and became the bending knee perceived as containing the speaker's heart, here turns into an unstrung lyre or harp representing the speaker's soul. While the speaker equates his spirit, cut off from the source of life, with a "nipt blossome," prosody concretely embodies the notion of separation by dividing the verb "hung" from its modifier. The penultimate line hangs—physically drooping, syntactically incomplete, and in a subjectified, affective sense, "discontented."

To the speaker, the breast seems "heartlesse" because the heart feels relocated to the knee and because the soul is hidden. The image suggests a sense of emptiness and inertia in the Other's absence. Having already shown signs of quickness, the prosodic subject in the last stanza gives clear indication that the Other is present and responsive. As recipient of God's "favours," the prosodic subject shows that the heart has been mended with the chime/rhyme closure of the final verse, signifying the reunion of all the separated "parts" of the poem. God and the self are reunited; soul and body are reintegrated; the heart is healed, and harmony restored.

Thus at the level of form, the self as broken object is made whole and resubjectified in the final lines. To the extent the speaker feels separate from God, the prosodic subject remains apart from the speaker, validating the speaker's feelings but at the same time offering reassurance—to the reader at least—that as the speaker himself asserts in "Discipline," "Love will do the deed: / For with love / Stonie hearts will bleed." (18–20) The chaos in "Deniall" is not so impenetrable as the speaker believes. Whether the speaker realizes it or not—and it is disputable whether he recognizes it even at the end of the poem—the holding Other is there; heart, verse, and self are not so broken that the Other cannot give them life, a fact the prosodic subject recognizes early on.[75]

"Jesu" explores the way in which the Word of God is made flesh, even after Christ's resurrection, through being written on the human heart:

> J ESU is in my heart, his sacred name
>   Is deeply carved there: but th'other week
> A great affliction broke the little frame,
> Ev'n all to pieces: which I went to seek:
> And first I found the corner, where was *J*,
> After, where *ES,* and next where *U* was graved.
> When I had got these parcels, instantly
> I sat me down to spell them, and perceived
> That to my broken heart he was *I ease you,*
>   And to my whole is *J E S U.*

Here as in "Deniall" prosody represents the speaker's heart, where Christ dwells in and with the speaker. But in "Jesu," the heart is not a self outside of the speaker's awareness; rather it is a self which the speaker can read as God's text; by reading the heart, the speaker discovers God's holding relation to the self.

The image hieroglyphically represented by verse is ultimately one of restored wholeness since the word *JESU,* the first and last word of the poem, ties the whole together as well as resolving the final couplet. Thus form enacts Christ's holding and represents the heart as the holding environment where "Jesu"—the Word made flesh—resides. But the brokenness the speaker refers to comes across as "J" appears in the "corner" of line five, split off from "ES," which follows after in line six. Next comes "U," "graved" toward the end of the line.

The verb "graved" suggests death as well as engraving. And the stone-like block constituted by the form in lines one through nine very nearly images a tombstone, though the final trimeter line ten restores liveliness to the prosodic body. "Graved" appropriately follows "U" (that is, "you") since this pronoun refers to the self separated from "J," which refers to Jesus.[76] While such separation could mean death to the self, Jesus remains whole, a viable subject, an "I" even when his name is broken with the speaker's heart.

Separated from the Divine "I," the self is rendered an object in two senses: first, he stands as a broken thing before his God; second, he becomes the grammatical object of "J," or Jesu.[77] This grammar illustrates the speaker's absolute dependence on Christ; and although one can be dependent on a male figure, in this case the poem underscores the maternal action of God's grace. Christ's action turns out to be one of easing the speaker, of holding him in his fragmentation and bringing him together as a revitalized subject. The letter of Love thus replaces the letter of the law, the Divine "I" resubjectifying the broken self and restoring him to wholeness within the prosodic body.

In Herbert's poems in general, the action of grace is as much maternal as paternal or patriarchal, and the self's experience of Christ's mothering is rendered with greatest power—made flesh for readers—through the poems' form. At the same time that, in some Herbert texts, form supports the I-speaker's fears—of punishment by an absolutist Father who is wrathful and unforgiving, or of abandonment by a divine Mother who is not good-enough—in almost all of *The Temple*'s formal spaces, prosody enacts a self's psychosomatic unification in relation to a God of mercy, who restores a sense of security and personal wholeness as he nurses, nurtures, soothes, comforts, holds the emerging self. Thus, though subject to God as ruler of the universe, the new man is subjectified, made human, by the indwelling presence of God as Love.

3

"Betwixt this world and that of grace": Herbert's Interpersonal and Potential Spaces

I

IN LINE TWO OF "AFFLICTION" (IV), HERBERT'S SPEAKER BEGS, "LORD, hunt me not," apparently addressing a rather aggressive deity. If the word "hunt" is to be taken literally, God is closing in on the speaker. By line three, without even a single word transition, the speaker claims to be "A thing forgot"—forgotten, one may assume, by a neglectful God.[1] In order to imagine himself from a God's-eye-view as a thing, the speaker must fear that the Other has distanced himself both physically and emotionally. After all, subject-object dualism is contingent on separation. So is God too close, hunting the speaker, or is he too far away, either forgetting the speaker altogether or perceiving him as a mere object? The speaker seems unsure.[2] In either case, the speaker concludes the stanza calling himself "A wonder tortur'd in the space / Betwixt this world and that of grace," a diagnosis of problematic interpersonal space which fits both situations (5–6).

Modern research indicates that interpersonal space is both a social convention and a gauge of personality. People's senses of interpersonal space typically differ according to culture, gender, and prior experience, but in general we understand physical proximity to others as a measure of intimacy or aggression. The way people react to and attempt to modify the space between themselves and others and the way that they respond to nonverbal cues of others regarding interpersonal space is a sign not only of their backgrounds but also of their interpersonal limits and capacities.[3]

In Herbert's poetry, interpersonal space is denoted not only by the speaker's frequent references to God's presence or absence, nearness or distance, but also by the prosodic subject's spatial form. The dynamics of interpersonal space between God and humanity in *The Temple* are more complex than those of inter-human spaces. After all, God is everywhere and able to control all events, including his encounters with his creation. Further-more, God co-occupies with believers not only objective but also subjective spaces. Finally, while among most adults, attempts to adjust interpersonal space assert a person's "bounded body ego" and "ego boundaries" (a person's sense of bodily and psychic integrity and of intersubjective relation), in *The Temple* the correlation between space and boundaries is more direct.[4] The speaker and prosodic subject do not merely express themselves through attempts to control interpersonal space; they are al-tered within and through that space. Their boundaries, like those of young children, are "soft and supple to [God's] will" ("H. Baptisme" (II), 8).

"The Temper" (I) illustrates the dynamics of interpersonal space between Herbert's speaker and God and the fluctuation of the speaker's boundaries in relation to God:

> HOw should I praise thee, Lord! how should my rymes
>   Gladly engrave thy love in steel,
>   If what my soul doth feel sometimes,
>   My soul might ever feel!
>
> Although there were some fourtie heav'ns, or more,
>   Sometimes I peere above them all;
>   Sometimes I hardly reach a score,
>   Sometimes to hell I fall.
>
> O rack me not to such a vast extent;
>   Those distances belong to thee:
>   The world's too little for thy tent,
>   A grave too big for me.
>
> Wilt thou meet arms with man, that thou dost stretch
>   A crumme of dust from heav'n to hell?
>   Will great God measure with a wretch?
>   Shall he thy stature spell?
>
> O let me, when thy roof my soul hath hid,
>   O let me roost and nestle there:
>   Then of a sinner thou art rid
>   And I of hope and fear.

Yet take thy way; for sure thy way is best:
    Stretch or contract me, thy poore debter:
    This is but tuning of my breast,
      To make the musick better.

Whether I flie with angels, fall with dust,
    Thy hands made both, and I am there:
    Thy power and love, my love and trust
      Make one place ev'ry where.

In the first stanza the speaker wants to feel God's love—and by implication God's presence—"ever." Instead, his occasional sense of God's nearness is fleeting. Thus he does not engrave God's love in steel, a material most notable for its durability. With this image, the speaker leaves open the question of whether God's love or only his sense of God's love vacillates. The speaker does not assert any reality beyond subjective experience ("what my soul doth feel sometimes"). If the speaker were addressing a human being, his implicit request that the Other effect a change in his feelings would reflect a confusion of self/Other boundaries. But unlike a human Other, Herbert's God could directly influence the speaker's subjective state since God's presence is as much internal as external.[5]

In subsequent stanzas, the speaker represents himself as the one in flux, but he also blames God more overtly for his internal instability. Figuring his profound mood swings in images of absolute ascent (to highest heaven) and descent (to hell), the speaker accuses the Lord of Hosts, for whom the world is too small even for a tent, of torture (racking the speaker) and militaristic aggression (meting arms with the speaker). These torments initially seem completely gratuitous. The speaker, in figuring himself as a mere "crumme of dust," and "a wretch" demonstrates how little he has to learn from being humiliated.

The speaker's question, "Will Great God measure with a wretch?" is the subtle turning point of the poem. Arguably the question ameliorates its own implicit allegation that God has not stopped to consider what he is doing by punning on the auxiliary verb; this measuring may be a manifestation of God's (essentially unquestionable) "will."[6] But why would a Great God "will" such a thing? As the speaker explicates his first impression in the next line, God is measuring himself against a human being in order to "spell" his own stature. Perhaps God needs no better reason than to exhibit his unconditional sovereignty, at the same time dramatically disproving the notion that "man is

the measure of all things." Calvin's God might well behave in
such a way. But Herbert's God finally does not. Herbert's speaker
continues, praying for God's protection, asking that he may
"roost and nestle" under God's roof. That is, he requests a space
of security, of holding, rather than one of conflict. Finally, he
surrenders, placing himself in God's hands. As he does so, he
rereads the whole idea of God's "measuring." As it turns out,
God may be "measuring" the speaker primarily in the musical
sense just as he is tuning the speaker's breast (or "measuring"
his heart strings) to improve the music (both the speaker himself as God's instrument and the speaker's poetry).

The prosodic subject's stretching and contracting lines parallel the speaker's sense of psychic torture in this poem. Each
quatrain stretches to five feet in the first line, contracts to four
feet in the middle two lines, then to three feet in the final line.
Since the rhyme scheme is *abab,* rhyming lines are of uneven
length and must, in some abstract spatial sense, stretch or contract to meet each other as they are joined through rhyme. But
with these "contrapuntal stanzas," the prosodic subject also
demonstrates how God can "make the musick better" through
such contortion.[7] Hence, the prosodic subject both demonstrates how God brings harmony out of apparent discord and
renders the speaker's suffering more vivid by giving it physical
expression.

And indeed, more than affective states are being reshaped in
this poem. The speaker's relationship to a God whose capacities
far exceed his own causes extreme fluctuation not only of feelings but also of self-image and ego boundaries. At times, supported by God, the speaker feels tall enough to peer above forty
heavens or more. At other times, he feels small; his God seems
too big, and God is in absolute control of the space between the
two of them. The speaker's whole self is being tempered here—
stretched, contracted, tuned. Hence, God's great distances
threaten to destroy the speaker's very sense of self. Yet God's
greatness, particularly his omnipresence, is also the speaker's
cure. Though the space of desire is felt as a space where the self
gets distorted, it is also the space of self-formation. As Anna K.
Nardo points out, "an enlargement of self occurs ... when the
complaining self meets the internal other in arms."[8] Even more
importantly, the speaker's intense desire for God serves to
deepen the *relationship* between the speaker and God, extending it to the lowest depths of the speaker's despair. "If I
make my bed in hell, behold, thou art there," the psalmist writes

(Ps. 139:8 AV). By the end of "The Temper" (I) Herbert's speaker seems to agree.[9]

Arnold Stein has cogently noted that "The Temper" (I) is centrally concerned with "movements up and down of actual and psychological space."[10] Interpersonal space is, after all, the intersection between the two, an actual space affectively filled as persons interrelate. Richard Strier, on the other hand, argues that the poem's last stanza "replaces the spatial terms of flying and falling and the whole vocabulary of places with terms denoting qualities of personal relationship—love and trust." Strier thus separates "ontological and spatial terms" from "personalistic and qualitative ones."[11] Where Strier perceives a contradiction between spatial and relational terms, I perceive a culmination in Herbert's figuration of interpersonal space. Space closes inward at the end of the poem as the speaker realizes that God is with him even through the dark night of the soul. Though Strier is right that the poem is more concerned with a relationship than with places, this conclusion can be drawn well before the last stanza. Herbert's representation of *space* rarely has much to do with *places;* it has everything to do with persons.

"The Agonie" further illustrates the complex interworkings of spatial and interpersonal boundaries in *The Temple,* and illustrates, in addition, the separate yet interpenetrating sensibilities of the speaker and the prosodic subject. The speaker begins with a seemingly logical introduction to the topic of what sorts of knowledge human beings can arrive at through ostensibly empirical devices:

> PHilosophers have measur'd mountains,
> Fathom'd the depths of seas, of states, and kings,
> Walk'd with a staffe to heav'n, and traced fountains:
> But there are two vast, spacious things,
> The which to measure it doth more behove:
> Yet few there are that sound them; Sinne and Love.
>
> (1–6)

Here is pre-rational insight forced charmingly into the mold of grown-up rhetoric. The speaker purports to dispense with the sum of human knowledge in three lines before introducing his own supposedly more modest topic. But the logical form of the speaker's argument is belied by childlike conflations.[12]

Even given that the term *philosopher* may refer generically to practitioners of various academic disciplines or to the metaphysician who mixes them in pursuit of fundamental questions, it may strike a twentieth-century reader as odd that Herbert's speaker makes no distinction, for example, between fathoming the depths of seas and fathoming the depths of kings. Rather he draws a Lear-like parallel between the measuring of physical bodies in geographic space and the measuring of human dimensions as embodied in a great man. The idea that kings have two bodies, the personal biological body and the political body delimited by the nation's territorial boundaries, is of course commonplace in Medieval and Renaissance writing, in literary and political texts alike. According to this theory, the land of a nation is not merely the king's property but an extension of the king's person. But the idea that the measurements of (or ways of measuring) the two have any correlation is a childlike literalization of Renaissance analogical thought.

Herbert's speaker refers at once to quantitative measurement as of the heights of mountains and the depths of seas and to qualitative measurement as of geopolitical bodies (states) and their heads (kings). In so doing, he suggests a fundamental and mysterious question. How does one fathom the affective, the intellectual, the spiritual depths of another person? What except a body—a natural body, a political body, a human body, the body of Christ—can be measured?

Measure here is also, as in other Herbert poems, a musical and prosodic term.[13] One may "measure" very different sorts of phenomena in the sense of singing or writing about them (that is, putting them to measure). Thus, though a mountain climber may "[walk] with a staffe to heav'n" in a literal sense, musicians rise heavenward with a different kind of "staffe," and in a musical or poetic sense one may "sound" any class of object, including the "two vast, spacious things" with which the speaker will concern himself: "Sinne and Love."

So the speaker will "measure" sin and love in spatial terms; the prosodic subject will "measure" them in formal terms. The reader, aware of both levels of meaning, may follow the speaker's rhetorical map, in the second stanza arriving, through a guided meditation, at a safely distanced image. Alternatively, the reader may "know" the wages of sin in a more immediate way, through experiencing the second stanza at the prosodic level:

> Who would know Sinne, let him repair
> Unto Mount Olivet; there shall he see
> A man so wrung with pains, that all his hair,
> His skinne, his garments bloudie be.
> Sinne is that presse and vice, which forceth pain
> To hunt his cruell food through ev'ry vein.
>
> (7–12)

While the speaker is distanced from the body of an Other, narrating a vision which he instructs his audience merely to *see*—and that, one may argue, from the twice removed distance of meditative re-imaging—the prosodic subject enters into Christ's consciousness.[14] The prosodic subject embodies both the psycho-somatic agony of Christ as he struggles in the Garden of Gethsemane to accept the coming crucifixion, literally sweating blood, and the physical agony of Christ on the cross.[15] The first two lines contort with bodily suffering signified by the metric irregularities of scarcely scannable overstressed lines; the next two lines throb with the highly regular pulse of pain and blood; the final couplet makes tangible the shock of pain pressed through the very veins of the dying savior. As Elizabeth Cook asserts, "The verb *hunt* brings the intelligible and conventional image of Christ and the wine press quite startlingly into the realm of the sensible."[16] The verb is all the more startling because of the enjambment. The tactile image of *pain* is syntactically forced through the white space "To hunt his cruell food." Inasmuch as the prosody *is* the body of Christ, the stanza hurts; the prosodic subject is *in* Christ; the speaker merely sees him.[17] Hence, the prosodic subject's way of knowing is more tactile than the speaker's.[18]

Of course, as represented in some Renaissance texts, the sense of sight is itself a tactile experience. In Donne's "The Extasie," for example, as the persona and his love look into each other's eyes, their gazes intertwine as their hands do: "Our eye-beames twisted, and did thread / Our eyes, upon one double string" (8–9). Similarly, in Herbert's own poem, "The Glance," the speaker claims that when God first looked at him he "felt a sugared strange delight / Passing all cordials made of any art" (5–6). The experience of being seen is *felt* here in terms of the sense of taste. In this text, there is little differentiation among sensory experiences.

But seeing or being seen in the context of a love relationship is a different matter from seeing a physically tormented stranger. And the speaker of "The Agonie" communicates his parable on sin in part by referring to Christ as "a man," identity unspecified, rather than as someone related to him or his audience—as "my God," the way he does in the stanza on love, for example. The reader may stand in a purely rhetorical relation to the image, "seeing" in the sense of understanding the speaker's point about an event that occurred long ago and far away; the reader may *see* more vividly, as if watching Christ at Mount Olivet, meditating on the image of another's suffering in a slightly less mediated way; or the reader may "know" with Christ, as the prosodic subject does, something of what it is to be at Gethsemane anticipating the cross.[19]

That a state of interpersonal merger is the goal of the poem is clarified even at the rhetorical level in the final stanza:

> Who knows not Love, let him assay
> And taste that juice, which on the crosse a pike
> Did set again abroach; then let him say
> If ever he did taste the like.
> Love is that liquour sweet and most divine,
> Which my God feels as bloud; but I, as wine.
>
> (13–18)

Those who can "know" sin only by "seeing" its consequences from the bounded off space of the self are here drawn into the mystery of love. Notably, the "two vast spacious things" opposed in the poem are both defined relative to Christ's suffering body.[20] Sin and love are measured in terms of the interpersonal space between humankind and Christ. Sin involves separation from the incarnate Christ as he looks ahead to and projectively experiences the crucifixion, feeling it as blood, whereas love involves merger with Christ through the eucharist, which (in one way or another) looks backward to the crucifixion, re-presenting blood as wine. While the speaker implies that one may "know" sin indirectly, by means of sight or intellectual comprehension, he suggests that one must "know" love directly—by tasting the blood of Christ eucharistically.

The reader "who would know Sinne" may remain separate. But the reader "who knows not Love" can learn it only by intimate experience. The prosodic subject has already bypassed an enactment of sin and manifested a knowledge of love through merging with Christ in his suffering. But the prosodic subject also experiences the ecstatic upswing of the final stanza, in the first line metrically rising for the first two feet, then falling, rising, and swinging into the strongly delineated iambic beat of the second line; next rhythmically speeding across the longer middle lines to a rest at the end of line four; and finally, dancing (metrically down with a trochee, up with an iamb and across line five) to an intoxicated close, the most strongly stressed phrase of the last line echoing behind: "my G̊od feels."

In short, while the speaker progresses from seeing to tasting (regressing from separation to merger as he is converted from sin to love), the prosodic subject exhibits feeling, a form of love, in both stanzas. The reader may draw two conclusions: first, some form of merger between the human subject and Christ is inevitably the goal of the poem; second, the amount of space a person maintains between the self and Christ is the primary distinction the poem makes between the egocentric state of sin and the interpersonal relationship of love.

The prosodic subject *feels* both in the sense of physically undergoing Christ's pain and in the sense of entering into it psychologically. As a bodily self closely identified with Christ but still connected to the speaker, the prosodic subject in "The Agonie" is the answer to the speaker's request in "Repentance": "O let thy height of mercie then / Compassionate short-breathed men" (13–14). *Compassionate,* an invented verb, points in the same two directions in which "The Agonie" moves. Psychoanalytically speaking, a developmentally mature form of *compassion* might be defined as the capacity to understand, to have pity on, or to sympathize with another, all the while remaining a separate individual. But especially in a religious context, *compassion* literally suggests something far deeper—the capacity to suffer the Passion with Christ, to enter into the experience as the prosodic subject does, in the words of Paul to be "crucified with Christ" (Gal. 2:20 AV). Beyond that, it means to understand the final words of Saint Francis' prayer as a present tense proposition: "It is in dying that we are born to eternal life."

The death most frequently dramatized in Herbert's poetry is not the death of Christ, but rather the death of a self and a way of seeing. All sorts of boundaries disintegrate when the speaker's ego breaks. Time and space collide. Thoughts become things with sharp edges. Threatening voices retaliate from a no longer safely interior psychic realm. Dreamlike images merge in bizarre reconfigurations of human experience. Again and again, *The Temple*'s I-speaker represents the experience of ultimate loss: the annihilation of the societally sanctioned categories which keep life ordinary and sensible (that is, the Lacanian Symbolic), the disintegration of a familiar, if not loved, imaginary self. "Mere anarchy is loosed upon the world" (Yeats, "The Second Coming," 4). When the speaker loses his sense of self, of separateness, *The Temple* itself—as text, as church, as world, as the body of the believer and the Body of Christ—is undone. Yet it is also remade, "raz'd and raised as before" ("The Sacrifice," 66). All the chaos of self-abandon is merely a moment in God's answering of the speaker's prayer:

> Lord, mend or rather make us: one creation
> Will not suffice our turn:
> Except thou make us dayly, we shall spurn
> Our own salvation.
>
> ("Giddinesse," 25–28)

II

In *The Temple* interpersonal space is important not only because it signifies the status of a relationship, but also because it is the ground from which the prosodic subject emerges as a new self in the image of God. In this regard, "The Agonie" illustrates an important conflict between the two Herberts. While the prosodic subject merges with the Divine Other, the speaker directs his audience to approach from a greater distance, at least initially. In other Herbert poems, the speaker and the prosodic subject are even more at odds with each other in how they perceive and attempt to modify interpersonal space; the prosodic subject's sense of God's closeness tugs against the speaker's sense of separation from God, whether the speaker perceives that separation as a form of independence to be fought for or a form of punishment to be endured. Their conflict may be read as representing an intra-psychic dependency struggle, possibly attributable to the historical author, almost certainly attributable to some people of Herbert's day.

The ambivalence between a desire for oneness with, or absolute dependence on, another and the desire for autonomy is also characteristic of toddlers grappling with their first awareness of separateness from their mothers. This fact makes it possible to identify the interpersonal space in "The Agonie"—as well as that in "Affliction" (IV), "The Temper," and other Herbert poems—as of a particular type which Winnicott calls *"potential space."*[21] Understanding the concept of *potential space* and the closely related concept of *transitional objects* will enable Herbert's readers to appreciate more fully the developmental function of Christianity for some believers of Herbert's day and the deeply human significance of Herbert's utmost art.

"Potential space" is the prototype for later interpersonal spaces and like them is a "space" constructed and occupied by both self and other, but potential space differs from other interpersonal spaces in being not so much a physical as an imaginary "space," one which originates in the mother-infant relationship. As the toddler becomes aware of the mother's separateness, of her capacity to go away and to resist the child's omnipotent control, the child attempts to fill the space between self and other with a "transitional object"—a blanket, a pillow, a piece of cloth, perhaps even a teddy bear. This object serves as a symbol both of the actual mother in her absence and of the lost mother-as-connected-to-the-self. "Potential space," then, is the psychic space filled by the child's representation of the mother-infant relationship and played out in reality with the transitional object. Potential space compensates for the gap between mother and child as real space opens up between them.[22]

Potential space is the precursor not only of later interpersonal spaces but also of later psychic spaces to be populated by introjects, internalized representations of important others.[23] The quality and durability of potential space contribute to the child's formation of boundaries and to his or her capacities to be alone (at first with the aid of the transitional object), to be intimate with others (as with the transitional object and the mother it represents), to play, and later to participate in cultural phenomena like theater, art, and literature (capacities contingent on the survival of the *as if* attitude first available in potential space).[24]

Potential space is also the space of the sacraments, particularly the eucharist, in which material objects, namely bread and wine, are believed to embody Christ's presence or in radical Prot-

estant interpretations to *represent* his presence, even though
Christ is believed to be physically absent. Whether construed as
the extension of Christ's incarnation or as a memento of Christ's
former bodily presence, the bread and wine are "transitional
objects" as Winnicott interprets them. Whatever their ontological status, they are symbols of the Other which enable believers
to retain faith in his continuing existence and eventual return.[25]

Other aspects of Christian belief also parallel transitional phenomena. To facilitate her child's transition from merger to separateness, a mother has an important job to do: she must survive
the child's psychic destruction of her, not only tolerating the
child's ambivalence, but also continuing to be a good-enough
mother through one moment's kicking and the next moment's
clinging. In surviving the child's destruction, the mother comes
to seem more real to the child, more permanent, less susceptible
to alteration by the child's positive or negative wishes or behavior; thus the child's image of the mother in relation to the self
becomes more stable.[26] Analogously, in conventional Christian
belief, Christ survives destruction by his children in his death
and resurrection. His survival solidifies for believers his permanence and reliability as the object of their love and worship and
firmly establishes his identity as their messiah.[27]

In "The Dawning," Herbert's speaker grieves over Christ's absence not so much because of Christ's death as because of his
resurrection and ascension. The speaker comforts his "sad
heart" with a relic the Other has left behind:

> Arise, arise;
> And with his buriall-linen drie thine eyes:
> Christ left his grave-clothes, that we might, when grief
> Draws tears, or bloud, not want a handkerchief.
>
> (13–16)

As Debora K. Shuger asserts, "the strips of burial cloth . . . signify
both [Christ's] triumph and His absence."[28] At the same time
they signify an extended sense of Christ's presence. The shroud
or handkerchief is a transitional object, a symbol that the Other
survives, a piece of evidence that he will return.

One might say the same of the Bible in "The H. Scriptures"
(I). In the poem's first lines, the speaker addresses his Bible:
"Oh Book! infinite sweetnesse! let my heart / Suck ev'ry letter,
and a hony gain" (1–2). Although the image is of honey, the lines
draw upon a well-established tradition of envisioning Christ as
a nursing mother.[29] But here, the scriptures serve Christ's ma-

ternal function.[30] Later in the poem, the speaker further indicates the Bible's significance as an object which stands in the place of the Other:

> Ladies, look here; this is the thankfull glasse,
> That mends the lookers eyes; this is the well
>   That washes what it shows. Who can indeare
>   Thy praise too much? thou art heav'ns Lidger here,
> Working against the states of death and hell.
>   Thou art joyes handsell: heav'n lies flat in thee,
>   Subject to ev'ry mounters bended knee.
>
> (8–14)

In this passage, scriptures not only constitute a mode of God's continuing presence in the world, specifically by being "heav'ns Lidger here"; they also serve the maternal function of mirroring God's children, enabling believers to establish their identities in relation to God even in the absence of the incarnate Other.[31] Furthermore, the scriptures represent God's caretaking function, specifically emblematized here by washing.

As these examples demonstrate, transitional phenomena in Herbert's poems serve significant functions. They enable the believer to retain faith in a Lord who sometimes seems absent. They also serve *in loco parentis* after Christ's resurrection—as objects which, occupying the Other's place, further the Other's influence on the believer's development. "The Collar" further illustrates the importance of transitional phenomena in *The Temple,* showing how they serve to remind Herbert's speaker who he is when he has forgotten.

In "The Collar," Herbert's speaker attempts, like a rebellious child, to free himself from the constraints of religious life, as emblematized by the collar.[32] Striking the communion table, he vows to abandon his former service:

> What? shall I ever sigh and pine?
> My lines and life are free; free as the rode,
>   Loose as the winde, as large as store.
>   Shall I be still in suit?
>   Have I no harvest but a thorn
>   To let me bloud, and not restore
> What I have lost with cordiall fruit?
>
> (3–9)

As Jeffrey Hart points out, the speaker refers ironically to a number of eucharistic objects. Believing that, through his tan-

trum, he will free himself to seize the fruits of "double pleasures," he fails to appreciate the way in which his references to
"bloud," to "cordiall fruit," and, in ensuing passages, to "wine,"
"corn," and the "fruit" of pleasure tie him to the "board" he is
attempting to desert (20, 8–11, 17, 1). These images of wine
and grain hold the speaker's words inside a metaphorical frame
ultimately signifying the body and blood of the Other.[33] Even
proclaiming his separateness, the speaker speaks through the
Other's language, and he speaks of objects intrinsic to the potential space between himself and the Other.

Oblivious to this fact, the speaker swears, "He that forbears /
To suit and serve his need, / Deserves his load" (30–32). He
vows, that is, that the man who remains dependent on another
rather than seizing his independence suffers pain of his own
making. Michael Schoenfeldt argues that "the speaker here
imagines a solipsistic and isolated social economy."[34] If so, the
speaker momentarily grasps for the pseudo-autonomy of a false
self.[35] No struggle for genuine autonomy can be waged on solipsistic ground. Healthy autonomy must be learned and maintained inside of a relational context. Hence the Other's
continuing intrapsychic presence as posited, however inadvert-
ently, in the speaker's language facilitates more than undermines the speaker's aspirations for selfhood.

Prosody further evidences the fact that the speaker remains
under the Other's protection even as he raves. As is common
in Herbert's poems, the prosodic subject in "The Collar" both
mimetically reinforces the speaker's affect and demonstrates an
awareness which transcends the speaker's more limited point
of view. Although formal experimentation pushes the limits of
order—at least as those limits would have been understood in
an age in which free verse was not yet invented—the form nevertheless brings order out of chaos by preserving some boundaries. While line lengths vary somewhat unpredictably, no line
shrinks to less than two feet or swells to more than five, and
while the rhymes come in no set order, all the lines rhyme.[36] As
the speaker calms down, the last four lines of the poem clarify
the prosodic boundaries (the full range of line lengths) in which
his words have been contained:

> But as I rav'd and grew more fierce and wilde
> At every word,
> Me thoughts I heard one calling, *Child!*
> And I reply'd, *My Lord.*

> (33–36)

In saying "Me thoughts I heard one calling," the speaker makes no objective assertion about the Lord's presence. Hence, these words place the events of the poem more in potential space, where the Other's presence is subjectively real whether the Other is objectively there or not, than in a physical interpersonal space. Schoenfeldt claims that the speaker's "uncertainty about the nature of this voice . . . records a lingering solipsism, where inner and outer, imagination and reality are difficult to distinguish."[37] This comment insightfully summarizes the essence of the transitional phase—by definition a stage when the distinction between internal and external phenomena is not yet clear—but, here especially, the word *solipsism* misses the mark. Far from being solipsistic, transitional phenomena are a *defense* against the threat of separation at a time when the child is unable to cope with it.

Thus, as Richard Strier asserts, "Whether the call to which Herbert presents himself responding is objective or subjective does not matter."[38] The speaker's need for an Other prevails in any case, his own psyche scripting the inevitability of his return to his Lord and itself functioning as the machinery through which the Divine Other intervenes.[39] In threatening to separate from his Lord, the speaker terrifies himself, his terror being evidenced by his falling apart. As Roger B. Rollin points out, at the height of his rage the speaker manifests all the symptoms of what Erik Erikson calls "identity confusion—a split of self images" in a "loss of centrality, a sense of dispersion, and a fear of dissolution."[40] This speaker is simply not ready to stand alone; he must invoke the presence of the Other psychically as the antidote to the loss of self his declaration of independence has entailed. The mere thought of the Other's voice restores a sense of identity—and ego integrity—to the speaker by reminding him of an interpersonal order in which he is child to his Lord.[41]

Although it seems accurate to say that the child-persona's passing flirtation with solipsism has temporarily undermined his desire to be a self, Barbara Leah Harman overlooks an important half of developmental truth in implying that the speaker gives over the self he has fought for when he submits to the Other's voice.[42] The return to the Other is as essential to the child's eventual selfhood as the initial rebellion was. If the Other survives and does not retaliate for the tantrum, the child moves one step closer to understanding that being a self does not entail abandoning or being abandoned by others.

In "The Collar," the speaker's frenzied attempt to achieve separation from the Other is quite characteristic of a child in transition. So is his sudden desire for reunion. In fact, the vacillation between these extremes epitomizes the transitional phase. Also, the poem itself, as a material reenactment of a relationship in which the actual Other may be absent, may be construed as a sort of transitional object.

Transitional phenomena, then, are intrinsic to Christian beliefs and serve important functions in *The Temple*. Some difference does exist, of course, in denominational preferences regarding potential spaces. Particularly during the Reformation, Calvinists and other radical Protestants assaulted the potential spaces hallowed by sacramentalist religion. They redefined the meaning of the eucharist. They destroyed icons and sacramental objects, deeming them idolatrous.[43] They disapproved of a government which permitted theater and other material manifestations of culture. They repudiated England's leaders, also, for allowing certain sorts of recreation, particularly on Sundays.[44] Games believed to "build character and a spirit of teamwork" displaced more idle toys in their children's play.[45] The "Word of God," appreciated more for its "literal" spiritual meaning as preached by ministers than for its objective presence as a Holy Book to be handled with reverence—genuflected to, kissed—gradually, among radical Protestants, displaced the sacraments as the most important sign of Christ's presence in the world.[46]

It seems metaphorically appropriate at the very least and perhaps psychoanalytically meaningful that, to establish fully their separation from the "Mother church," seventeenth-century Reformers so adamantly condemned orthodox potential spaces. Their condemnation was not without irony, of course. As Stephen Greenblatt has shown, the boundaries between reality and the sort of consensual imagination or group hallucination that makes drama successful may not always have been clear to people of the Renaissance, Puritans included.[47] What looks like a progression from magical to scientific ways of thinking may have been a product as much of fear as of faith. Were the repudiation of priestly magic a matter of mere disbelief in inexplicable or mysterious phenomena, the Puritans in America would hardly have burned a number of Salem's citizens as witches, for example. This incapacity to distinguish what is empirically real from what is imagined or believed suggests that even Puritans continued to occupy a somewhat darkened potential space.

Unlike the Puritans, Herbert, I think, wrestles with God within conventional potential spaces: those of religion and those of art. Herbert's poems generally grapple with the problems that most people first encounter before age two, problems typically worked out inside potential space: how to love someone who makes one angry; how to deal with loss or separation; how to be a self and be pleasing to others at the same time; when and how to submit when what an important Other does is not what one desires or when what an important Other demands is not what one wants to do; how not to be too lonely when physically isolated; how not to be too lonely in a crowd.

These issues are as close to being fundamental human dilemmas as any can be, and their resolution is, for most people, a lifelong project. But the way these first dependency conflicts get resolved, the teleology of potential space, may differ from culture to culture. Whereas one society may value autonomy as an ideal—for men, for women, or for both sexes—another may encourage submissiveness to and dependence on authority. King James' strategy of representing himself as a mother feeding his subjects and sacrificing himself for their welfare was by no means psychologically unsophisticated.[48] Appealing to the anaclitic tendencies of his subjects, to their desire to be fed and protected, was a way of inclining them toward the merger side of the potential space between ruler and subject. Of course, events leading to and culminating in the civil war of 1640 prove that the strategy failed.

The conflict between a desire for closeness and a desire for distance evidenced in poems like "The Agonie" and "The Collar" is symptomatic not only of fundamental human struggle but also of the tensions of Herbert's day. While Herbert may have distanced himself from the demands of secular authority, proclaiming his intention to "plainly say, *My God, My King*" (either in that order or with God as his sole ruler), he nevertheless found comfort and a sense of identity in the potential spaces sanctioned by the established English church ("Jordan" (I), 15).[49] Herbert's speaker makes this point most clearly in "The British Church." Addressing his "deare Mother," the Anglican church, the speaker represents the Catholic extreme as a "painted" woman, the radical Protestant extreme as a female "undrest" (1, 11–12) Perhaps the implication is that the speaker feels seduced by other churches. But the maternal comforts offered in the potential spaces of his own church, in ceremonies "neither too mean nor yet too gay" finally seem more attractive (8).

III

We may now turn specifically to the potential space of art. I must clarify one technical point before proceeding. To argue that from the reader's perspective, prosody may be construed as a second persona in *The Temple* is somewhat different from arguing that verse functions for the speaker as a transitional object. Whereas the speaker *uses* his verse, his poetry, as a "subjective object" which enables him to practice his relationship to God, the reader may perceive, in addition, the way in which the verse form comes to constitute a sensibility not always under the speaker's imaginary control. The two perspectives are not identical. But they need not be construed as contradictory either. Both underscore the same fact: in *The Temple,* "verse" functions to facilitate the re-formation and development of the human self in relation to God.

If, from the speaker's perspective, Herbert's poems do indeed function as transitional objects, then the poems do much more than document the self-Other relationship; they further the speaker's growth in relation to the Other, contributing to his capacity to love.[50] This means that "art" in *The Temple* is a far more poignant endeavor than many critics' operative definitions of Herbert's art imply. Herbert's verse is a means for the speaker to become more human as he discovers himself in relation to an Other.[51]

Because *The Temple* includes so many poems about poetry, many of them raising serious questions about the legitimacy of religious art, debate over Herbert's disposition toward his verse has been a prevalent theme in Herbert criticism for generations. One of the more compelling arguments about whether Herbert's poems manifest a respect for ceremony and art or whether they reflect or enact a Calvinistic iconoclasm is Joost Daalder's. On surveying both the long term debate and Herbert's poems about poetry, Daalder concludes that Herbert's attitude is inconsistent, varying from one poem to another.[52]

Daalder's solution to a forty-year debate is inevitable and refreshingly honest. And indeed, the question for those who wish to argue for a "Herbert" who respected verse is not *whether* the I-speaker sometimes repudiates his verses but *why* he does so.

Even granting the vacillation which Daalder bluntly asserts, I believe that Herbert's author persona consistently *attempts* to place his poems in a sacramental frame, one which facilitates the speaker's growth in relation to the Other by demarcating a potential space where the relationship can be worked out. In treating his poetry like a transitional object, Herbert's speaker reveals a profound respect for verse. Destructive turns in his attitude toward his poetry occur only when he fails in his goal of including the Other, or when the Other's prolonged absence causes the potential space of the poem to collapse. Thus, as I will argue, the problem with the poems the speaker rejects is not that they are idolatrously presumptuous in attempting to embody the Other; it is that they fail to include the Other, often despite the speaker's wishes to the contrary. Precisely out of his reverence for the potential space of religious art, Herbert's speaker denounces, even destroys, his more solipsistic verses.

At first glance, the idea that Herbert's poems transpire in the potential space between the believer and God may appear merely tautological. Art by definition occupies an in-between space analogous to that of a small child, where an *as if* attitude mediates between what is and what is not. For the child, a piece of cloth may come to symbolize the self-Other relation, standing in for the real Other in periods of temporary separation and representing the Other as created by the self, even though the Other in reality operates outside the realm of the child's omnipotence. Analogously the words of poetry may mediate between presence and absence, standing as material signifiers for absent or imagined Others.

Herbert's poetry is a bit more complicated, however, in that it always involves at least two overlapping potential spaces: that of art and that of religion. More often than not, it combines with these a third: the potential space of a child persona, who relates to God as a primary parent. Ontological assumptions about these potential spaces differ. Most artists understand, at least on a rational level, the difference between representation and embodiment of the represented object. The potential space of religion is considerably more controversial. In sacramentalist religion—including, I think, Herbert's—the Other is believed to participate in the potential space to such a degree that he is really present. The toddler's experience of potential space falls in between the artist's and the communicant's, since the very origin of the space is a developmental stage when distinctions between interior and exterior phenomena, between desire and actuality, are still blurred. Is the child's transitional object a genuine embodiment of the self/Other unit and a real emissary of the mother in her absence? Yes and no.

Herbert's poems continually challenge critically imposed boundaries between art and enactment. In "Jordan" (I), for example, the speaker addresses the issue of poetic fictions: "Who sayes that fictions onely and false hair / Become a verse? Is there in truth no beautie?" (1–2). The speaker implies that he, as author, will seek to make his verse becoming by taking as his subject matter the "truth," in which there is inherent "beautie." But he also implies that he will cause "truth" to become a verse. He will seek to write lines which "do their dutie" to a "true" rather than a "painted chair" (4–5).[53] The Platonic references to the ontological vacuity of mundane art suggest that "Herbert" hopes to infuse verse with reality, to embody in a new kind of poetry (or to enact through it) an ontologically real relationship.[54]

So what does the speaker reject in poems which critics have called iconoclastic? Does he not critique the "idolatrous" assumption that God could be present in textual reality, that God would participate in the potential space of the poem? I think just the opposite is true. In "Jordan" (II) for example, the author-speaker reports on a failed poem or group of poems from his past:

> When first my lines of heav'nly joyes made mention,
> Such was their lustre, they did so excell,
> That I sought out quaint words, and trim invention;
> My thoughts began to burnish, sprout, and swell,
> Curling with metaphors a plain intention,
> Decking the sense, as if it were to sell.
>
> Thousands of notions in my brain did runne,
> Off'ring their service, if I were not sped:
> I often blotted what I had begunne;
> This was not quick enough, and that was dead.
> Nothing could seem too rich to clothe the sunne,
> Much lesse those joyes which trample on his head.
>
> (1–12)

Critics have noted how these stanzas enact some of the very mistakes they deride. The phrase "curling with metaphors" is itself metaphorical, for instance, and the prosodic subject joins in the fun, mimetically curling through enjambment the last three lines of the first stanza and "decking" lines on top of each other just as the speaker rhetorically decorates the "sense."[55]

But an even bigger joke is the presumption of a speaker so preoccupied with his gift to God that he hardly consults God in the process. The "I" in these stanzas is attending not to the mine/thine relationship so often reflected in *The Temple*, but to his own performance.[56] Thus, the most frequently recurring words are *I* and *my,* and when finally the speaker does mention "the sunne" in line eleven, the reference is metaphorical, hence indirect.[57] It is followed in line twelve by a third person pronoun (as if Christ were not there). The speaker of these stanzas parodies a former self who positioned himself outside of a relationship with the God he sought to honor. The speaker pinpoints this error in the last stanza:

> As flames do work and winde, when they ascend,
> So did I weave my self into the sense.
> But while I bustled, I might heare a friend
> Whisper, *how wide is all this long pretence!*
> *There is in love a sweetnesse readie penn'd:*
> *Copy out onely that, and save expense.*

> (13–18)

In the past the speaker sought to "clothe the sunne" in a verse into which he wove himself. Rather than putting on Christ as the Biblical injunction advises, he "bustled" to make himself the cloak of Christ, obscuring the light of the "sunne" in the false lustre of the self's creation.[58] Instead of seeking to further a genuine relationship (as he does in *this* poem when he voices the words of his friend, words which take the form of direct address) he sought to create a false relationship. The idol was not the artifact; the idol was the too self-conscious self cut off from God in the production of the artifact.[59]

The solution to this problem is not to negate art; it is to discover art in the space between self and Divine Other, the potential space where the self meets the Other psychically by remembering the Other in and remembering the Other through a transitional object.[60] As the speaker claims in "A true Hymne," the words "*My joy, my life, my crown,*" words of the self's direct address to God, "If truly said . . . may take part / Among the best in art" (5, 7–8). The point is not to destroy art as a merely external phenomenon; it is to bring "outward and visible signs" into

conjunction with "inward and invisible" realities: "The finenesse
which a hymne or psalme affords, / Is, when the soul unto the
lines accords" (9–10).[61]

The speaker clarifies his aesthetic in the last half of "A true
Hymne":

<blockquote>

He who craves all the minde,
And all the soul, and strength, and time,
If the words onely ryme,
Justly complains, that somewhat is behinde
To make his verse, or write a hymne in kinde.

Whereas if th' heart be moved,
Although the verse be somewhat scant,
God doth supplie the want.
As when th' heart sayes (sighing to be approved)
O could I love! and stops: God writeth, *Loved.*

</blockquote>

(11–20)

If a poet's words merely rhyme, God, who commands "Thou shalt
love the Lord thy God with all thy heart, and with all thy soul,
and with all thy strength, and with all thy mind" is right to
complain (Luke 10:27 AV).[62] But also, as Diane McColley points
out, if only the words rhyme while the self is in a disharmonious
relationship to God and the soul is in a discordant relationship
to the lines, the poet is putting the cart before the horse.[63] In
attending to craft (the outward sign) while neglecting emotion
(the inward reality), the poet leaves God "somewhat" behind in
making "his" verse. The pronoun reference is equivocal; if God
is abandoned as the poet prioritizes art over religion, then poems
meant to be God's are in fact only the poet's.

On the other hand, when the poet operates in relation to God,
writing out of a real desire to love, God coauthors the poem,
manifesting himself in and through it. God supplies a rhyme
word which denotes a restored relationship (*"Loved"*) and symbolizes through the fact of the rhyme restored harmony between
self and Other.[64] The outward sign is not displaced; rather it is
improved through God's participation.

In "The Quidditie," the Herbert speaker as author addresses
what verse is and how it serves a function in the relationship
between the self and God:

<blockquote>

MY God, a verse is not a crown,
No point of honour, or gay suit,

</blockquote>

> No hawk, or banquet, or renown,
> Nor a good sword, nor yet a lute:
>
> It cannot vault, or dance, or play;
> It never was in *France* or *Spain;*
> Nor can it entertain the day
> With my great stable or demain:
>
> It is no office, art, or news,
> Nor the Exchange, or busie Hall;
> But it is that which while I use
> I am with thee, and *most take all.*

A transitional object is both material and subjective, a thing infused with the presence of an Other. Here the speaker denies both the materiality of his verse (the verse is not a thing—a crown, a sword, a lute, and so forth) and its subjectivity (the verse cannot do what people can do—vault, dance, play, travel, and so forth). The very denial suggests that the speaker may have viewed his verse previously as a "subjective object." He may have even entered imaginatively into the textual premises I have already suggested *The Temple* sets up: that verse is a personality.[65] Arguably, even as the speaker denies the personality of verse, the prosodic subject dances and plays as before.[66] In any case, even after denying the materiality and subjectivity of his verse, the speaker asserts in the third stanza that verse can serve one key transitional function; it can be used to bring the self into genuine contact with God.[67]

"The Forerunners" not only illustrates that the speaker believes his verses facilitate his relationship to God; it also dramatizes how the speaker relates to his poetry as a transitional object per se. In stanza three the speaker grieves over the loss of his "sweet phrases" and "lovely metaphors." Though the words *Thou art still my God* are all the speaker's poems can say, "that dittie" is enough to please the Divine Other, and the speaker asserts "if I please him, I write fine and wittie" (6, 11–12). The rhyme itself is "wittie," in being so far from "fine."[68] But the point is that the poetry is not meant to be "fine and wittie" in a worldly sense. The poems are meant to serve as a means of furthering a relationship, not as a way of dazzling the Other with the self's verbal facility.

Of particular relevance to my argument that Herbert's poems transpire in the speaker's potential space is that the speaker's poetry in "The Forerunners" serves as the object of the speaker's affectionate address: "Lovely enchanting language, sugar-cane, / Hony of roses, whither wilt thou flie?" (19–20). The speaker addresses his language as one might address an object of romantic interest—and as Herbert's speaker sometimes addresses Christ.[69] In serving as a means for connecting self to Other, the poems themselves become, like the Other, love objects. Of course, in the same stanza, the speaker rebukes his poetry for abandoning him and treats it like an ungrateful inferior: "Fie, thou wilt soil thy broider'd coat, / And hurt thy self, and him that sings the note" (23–24). This fluctuation between treating the verse as a superior and treating it as an inferior may prove more than disprove the transitional nature of the verse. Transitional objects represent both the Other in relation to the self and the self in relation to the Other. Sometimes, a child treats the object as he or she would treat the parent, appealing to it for soothing. At other times, the child parents the object—caresses it, sings to it, or even gives it instructions—doing for the transitional object what the parent does for the self.[70]

There are, of course, some poems in which the speaker rejects his verse and that not because of any apparent fault of the speaker or poem but only because of a failed attempt at invoking God's participation. Paradoxically, the destruction of the transitional object sometimes falls within the province of transitional phenomena. For the toddler, a serious disturbance in the self-Other relationship threatens both the sense of self and the sense of the Other which the transitional object represents. According to Winnicott, if the mother abandons the child, whether deliberately or because of circumstances beyond her control, the transitional object loses its power prematurely.[71] Similarly in Herbert, God's perceived absences disrupt the speaker's ego boundaries, sometimes so much that the speaker attempts to destroy the poem because he no longer feels that it unites him to God. When God returns, however, poetry becomes meaningful again.

In a series of four poems beginning with "The Search" and ending with "The Flower," Herbert's speaker goes through several stages of grief over God's absence.[72] At first he uses his poetry to attempt to maintain contact with the Other; next he despairs of the Other's return and attempts to destroy this transitional object; then he attempts to address the Other again, in part by turning to other transitional objects; and finally he rejoices when the Other returns and again takes pleasure in his potential space.

"The Search" opens the sequence, cataloging among other problems the serious disturbances in the speaker's sense of self-boundaries and interpersonal space which are intrinsic to his experience of the Other's absence:

> My knees pierce th' earth, mine eies the skie;
> And yet the sphere
> And centre both to me denie
> That thou art there.
>
> (5–8)

In this, the second stanza, Herbert's speaker metaphorizes the magnitude of God's absence through an image which represents the self as stretched from earth to sky; the prosodic subject's stretching and contracting lines underscore the point.

In stanzas five and six the speaker seeks God by sending a sigh "Wing'd like an arrow" and another "tun'd . . . / Into a grone" (19, 21–22).[73] Grief, externalized as a sigh, becomes an arrow—a standard metaphorical transformation to be sure, but also a progression characteristic of a child's potential space, where distinctions between internal and external phenomena are unclear. Here the magical transformation of one kind of thing (a sigh) into another (an arrow) seems as possible as the transformation of felt emotion (grief) into expressed emotion (the sigh). Also characteristic is the aggressiveness suggested by the arrow image. Although he does not say it directly, the speaker is angry that God is gone.

Determining that it is God's will to be absent, the speaker offers in the last stanzas a detailed picture of the disturbance in intra-psychic and interpersonal space which results:

> Thy will such a strange distance is,
> As that to it
> East and West touch, the poles do kisse,
> And parallels meet.
>
> Since then my grief must be as large,
> As is thy space,
> Thy distance from me; see my charge,
> Lord, see my case.
>
> O take these barres, these lengths away;
> Turn, and restore me:
> Be not Almightie, let me say,
> Against, but for me.

> When thou dost turn, and wilt be neare;
>   What edge so keen,
> What point so piercing can appeare
>   To come between?
>
> For as thy absence doth excell
>   All distance known:
> So doth thy nearenesse bear the bell,
>   Making two one.
>
>   (41–60)

The absence of a deeply loved Other is quite traumatic for a small child. Perhaps it is even more so for Herbert's speaker, whose Other cannot be absent except by choice. God is everywhere, yet in this poem he is nowhere to be found. God's will itself seems here to be the epicenter of a spatial rupture. The speaker figures God's will as a "strange distance" where the geometrically impossible meeting of East and West, of parallels, expresses what Lacan might call "the impossible Real," the child's unspeakable sense of helplessness and of complete collapse of the self in the Other's absence.

The speaker attempts to fill the space between himself and God in two ways. Negatively, as he claims, his grief grows large enough to fill the gap created by God's immeasurable distance. Positively, though more implicitly, the poem itself fills the gap between self and Other, constituting a mode of imagined contact, perhaps even "Making two one," through entertaining the possibility that God is near enough to hear the speaker's complaint.[74]

But the transitional object cannot survive too long in the Other's absence. In "Grief," the speaker, no longer trying to address God, addresses the poem and does so in an attempt to silence it:

> Verses, ye are too fine a thing, too wise
> For my rough sorrows: cease, be dumbe and mute,
> Give up your feet and running to mine eyes,
> And keep your measures for some lovers lute,
> Whose grief allows him musick and a ryme:
> For mine excludes both measure, tune, and time.
>   Alas, my God!
>
>   (13–19)

In the earlier two thirds of the poem, the speaker has grieved over the absence not of the Other (who is not even mentioned until the last line) but of tears. Here the speaker personifies his verses not only by addressing them, but also by claiming the verses have "feet" which are capable of running. The speaker requests that the verse give this capacity of running to the speaker's eyes, which could then, ostensibly, run with tears.

Unless the reader looks to the previous poem, the cause of the speaker's grief will remain obscure. In the context of the sequence, the poem continues discussion of a grieving process over the Other's absence. The pain has become so severe that, to indicate how the speaker's heart is breaking, the prosodic subject's verse breaks, as signified in the last line by an abrupt departure from a line length which has not varied for sixteen lines and by an abandonment of rhyme.

Again it is necessary to make a distinction between verse from the speaker's point of view—an object to which the speaker ascribes personality but which he can abandon as a mere thing— and the prosodic subject—a personality who remains intact regardless of what the speaker does. In allowing the verse to break in the last line, the prosodic subject accomplishes what the speaker cannot accomplish on his own power, expressing the grief which "excludes both measure, tune, and time."[75] The verse as transitional object, a thing, gets broken; the prosodic subject as a persona transcends discursive limitation to express what the speaker cannot put into words.

And even the collapse of the speaker's potential space is temporary. In "The Crosse" the speaker turns to another sort of transitional object, a "strange and uncouth thing," specifically a cross (1). In stanza one the cross is a literal thing. As the poem proceeds, the cross also becomes a symbol for the speaker's personal suffering. Thus, the cross is a material object which binds the self to the Other whom it typically represents.

Perhaps because this transitional object enables him to do so, the speaker again addresses God directly, in order to argue with him. The speaker complains that he has entered himself and his family into God's service "after much delay, / Much wrastling, many a combate" and now "this deare end, / So much desir'd, is giv'n, to take away / My power to serve thee" (7–8, 8–10). Even having surrendered to the will of the Other at the behavioral level, the speaker continues to resist accepting the Other's will as appropriate.

Thus the poem continues the theme of grief developed in the previous two poems and returns to the conflict between God's will and the speaker's, a theme developed especially in "The

Search." However, the issue has changed somewhat. Here the conflict seems to be less over God's absence per se, than over God's refusal to ease the speaker's suffering. The speaker implies that, were it not for his bodily suffering, he could serve his lord better. A second "ague" is the speaker's memory of former beneficent intentions toward God which he now lacks the capacity to carry out (13–14). Except "in the sight thereof, where strength doth sting," in the "sight" of the cross and the presence of Christ which it represents, the speaker feels "weak" and "disabled" (18, 17). Yet Christ's condition, "If any man will come after me, let him deny himself, and take up his cross, and follow me," demands that the speaker surrender his strength in order to gain Christ's, moving backwards through potential space to a position of absolute dependence on an Other whose will seems, at times, inexplicable, even cruel (Matt. 16:24 AV). The speaker vocalizes his sense of God's cruelty in stanza four:

> Besides, things sort not to my will,
> Ev'n when my will doth studie thy renown:
> Thou turnest th' edge of all things on me still,
>   Taking me up to throw me down:
> So that, ev'n when my hopes seem to be sped,
> I am to grief alive, to them as dead.
>
> (19–24)

This struggle against an Other's will is precisely the struggle of a small child. The child's submission, while perhaps necessary from the parent's perspective, is likely to involve, from the child's perspective, the temporary loss of a newly discovered sense of self. At the same time, the refusal to submit risks, from the child's point of view, the loss of the Other who is the self's foundation. A toddler's tantrum thus expresses not merely rage but the terrified confusion of a double bind. In a Christian frame of reference, the imperative to be "crucified with Christ" makes the loss of self through submission an even more explicit demand on the Other's part (Gal. 2:20 AV). Herbert's speaker manifests the small child's perplexity when what an Other requires seems not only in conflict with the child's desires but manifestly painful. As Stanley Fish points out, "The only recourse is to turn to the very person whose action is the problem's cause."[76]

The speaker's sense of spiritual torture is expressed by the prosodic subject through the verse form. The relation between the speaker's and the prosodic subject's text becomes especially clear in the final verse:

> Ah my deare Father, ease my smart!
> These contrarieties crush me: these crosse actions
> Doe winde a rope about, and cut my heart:
> And yet since these thy contradictions
> Are properly a crosse felt by thy Sonne,
> With but foure words, my words, *Thy will be done.*
>
> (31–36)

Prosody simultaneously expresses the image of the winding rope and the image of the cross in lines which twist and become entangled. In each stanza, a tetrameter line one rhymes with a pentameter line three and a pentameter line two rhymes with a tetrameter line four; if the first and fourth lines were not indented, the "a" rhymes would slant right to left while the "b" rhymes slanted left to right, creating a chiasmic (x) shape; with these lines indented, the elongation of the middle lines visually suggests the horizontal beam of a crucifix. The rhyme of the first four lines is cross rhyme. Each six-line stanza resolves itself with a final heroic couplet, expressing perhaps the merger the speaker finally arrives at in the last line when he appropriates the Other's words as his own, surrendering entirely to the will of the Father. Another's words appropriated in such a way may constitute yet another sort of transitional phenomenon, one Herbert frequently exploits in the context of his verses.[77]

Having surrendered to absolute dependence on God in "The Crosse," the speaker reaps the benefits in "The Flower," which expresses the joy of reunion after a long separation:

> HOw fresh, O Lord, how sweet and clean
>   Are thy returns! ev'n as the flowers in spring;
>   To which, besides their own demean,
> The late-past frosts tributes of pleasure bring.
>   Grief melts away
>   Like snow in May,
>   As if there were no such cold thing.
>
> (1–7)

Though here the speaker compares the returns of his Lord to spring flowers, in the next stanza, it is his own "shrivel'd heart" which has "recover'd greennesse," having "gone / Quite under ground; as flowers depart / To see their mother-root" (8–9, 9–11). Thus self and a maternal Other (Christ as the mother-root) momentarily share an identity as flowers. The speaker's rebirth when his God returns parallels Christ's resurrection, a fact which suggests that the loss of self required in "The Crosse" is compensated for by the gain of a new self in "The Flower."[78] For the rest of the poem, the speaker remains the flower; God (specifically the Father) is both the gardener, his garden being Paradise, and, at times, the cause of his flowers' decline.

In stanza three, the speaker expresses God's wonders in spatial terms, attributing to the "Lord of power" the acts of "Killing and quickning, bringing down to hell / And up to heaven in an houre; / Making a chiming of a passing-bell" (15, 16–18). God's "word," synonymous with God's will or power, holds all things together, uniting opposites: "We say amisse, / This or that is: / Thy word is all, if we could spell" (19–21). The boundaries between things here collapse.[79] But though all things merge as part of the One will, the speaker is not "past changing" and therefore not past the experience of separation from God. Thus he remains vulnerable to God's anger:

> But while I grow in a straight line,
> Still upwards bent, as if heav'n were mine own,
> Thy anger comes, and I decline:
> What frost to that? what pole is not the zone,
> Where all things burn,
> When thou dost turn,
> And the least frown of thine is shown?
>
> (29–35)

God's anger alters the speaker's space, regardless of where the speaker is located. Even the poles burn, becoming hell-like, when God turns away. The speaker suggests that hell is less a place than a state of relation, or lack of relation, to God.[80] When the potential space between the self and God collapses, the speaker believes himself to be in a type of hell.

Once the relationship is restored, the space of celebrated presence, the space of writing, becomes viable again:

> And now in age I bud again,
> After so many deaths I live and write;
> I once more smell the dew and rain,
> And relish versing: O my onely light,
> It cannot be
> That I am he
> On whom thy tempests fell all night.
>
> (36–42)

The speaker's sense of renewal is so strong when God returns that he feels as if he cannot be the same man who suffered so severely in God's absence. The speaker's renewed relationship with the Other renews his relationship with "versing," a claim which suggests that the speaker's occasional temptation to destroy his verses does not signify an iconoclastic bent; rather it is a sign of his total participation in the potential space of religious art and his complete dependence on God to make that participation meaningful.

The fact that Herbert's poems serve as potential spaces for Herbert's speaker suggests that the poetry functions not merely to represent the self-Other relationship but to further it. The ultimate purpose of these potential spaces is not self-indulgence, not even worship only, but the transformation of the believer in relation to his God. While art for art's sake may be devalued as an exercise in vanity, and while art for the sake of impressing an Other may be deemed presumptuous—especially when that Other is the creator of all things—art for the sake of rehumanizing the self in relation to an Other, for the sake of discovering and practicing the capacity to love, must be understood as an eminently ethical and courageous enterprise.

4

"To God, His Neighbour, and Himself Most True"

I

Perhaps objectivity as invented by bacon, descartes, and others in the early modern age is a collective illusion. Whether it is or not, it may not far outlast the twentieth century—in literary studies at least. And such a loss need not be altogether tragic. But at the same time when some in our profession deny the possibility that people can make "objective" judgments based on unmitigated "facts," some (and the two groups overlap) deny the possibility that people can base subjective perceptions and intersubjective decisions on anything at all. The self, they say, is an illusion perpetrated on infants in accordance with the fantasies, needs, and desires of other illusory selves. We, the sole creators of human culture, are ourselves unreal.

While such arguments may be philosophically valid, they are psychologically unsound. It is one thing if the belief that human identities are constructed in accordance with the exigencies of social contexts determines a critic's approach to texts or cultures. The result is the demythologizing of "culture," the insight that people are historical beings and that our priorities, like our clothes, may be subject to changes of fashion. It is quite another matter if the sense that selves are illusory pervades an individual's or group's actual self-experience. From a Winnicottian perspective, this way of being (or *not* being) in the world leads at best to a profound sense of futility and paralysis.

Shakespeare's Macbeth manifests this extreme disengagement with life and self when he reacts to news of his wife's death:

> Life's but a walking shadow, a poor player,
> That struts and frets his hour upon the stage,
> And then is heard no more. It is a tale

Told by an idiot, full of sound and fury,
Signifying nothing.

(V.v.23–28)

Macbeth is himself a "walking shadow," of course, not only because he does not exist except as a theatrical character but also
because within the play he is a man driven by others, Lady Macbeth foremost among them. Appropriately he conceives of life
in the passive voice, experiencing his own "tale" as "told by an
idiot," a grand and meaningless spectacle. Macbeth's observations on life epitomize the psychological experience of a person
who habitually relates to his or her own actions, feelings, and
thoughts more as scripts that have been authored—by others or
an estranged self—than as experiences that have emerged from
her or his own bodily/affective core.[1] Macbeth's words shadow a
historical experience of self as shadow, unreal.[2]

As Winnicott charts the course of healthy human development, a child progresses from a sense of being a self, through a
sense of continuity of individual being, to a sense of personal
agency, from "I" to "I am" to "I do."[3] Prior to historical democracy,
the majority of human beings never completed the course. Until
the seventeenth century, the average person's identity derived
primarily from his or her relation to an extended family, not
from a sense of self per se. Even physical separations from others
were rare. The poor lived in two-room houses; the rich had many
servants, and their homes had no hallways to isolate private
rooms.[4] It is true that a new sense of self definable not merely
in terms of communal ties but also in terms of divinely created
nature and purpose and personal relation to God was emerging
during the Renaissance.[5] But even those people who had a sense
of themselves as "I" were liable never to complete Winnicott's
second step. Continuity of being is contingent on a good-enough
beginning in life, and in the Renaissance, as I will argue, the
likelihood of being traumatized early in life was statistically
high.[6] And even at the end of the Renaissance, a sense of personal agency was reserved for the privileged few. In seventeenth-
century British and American political usage, references to "the
people" were understood to signify only male heads of households—not women, not children, not the poor.[7]

Stephen Greenblatt provides evidence that one consequence
of this state of affairs was a not infrequent sense of life as theater. Lacking an experience of self as a potentially effective agent
in sociopolitical life, many, especially the younger sons of middle

and upper class families, resigned themselves to playing their parts in the fantasies of those in power. Questions of how to fashion a self pervade Renaissance texts—those of Castiglione, Machiavelli, Erasmus, Ascham, and Elyot to name only a few. Yet human personality was understood as more an affect than an agency. According to Greenblatt, in order to fashion an "I," Renaissance individuals had to have an authority whose desires they could follow; they also had to scapegoat an Alien, defining themselves as much by what they were not as by what they were.[8] One implication of this authoritarian binary model for human subjectivity is that the possibility of personal agency was subverted by the very process which delimited Renaissance selves. Self was defined in deference to and in reaction against others.

Winnicott claims that many people learn very early in life to live reactively, to abandon healthy needs, genuine potentials, and valid insights and fashion false selves which can live on the basis of compliance to others. Following Winnicott, I will argue that Greenblatt's insights about Renaissance self-fashioning indicate a collective tendency in the early modern age toward false-self organization, a consequence of authoritarian child rearing, restrictive education, and absolutist politics.[9]

To some extent all human beings have false selves, and all societies promote them. Most human beings cultivate capacities to observe just laws, exhibit good manners, and participate, as the true self desires, in cultural trends or fashions. The problem arises when a person's false self deposes his or her true self and sets itself up as real. In some such cases, the person knows that the true self exists and allows it a secret life. In others, the person remains for a lifetime completely oblivious to his or her own reality and therefore experiences life itself as if it were unreal.[10]

One may define the Winnicottian true self as the core of a person whose identification with the qualities that his or her natural potential drives toward has been secured through relationship to a good-enough mother prior to socialization.[11] The true self begins not as an inside but rather as an awareness infusing the living body, not as a source of agency but rather as "the summation of sensori-motor aliveness."[12] Over time, the true self may become "a living reality," a personal way of being in the world, if the mother adapts herself and the environment to "the infant's living needs."[13] By this definition, true selves, though easily subverted, are potentially as universal as human bodies. They are also as individual. Winnicott insists that only a true self can feel real; only a true self can initiate action; only a true self can genuinely serve.[14] Greenblatt, on the other hand, suggests that it is wise to put quotation marks around the words "true self."[15]

To signify a working hypothesis, I will omit this punctuation. My discussion of false and true selves in Herbert will be grounded on the premise that true selves are a biological fact of human existence, while false selves are culturally determined. Skepticism about true selves easily predates their historical liberation, as I will demonstrate. Yet in spite of profound ambivalence on the part of Renaissance poets, traces of true selves are manifest in Renaissance texts.

Ambivalence about the self ran deep in Herbert's day. As Jean Delumeau observes, "the fear of one's self . . . crested during the early modern era."[16] Arising in a sociopolitical context in which the majority did not have the last word regarding their careers, their spouses, their property, or even their religion, the authoritarian relational mode which underlies many false–self disorders generated and was sustained by much of the theology of the age; yet at the same time, seventeenth-century Protestantism prepared the way for true selves to emerge first as souls in relation to God and later as historical individuals.

On the one hand, Reformers devalued human beings in relation to the Almighty. Contra the Humanists, Calvinists especially considered fallen human beings to be worthless and incapable of self-improvement and believed that God was the sole agent of the believer's redemption and sole author of the faith which led to salvation. Thus frequently in Reformation as in Augustinian and Pauline terms, *self* is pejorative, denoting the sinful human agent who is the opponent of grace; redeemed subjectivity is characterized by selflessness and passive dependence on God. In Paul's words, the self is "crucified with Christ" so that "Not I but Christ liveth in me" (Gal. 2:20 AV). In Herbert's words, "to have nought is ours, not to confesse / That we have nought" ("The Holdfast," 9–10).

On the other hand, Reformation Protestants may be said to have discovered the true self. Emphasizing personal faith and relationship to God as more essential to salvation than communal worship or sacramental participation, they directed Christian attention inward.[17] In theory at least, Protestants vested authority in the divinely guided individual conscience, proclaiming the priesthood of the believer rather than the su-

periority of the clergy in regard to matters of faith.[18] Finally
(unbeknownst to them) Reformation Protestants prepared the
way for a later historical sense of self-determination by advancing the notion that a young person's vocation is for him (or more
rarely her) to determine in obedience to God's will rather than
in deference to a parent's wishes.[19]

Natalie Zemon Davis challenges Jacob Burkhardt's controversial thesis that in the Renaissance "man became a spiritual individual" rather than a self defined by a familial and communal
context, pointing out that the Romantic strategy of defining an
isolate self in opposition to society did not exist in the Renaissance.[20] Nevertheless, she notes, in sixteenth-century France,
the self in relation to God became theoretically separable from—
and gained ideological priority over—the self subordinate to familial authority. The concept of *naturel,* "'nature'—a wide-
ranging word which could include temperament, character and
talent," marks, I would argue, an emergent historical conception
of a true self.[21] While the self in and of the family was still
tangled up in the patriarchal structure which, from a Winnicottian standpoint, makes a false self dominant, the self defined as
naturel, the divinely created self, was redeemed by Love and
liberated from Law—at least to the extent that this Protestant
doctrine prevailed over other Protestant doctrines more conge-
nial to authoritarian interpersonal or intrapersonal dynamics.[22]

Greenblatt also challenges Burckhardt's thesis, arguing that
"uniqueness," a definitive quality of the Romantic individual,
was beside the point of Renaissance selfhood: "individual identity in the early modern period served less as a final goal than
as a way station on the road to a firm and decisive identification
with normative structures."[23] Yet, Greenblatt points out, some
Renaissance selves ("prodigies") could not be accommodated by
normative structures.[24] I agree with Greenblatt as far as he goes,
but would like to go a step further. An outwardly "normal" person becomes "A wonder tortur'd in the space / Betwixt this world
and that of grace" in a society which renders potentially adaptive
aspects of experience prodigious ("Affliction" (IV), 5–6). By using
the term *true self,* I do not mean to imply that any part of Herbert's text represents a unique "Herbert" who differs in any *particular* way from others of his day. Like Greenblatt I am on a
quest for a Renaissance mode of self-experience, not for a historical author. But I do mean that Herbert's text, especially at
the level of form, encompasses aspects of self which Renaissance
"normative structures" disallowed.

One conscious sense of a true self falls very much inside the pale of normative seventeenth-century religious thought and finds expression at the discursive level of *The Temple*. In Herbert's "The Sinner," the speaker claims that "The spirit and good extract of [his] heart / Comes to about the many hundred part"— less than one percent of his being—and prays, "Lord restore thine image" (10–12). The speaker asks for his true nature— Adam, Christ—his "quintessence" to be sorted from the "dregs" of his worldly identity (11). Like Winnicott, the speaker believes in a true self at odds with an environmental self. Unlike Winnicott, he ties his sense of the environmental self to the notion of sin and believes that the true self is universal rather than individual. Also, the speaker believes that the true self is spiritual, though his reference to "the spirit and good extract of [his] heart" follows Renaissance rather than modern usage, *spirit* denoting a substance which mediates between body and soul, not an incorporeal essence. In this sense, the quintessential self Herbert's speaker discusses is not unlike the Winnicottian self based in the body.

More frequently in *The Temple*, a true self exists outside of the speaker's awareness, emerging in the non-discursive dimension of form. As we have seen, Herbert's form typically stands for his speaker's heart and often figures a second sensibility within the text. Herbert might have called it a soul; Winnicott labels it a true self and claims that, in the beginning, it is ineffable—that nebulous but very real potential which characterizes each person as personal. "The spontaneous gesture is the True Self in action," yet the true self cannot in itself be known:[25]

> The True Self comes from the aliveness of the body tissues and the working of body-functions, including the heart's action and breathing. It is closely linked with the idea of the Primary Process, and is, at the beginning, essentially not reactive to external stimuli, but primary. There is but little point in formulating a True Self idea except for the purpose of trying to understand the False Self, because it does no more than collect together the details of the experience of aliveness.[26]

Winnicott links the true self to primary process. Heinz Kohut links primary process to poetic form:

> The meaningful content of poetry is the secondary-process surface of the phenomenon; the form, however, with the *Klangassoziation* rhymes and the rhythm of the words, belongs to the primary proc-

ess, the primitive psychic forms of the unconscious. In poetry a verbal secondary-process layer (content) may cover a deeper musical primary-process layer (rhythm, rhyme).[27]

Adding Kohut's premise to Winnicott's, we may hypothesize that prosody in Herbert represents an infantile true self and further-more that when prosodic signification (primary-process mean-ing) contradicts or exceeds discursive content (secondary-process meaning) a true self and false self are split off from each other. This split suggests that in Herbert's day, some needs were unmet, some desires unfulfilled, and some potentials unreal-ized; Renaissance selves exceeded the institutions, the relation-ships, the conventions, which were meant to define and contain them. To the extent that Herbert's form preserves indicators of these needs, desires, and potentials, it figures a *negative* of the Renaissance social contract. According to this hypothesis, Her-bert's form represents the speaker's repressed humanity, a core self who, having survived socialization in an absolutist cul-ture, gestures toward the possibility of personal and historical change.[28]

Herbert's speaker *is* the poststructuralist, historical self. He defines himself according to a number of culturally available roles: the Reformation believer, the English priest, the Renais-sance courtier, various Biblical types, and so on; he is adept at the sort of negotiations that his class, education, and social connections facilitated. The prosodic subject is a self left over. From a Winnicottian standpoint this excess of self may be attrib-utable to core potential; a poststructuralist may prefer to view it as indicative of a historically overdetermined self. In any case, within *The Temple*'s form, aspects of self not fully expressible within the matrices of Renaissance society are integrated into the Body of Christ. The individual who emerges in the interplay between form and content is neither a set of unique qualities nor an entity who exists and acts in isolation. In fact, we may view Herbert's representation of his assimilation by faith into the Body of Christ as a strategy for avoiding felt uniqueness and isolation. Herbert discovers through poetic form a structure which is at once normative and inclusive of all his parts. The Reformation "individual" then, as represented in *The Temple,* is a self whose totality emerges and gains meaning, place, and value in relation to his creator. Through dependence on an Other who knows and understands all the pieces, the Herbertian self comes together as a whole and viable person.

Perhaps, to the extent the historical Herbert was aware of what he was doing, his intention was to create with his prosody a representation of the "new man" at odds with the "old Adam" the speaker often represents. Perhaps he intended form to represent divine rather than human presence or agency. Or maybe both; perhaps Herbert meant for verse to dramatize the redeemed self's emergence in Christ's presence and through Christ's agency. In any case, as I will show, while the I-speaker of *The Temple* shows multiple signs of false-self organization, Herbert's prosodic subtext registers the unarticulated realities of a true self for whom psyche and soma exist in harmony.

In *Discipline and Punish*, Foucault puts forth the thesis that, historically speaking, the human soul (the psyche) is born of punishment and repression.[29] Perhaps some version of it is. But a body that is tortured has a prior potential to thrive; a mind that is repressed has a prior capacity to be aware; abuses can be defined only with reference to potentials they subvert. If the soul, as Foucault understands it, is a split off consciousness born of abuse, then the true self is a potential which pre-exists the abuse, perhaps less self-conscious than the soul Foucault defines but conscious nevertheless. The true self is the soul (or whole) that emerges from and dwells within the human body. The soul humankind has created through cruelty is the soul of a false self: the true self isolated, disembodied, lost, looking elsewhere.

II

D. W. Winnicott typically developed his ideas in multiple texts, written or spoken at different times to audiences which varied widely in levels of theoretical sophistication. At times even within texts, Winnicott left the connections between his ideas implicit or open to conjecture. Other writers who follow Winnicott sometimes alter the theory slightly as they apply it to the contexts which preoccupy them. Often, in the process, they combine Winnicott's ideas with other theories of child development. For all these reasons, a theoretical survey seems in order prior to my applying Winnicott's idea of true and false selves to Renaissance life and literature.

Winnicott's most condensed statement about true and false selves exists in the form of a clinical definition recorded in the early 1950s. There Winnicott notes that a false self results from "a premature taking over of the nursing functions of the mother, so that the infant or child adapts to the environment while at the same time protecting and hiding the true self, or source of personal impulses."[30] Winnicott does not specify precisely how early or late in life a false self may usurp the place of the true self. In referring to the mother's "nursing function," he does limit the period in question to infancy or early childhood, however.

In a 1960 essay, Winnicott develops his ideas in more detail, defining five possible levels of false-self organization, which range from extreme illness to health. The most extreme form of false self "sets up as real" and is often mistaken by others for the real person. The second most extreme form of false self "defends the true self," which is "acknowledged as a potential and is allowed a secret life." The third form of false self "has as its main concern a search for conditions which will make it possible for the true self to come into its own." The fourth, almost healthy, form of false self is "built on identifications." The fifth form, a genuinely healthy false self, "is represented by the whole organization of the polite and mannered social attitude."[31]

In this essay, Winnicott defines the origin of the most extreme form of false self as the mother-child relationship of early infancy. According to him, "periodically the infant's gesture gives expression to a spontaneous impulse; the source of the gesture is the true self, and the gesture indicates the existence of a potential true self."[32] A good-enough mother gives the true self life by "meeting the infant's spontaneous gesture or sensory hallucination."[33] (The mother feeds an infant whose sucking movements suggest that the baby is imagining being fed, or picks up an infant whose agitation suggests that the baby desires to be held.) A not-good-enough mother, rather than responding to the infant's cues, "substitutes her own gesture which is to be given sense by the compliance of the infant."[34]

In short, Winnicott states that the aetiology of the severest form of false self precedes the mirror stage, its origin being the first stage of object relations when a mother who is not good enough fails to empathize with her infant. He leaves somewhat ambiguous his ideas about whether less severe forms of false self originate at the same time. In one passage, Winnicott implies that some of the false selves born in earliest infancy are closer than others to the true selves they replace.[35] In another, he suggests that some false selves may come about at later stages.[36]

In a 1964 speech, Winnicott discusses a case example of a ten-year-old boy who, having been a bad student, developed a false self to comply with the demands of an educational curriculum and consequently suffered nightmares of persecution. Insisting that the boy was from a good home and that he was essentially normal, Winnicott suggests that false selves may become problematic at any point in life when a person is faced with an insoluble conflict between conformity and self-assertion. But what for infants and small children may become a manifestation of personality disorder exists for older children and adults as a situational crisis.[37]

Other theorists offer their own perspectives on how and when pathologically false selves may become established. Summarizing the results of an experiment in which small children were asked to imagine various scenes of separation from parents, John Bowlby reports that "children who have experienced long and repeated separations or who come from unhappy homes" sometimes give "responses that indicate that the child will do his best to get along on his own or that he will be happier as a result of the event."[38] Bowlby interprets these responses as manifestations of the Winnicottian false self, which he defines as "a forced and premature attempt at autonomy that will prove brittle."[39] Thus he implies that a false self may originate at any age prior to the times of life when various manifestations of autonomy become age appropriate.

Daniel Stern argues that the process of splitting the false from the true self begins early in infancy, but tends to recur later through the mother's selective "attunement, misattunement and nonattunement" of her child's affects and behavior (*attunement* being roughly synonymous with the psychoanalytic term *mirroring*). Stern explains this process quite clearly:

> Some self-experiences are selected and enhanced because they meet the needs and wishes of someone else (the false self), regardless of the fact that they may diverge from the self-experiences that are more closely determined by "internal design" (the true self).[40]

Stern argues that the false self is later afforded a privileged status in language as well:

> Gradually with the cooperation between the parent and the child, the false self becomes established as a semantic construction made of linguistic propositions about who one is and what one does and experiences. The true self becomes a conglomerate of disavowed experiences of self which cannot be linguistically encoded.[41]

Thus Stern suggests that false selves have multiple points of origin, given that they must be established on multiple levels of self-experience.

One of Alice Miller's recurrent themes is the way in which parents force false selves on their children in part because of the bad parenting the parents themselves received when they were young. In *Prisoners of Childhood,* Miller focuses primarily on early childhood, combining Winnicott's ideas about true self development with Heinz Kohut's insights about early childhood narcissism and about the pathological narcissism of adults arrested in that developmental phase.[42] True to an agenda which disdains all pedagogical approaches to child rearing, even in their mildest and most conventional forms, Miller's applications of Winnicott and Kohut occasionally seem more passionate than disciplined in an academic or professional sense. Nevertheless, her synthesis of the two theories seems quite valid.

To understand Miller, one must first understand Kohut. In the spirit of the myth after which Freud named the condition, and because of the effects adult narcissism has on others, psychoanalysts have traditionally treated childhood narcissism as a manifestation of natural human depravity. If Kohut's theory is correct, many ironies are inherent in this stance. According to Kohut, narcissism is not only a healthy and normal developmental phase; it is also the psychic foundation for the best humankind has to offer. Once successfully gotten through, narcissism transforms itself into mature human capacities for humor, wisdom, creativity, empathy, and self-sacrifice.

Untransformed, narcissism manifests itself in two ways: an unrealistic overvaluation of the self, and unrealistic attributions of power to others who, from the narcissist's point of view, belong to, extend from, or, by some magical equation, are identical to the self. Pathological narcissism, that which persists beyond the age of two or three and comes to characterize a lifelong mode of relating to the world, results not from parental overindulgence, as one might expect, but from severe narcissistic traumatization of a child after the narcissistic phase has been successfully initiated but before it has been successfully completed. To put the matter concretely, a two-year-old needs to be let down slowly, gently from the reciprocal delusions that his or her parent possesses superhuman powers and that he or she has God-like importance.[43]

Miller reasons that one common form of false-self pathology finds its genesis in the competing narcissistic needs of a normal toddler and a narcissistically fixated adult. In a healthy parent-child relationship, as Winnicott implies, the adult mirrors the child's true self, responding to the child's first intimations of personal potency with approval, admiration, and apparent credulity. If a mother or father is not healthy, the parent may need a child who can mirror her or him and who can become the person that the parent desires either to be or to have.[44]

The consensus seems to be that the more pathological forms of false-self organization begin quite early in life as a response to failure on the part of a primary caretaker and consequently affect the whole personality. Whether the false self is born in earliest infancy or later during the mirror stage, the child who grows up following a script implicit in a parent's gestures bypasses the developmental path whereby separation leads to autonomy, experiencing the self as an extension of another rather than as a whole. In Kohut's terms, the child becomes the self-object of another. Hence, as Winnicott points out, one symptom of false-self problems is the person's awareness that she or he lacks something. Also, given that false-self actions are originally initiated from the outside, a common manifestation of false-self living is the loss of psychosomatic indwelling as the person comes to rely too heavily on the split off intellect.[45]

The story of Pinocchio may clarify these points. As a puppet, Pinocchio may be understood to symbolize a false self, one who, in performing actions not authored by himself, is alienated from possession of his own body. Pinocchio is a self-object (that of his father and maker) rather than a self. Once brought to life by a fairy, Pinocchio wants to be a real boy. This desire, a manifestation of true self, exists prior to the true self's actualization. Among other limitations the fairy places on him, Pinocchio must never lie or else his nose will grow. Lying, one might argue, is a manifestation of false self in the realm of the Lacanian symbolic; it is a verbal act performed both to protect the self and to create a self in compliance with the demands of others, one which does not square with the self's real experience. Pinocchio's body comes to betray his infidelity to a true self who might otherwise live in undetected isolation from the realm of shared experience.

Pinocchio may be luckier than we think. Historically, many children have been taught the opposite lesson, often in the name of what is good. They have been taught not merely to tell a lie, but to live a lie, to become the lie that others want to hear.[46] In the Renaissance such education may have started early. As

Lawrence Stone paints the picture, infants in the sixteenth and early seventeenth centuries were liable to four common traumas in the first two years of life (some but not all of these traumas contingent on various accidents of birth or fortune).

First, infants born to aristocratic mothers were frequently sent to nurses who often were not "good-enough" mother figures in Winnicott's sense of the term. Even those babies who had good-enough nurses were liable to lose them if the nurses ran out of milk. Those infants lucky enough to bond with a single nurse were sure to lose this mothering figure at the time of weaning, except in those extremely rare cases in which the nurse lived in the parents' household and continued her mothering function throughout the child's early life.[47]

Second, one in ten children lost one or both parents to premature death before the children were three years old. Two in ten lost parents before the children left home, around the age of seven. Even those who did not lose parents were liable to face intense grief early in life upon the loss of siblings, friends, or others close to the family. While such losses were inevitable and from a mature standpoint nobody's fault, it is likely that small children experienced them as a form of abandonment.[48]

Third, all infants in England and elsewhere in Renaissance Europe were wrapped in tight swaddling clothes, a practice believed to protect them from injury and to make their limbs grow straight. Swaddling enabled mothering figures to pay less attention to babies, who could be left in a corner or even hung on a peg on the wall while the women pursued their daily routines. Infants were thus deprived of both sensori-motor stimulation and human contact.[49]

Fourth, according to Stone, especially Puritan parents but others to lesser degrees manifested "a fierce determination to break the will of the child and to enforce his utter subjection to the authority of his elders and superiors, and most especially of his parents." Conceived in a state of original sin, the child was born to be broken; self-assertion, now construed to be the beginnings of health, was then construed as evidence of human depravity, and it was the job of the solicitous parent not to pamper or coddle the child but to fit the child for God's kingdom by enforcing a relational model of dominance and submission in accordance with the authoritarian ideology of the day.[50]

Recent historians argue against a number of Stone's contentions. Linda Pollock, for instance, appeals to primary evidence, especially journals and autobiographies available from Renaissance parents and children, to argue that most Renaissance parents valued their children highly, seeking both to protect them and to socialize them in accordance with the values of the day.[51] As Pollock herself recognizes, her evidence has some drawbacks, since only a limited number of early modern diaries are available and most come from people of the upper or middle classes.[52] Nevertheless, Pollock persuasively argues through a number of counterexamples that Stone and other historians (Lloyd deMause and Philippe Aries, for example) exaggerate the pervasiveness of Renaissance child-abuse and draw hasty generalizations from secondary sources to portray typical Renaissance parents as deliberately indifferent, cruel, or negligent.[53]

At the same time, from the standpoint of the child-centered perspective I am seeking to develop here, Pollock too often seeks to vindicate Renaissance parents on the basis of their intentions rather than their actual effects on children. For example, in regard to parents' sending infants away to nurses, Pollock argues that people in the Renaissance believed that nursing mothers should not sleep with their husbands because sex could curdle a mother's milk. Thus parents who wanted more children thought that they had to hire wet nurses for their babies.[54] But primary evidence cited by Alan Macfarlane suggests that a more realistic viewpoint was available to people in the Renaissance. Not all parents believed that nursing and sexual relations were mutually exclusive; in fact, some knew better by experience, as the fact that some mothers conceived while nursing demonstrates.[55] And as Pollock herself points out, in spite of parents' care to choose good nurses, some families found bad ones.[56] Nurses did sometimes run out of milk, and eventual separation from nurses was the inevitable fate of most Renaissance babies. Although Pollock argues that infants sent to wet nurses formed lasting bonds with their visiting parents, she does not directly confront the traumatic effects of the infant's losing the nurse at the time of weaning.[57] To say that a child deeply loves one caretaker is not to prove that the child does not deeply grieve over the loss of another caretaker, especially one who has been with the child on a daily basis for most of the child's life.

Similarly, in response to arguments that the practice of swaddling was detrimental, Pollock emphasizes that Renaissance parents believed that swaddling was a protective measure; furthermore, the practice of swaddling may have prevented infants from crawling too rapidly toward open fires.[58] And she may well be right. But particularly during the summer months, the woolen cloth used to make swaddling clothes could not have duplicated the well-regulated temperature of the womb, as some writers on the subject have claimed, and whatever womblike holding effect swaddling produced for the baby substituted for intimate human contact that primary caretakers might otherwise have provided; furthermore, the extension of a womb-like experience into the first year of life may have retarded the infant's progress toward a sense of self, both as a bodily reality and as a potentially autonomous being.[59] To argue that these unfortunate effects may have been necessary to keep infants from crawling into open fires is to assume both that the lesser of two evils does not affect human infants badly at all and that a better means of protecting infants (close adult supervision) was unimaginable. It also raises the question of why caretakers gradually removed swaddling bands when the child was between one and two.[60] Did Renaissance parents believe that one- to three-year-olds, in spite of being more mobile, were less at risk of accidental burning?

In addition, Pollock seeks to vindicate mothers and nurses who overlaid infants (that is, slept on top of them in bed) from the charge of deliberate infanticide or extreme negligence by claiming that primary caretakers intended to watch babies more closely at night because Renaissance adults were concerned about infant mortality. Again her argument seems plausible, but it misses the point: a number of babies died—and probably many more suffered moments of near suffocation that may have affected their capacities for human closeness later in life.

Thus, while I agree with Pollock that probably most Renaissance parents sought to rear their children in ways that seemed likely to ensure the children's safety, growth, education, and eventual economic well-being, I continue to agree with Stone that the majority of Renaissance children probably suffered some form of trauma early in life, however inadvertent that trauma may have been on the parents' part.

Any one of the four traumas Stone discusses might be sufficient to bring about a false self. In fact, it is hard to imagine how the universal practice of swaddling would not in itself have limited infantile expressions of "omnipotence," even if a mothering figure were available to respond. The infant, tightly wrapped, was liable to sleep most of the time and to be, from the beginning, out of touch with her or his own body.[61] Those infants further traumatized by cruel or neglectful nurses or the loss of beloved nurses, by the deaths of important others, or by attempts to quell self-assertion perhaps only relearned at later stages of infancy what they had already gleaned from the beginning.

The lesson that "compliance is best" served children after age two as well, though historians disagree about how Renaissance adults sought to inculcate this value in children. Stone claims that corporal punishment, sometimes abusive in severity, was common not only in Renaissance homes but also in schools.[62] Pollock disagrees, offering evidence that some Renaissance parents preferred other disciplinary measures over corporal punishment.[63] Furthermore, she demonstrates that, while in theory paternal authority was absolute, in practice fathers were sometimes lenient toward their rebellious offspring.[64] Although Pollock concedes that Renaissance teachers were occasionally abusive, she points out that not all children suffered corporal punishment at school, and shows that when educators were too severe, some parents intervened.[65]

Steven Ozment asserts that, even in theory, Renaissance discipline was not to be excessively harsh, and though in reality it sometimes was, "both children and adults . . . viewed harsh and arbitrary discipline as exceptional and condemned it, while outright brutality brought firings and fines and even deep personal remorse."[66] Still, Ozment admits that leniency rather than harshness was considered to be "the cardinal sin of child rearing," and asserts that among the duties of childhood, the child's honoring of parental authority and his or her submission to parental commands were high priorities.[67]

Winnicottian theory implies that a society which rewards a child's reverence for, and submission to, authority more highly than the child's self-discovery and self-expression privileges the false self over the true. Also, a society which values maturity more than childlike qualities risks alienating children from themselves. Even if Renaissance parents and educators were not physically abusive, they tended to be very adult-centered as Jean Delumeau asserts:

> In early modern Europe . . . interest in children did not always mean admiration for their freshness or recognition of their otherness— far from it. The schoolmasters . . . did certainly place a high value on education and instruction, but they had only one objective: to shape grown men. Applying adult criteria, they did not reflect on the child's own gradual development.[68]

Parental desire to begin educating children early, teaching such skills as Biblical memorization, reading, and spelling before the age of five, may further illustrate a Renaissance tendency to value children more for their pseudo-adult (false–self) qualities than for themselves.[69]

And of course the need to comply was not a lesson reserved for educated children. Lower-class children, who rarely went to school, had to comply with their masters or risk corporal punishment. It seems likely that Renaissance masters would have even less inclination than educators to empathize with a child's point of view prior to disciplining a child-servant for failure to meet adult needs or desires. And in fact, servants never outgrew the threat of possible beatings, at least so far as the law was concerned.[70]

Grown women also were subject to physical blows from their husbands, who had a legal right to batter them.[71] Renaissance rulers and magistrates meted out physical punishments as well, often torturous ones, to those who broke the law.[72] As Delumeau points out, "executions accompanied by torture were considered to be just so many moral lessons, and children were brought to them so that they would be suitably edified."[73] Such socially acceptable threats of violence could only have underscored in the minds of most Renaissance human beings the necessity of maintaining a false self who could get through life without offending more powerful others.

Even if Stone overgeneralizes about the plight of early modern children, Herbert's poems substantiate Stone's account to some degree. All four of the traumas that Stone discusses are implicit in some Herbert poems. Suspicions that Christ may be a bad mother often hover over the speaker's attempts to establish intimacy with the maternal Christ. If in poems like "Redemption," the empathic Other knows and meets the persona's needs before the speaker can even ask, in poems like "Deniall," Christ waits too long to answer the speaker's cries. In "Longing," infantile fears of abandonment vie with images of Christ as a good-enough mother. Although the speaker approaches Christ as the very "Bowels of pitie," he remains terrified, at one point complaining, "Thou tarriest, while I die, / And fall to nothing" (19, 55–56). Deep annihilation panic evidences real maternal failure, though in this instance the speaker's desperation may be read as transferential, its cause based in previous experience with an other rather than in his present relationship.[74]

The effects of infant swaddling are vividly realized in "Mortification," where the speaker and the prosodic subject figure swaddling as a type of death:

> HOw soon doth man decay!
>   When clothes are taken from a
>   chest of sweets
> To swaddle infants, whose young breath
>   Scarce knows the way;
> Those clouts are little winding sheets,
> Which do consigne and send them unto death.
>
> (1–6)

Helen Vendler argues that the speaker's equation between swaddling and death is subjective and idiosyncratic, certainly not an equation babies, mothers, or nurses would share.[75] Given historical and psychological data about the negative effects of swaddling, the opposite may be the case. The speaker's equation between swaddling and death may emerge from earliest memories, evoking in Herbert's original audience an infantile sense of psychic dying as much as it constitutes a metaphor for the end of life. The running on of the first five lines suggests a degenerative motion, mirroring the speaker's emphasis on decay. Such decay occurs literally after death but can occur psychically in moments of ego disintegration. The winding of the lines images both swaddling bands and "winding sheets." The end stop after the word *death* suggests not only bodily termination but also the arrest of physical movement which results from swaddling.

Throughout *The Temple,* the speaker's preoccupation with death and his fears of separation from the Other suggest that early losses (in the author's case the loss of his father at the age of three and a possible separation from his mother preceding that) affect the speaker later in life.[76] Not only "Mortification," but "Church-monuments," "Grace," and many other poems deal with physical dying and decay in vivid *memento mori* terms; anaclitic depression (an infantile form of mourning) characterizes such poems as "Longing," "Deniall," and "The Search."

Finally, a number of Herbert's poems emphasize God's wrath and power, the Father's inclination (from the speaker's point of view) to break the human will. "Sighs and Grones" and "The Method" are only two examples of the way in which Herbert's speaker sometimes interprets his suffering as evidence of divine punishment. In "Discipline," the speaker recognizes the power of God's "rod" and "wrath" even as he states a preference for "the gentle path" (1, 2, 4). God's inexorable will is the subject of many poems—of "The Search," "The Crosse," and "The Flower" to name only a few examples.

Perhaps the most poignant example of the speaker's fear of God occurs in the first stanza of "Complaining":

> D O not beguile my heart,
> Because thou art
> My power and wisdome. Put me not to shame,
> Because I am
> Thy clay that weeps, thy dust that calls.
>
> (1–5)

When the stanza is considered whole, the reader is only vaguely aware that God might be doing what the speaker asks him not to do. The speaker's argument seems fairly calm, quite rational. The reason that God should not "beguile [the speaker's] heart" (or exploit his true self) is that God is the speaker's power and wisdom.[77] The reason that God should not put the speaker to shame is that the speaker is God's clay and dust, God's creation. But the prosodic subject's line breaks suggest a more painful message. Taken in isolation, the first two lines show the speaker begging God not to betray him simply because God is; lines four and five show the speaker begging God not to shame him simply because the speaker exists. Embedded in the whole, a suffering child assigns existential causes to gratuitous betrayal.

On the other hand, some Herbert poems evidence trust in the Divine parent as well as implicit admiration for childlike attitudes. Leah Marcus points out that some Protestants, especially Anabaptists, and, in England, Anglicans more than Calvinists, embraced a positive outlook on childhood for religious reasons. The Christian imperative to become as a little child to some degree ameliorated the harshness of adult attitudes toward immaturity.[78] Certainly this seems to be the case in Herbert's "H. Baptisme" (II), a poem in which the speaker prays to be as innocent as he was when he was baptized:

> O let me still
> Write thee great God, and me a childe:
> Let me be soft and supple to thy will,
> Small to my self, to others milde,
> Behither ill.
>
> (6–10)

Though compliance to God's will is the goal, the speaker's words imply not a rigidly fixed, depraved human will to be broken by divine punishment but an organic softness, the suppleness of an infantile self who can be molded to fit the Divine plan.

The antithesis is articulated by John Donne's speaker in "Holy Sonnet XIV":

> Batter my heart, three person'd God; for, you
> As yet but knocke, breathe, shine, and seeke to mend;
> That I may rise, and stand, o'erthrow mee, 'and bend
> Your force, to breake, blowe, burn and make me new.
>
> (1–4)

Herbert's speaker believes that his infantile (true) self, once baptized and freed from the bondage of original sin, is the form of subjectivity to which he should aspire. Donne's speaker, on the other hand, believes that no trace of potential goodness exists in him to be revitalized. Thus Herbert's speaker prays to be restored to his childhood state, whereas Donne's prays to be broken and made new. These differing desires are expressed on the poems' prosodic levels as well. Donne's overstressed lines strain against the limits of sonnet form, mimetically suggesting the struggle of the fallen will against Divine force. Herbert's prosody seems supple, with variable line lengths and a comparatively smooth cadence, mimetically suggesting a cooperative relationship between the true self and Divine grace.[79]

Of course it is not sonnet form per se, but the interplay between conventional sonnet form and the form of Donne's particular sonnet which creates mimetic effects suggestive of a struggle. Like Donne's sonnet, Herbert's fifteen-line poem establishes and often departs from an iambic base meter. But perhaps in part because Herbert's nonce form defines itself in the process of its development, prosodic substitutions operate differently within the two poems.

Metrically speaking, Donne's sonnet begins with a trochaic substitution; the rhythm is reversed by an iamb in the second foot, then thrown again into arrears by a spondee in the third before the first line ends on two iambs. Extreme substitution so early in the poem prosodically mimes God's battering of the verse, which, like Herbert's, may be read as representing the speaker's "heart." Line two proceeds primarily by an accumulation of verbs; although the third foot ("breathe, shine") may be resolved as an iamb, a spondaic heaviness nevertheless echoes in this sensitive mid-line position. Line three does "rise, and stand" in its first three iambic feet, but a spondaic (or near spondaic) substitution in the fourth foot and an anapest in the fifth "o'erthrow" the tenuously established rising meter and, along with strong enjambment, "bend" the line into the next. The fourth line embodies "force" with a further accumulation of strong, monosyllabic verbs which overload the quatrain with stressed (or stressable) syllables, suggesting violence.

Herbert's second stanza begins with a short, iambic line. In the first half of its second line (line 7 of the poem), the only overstressed phrase of the stanza suggests the magnitude of God's greatness; this rhythmic effect is balanced by an easy return to the iambic norm in the second half of the line. The stanza's third line (line 8) begins with a stressed syllable, as does its fourth (line 9). Given that each of these lines is preceded by an interlinear pause which may be counted as an unstressed syllable, these initial stresses may be read as truncated iambs, followed by anapests. Alternatively, the first foot of each line may be read as an initial trochaic substitution, rendered more graceful by the pause which precedes it and by the transition it facilitates from one line length to another.

If one extends the notion of prosodic subjectivity to Donne's stanza, the experience of Donne's prosodic subject is a desperate case: intense desire frustrated by violent constraint, whether that constraint is to be understood as coming from the Divine Other or as registering the subjective experience of a prosodic (bodily) self who anticipates being battered, broken, undone. In contrast, Herbert's prosodic subject exists in a nonrestrictive prosodic environment (metaphorically a holding environment). This environment allows for freedom of movement and self-expression, for a formal dance that can change a little line by line. At the same time, the rhymes (*ababa*), the symmetrical crescendo and decrescendo of line lengths (counting feet: 24542) and the stanzaic consistency within the poem as a whole indicate that God is holding the prosodic subject, keeping this persona together as a coherent affective and bodily whole.

As a persona whose psychic and physical processes are closely linked, the prosodic subject in Herbert's poems may be said to enact the true self. However, the I-speaker of "H. Baptisme" (II) remains oblivious to the fact. As the poem's last stanza makes clear, the speaker does not ultimately believe that his true self can be embodied in a fallen world:

> Although by stealth
> My flesh get on, yet let her sister
> My soul bid nothing, but preserve her wealth:
> The growth of flesh is but a blister;
> Childhood is health.
>
> (11–15)

While the Winnicottian true self, like Herbert's prosodic subject, is the self in and of the body, the true self for whom Herbert's speaker prays is the "soul," apart from the "flesh." Perhaps here as elsewhere, the speaker follows Luther in construing the Pauline dichotomy between flesh and spirit as a division not between two parts of the self (material body and immaterial soul) but between two selves (the self born of the flesh and the self born of the Spirit—the soul).[80] The Lutheran idea might explain why the poem's speaker implies that the "soul" is distinguishable from the "flesh" as two sisters are distinguishable from each other—as separate personalities.

But if the I-speaker thinks of his soul as a child cut off from the growth of the flesh, it makes little difference whether *flesh* means the body or the worldly personality or both. In either case, the speaker is a man divided against himself; the "soul" is a merely potential true self. Furthermore, we oversimplify the issue if we agree too quickly with the speaker that the false self of the poem is the "flesh." In seeking to disavow part of his experience as "not-me," (or as "but a blister"), the speaker employs a false-self strategy. Thus, the false self of the poem is the speaking "I," who seeks in the context of a relationship with God to repudiate a part of himself different from that he apparently repudiated in growing up.[81] As a false self, he still hopes to protect his true self from exploitation, praying that his soul will take no risks, will "bid nothing, but preserve her wealth." Meanwhile, the prosodic subject risks being exposed not only to the Divine Other but also, at another level, to the poem's reader.

Given the configuration of relationships in Renaissance England, if the Other addressed were anyone but God, the result of the speaker's petition might be the displacement of one false self by another. However, as the author of the true self, the God of *The Temple* has the capacity to help actualize the true self *through* the false self's defense of compliance. In submitting to

his creator, the Herbertian subject (a whole person usually split
into two agencies: the speaker and the prosodic subject) discovers who he really is, and, contrary to the expectations the
speaker articulates in "H. Baptisme" (II), he begins to express
his true self more in some poems, as I will argue. Legitimate
authority thus undoes the damage done by parental or political
authoritarianism.[82]

Of course, to psychoanalyze the text in these terms, we must
enter into the text's mythos. From another angle, one might
argue that George Herbert's representation of the self-Other relationship is a function of two historically determined factors:
first, the experiences with others the historical author had—
experiences we can only glean from our understanding of the
relational models available in the British Renaissance and from
rather scanty biographical evidence; second, the experiences
with an Other the historical author needed or desired, needs or
desires the expressions of which we may locate in Herbert's
poems and the understanding of which we can derive from psy-
choanalyzing relationships among the speaker, the prosodic
subject, and God (each representing some part of Herbert's psyche) within the relational matrices of historical Renaissance
society.[83]

Must postulating a correlation between Herbert's needs and
Herbert's understanding of God compromise the reader's capacity to understand Herbert's faith on its own terms? Not necessarily. Rene Pascal argues that within every human being, there is
a God-shaped vacuum. George Herbert might well have agreed.
Some twentieth-century readers will prefer to say that within
many human beings there are vacuums (needs of various types)
which shape various personal and cultural understandings of
God. In either case, God may be defined as the Other who is
needed to fulfill the self. Herbert's God may be understood to
function in relation to the Herbertian subject much as a Winnicottian psychoanalyst might. He takes over the protective (essentially parental) function of the false self in order to facilitate the
emergence of the true self.

III

Before examining the relational dynamic whereby the Divine
Other reclaims the Herbertian true self, I want to establish the
significance of the true self's emergence more fully by analyzing

skepticism about true selves in Renaissance literature generally
and *The Temple* in particular. To further the case for the existence of a false-self dilemma in Herbert's poems, I will note, in
passing, evidence of the I-speaker's sense of unreality, his sense
of being divided, his sense of alienation from the body, and his
compliant approach to authority, especially God's. More intriguing questions will arise. How is the false self/true self relationship enacted in the interplay between content and form in *The
Temple?* How can the true self's appearance be reconciled with
the speaker's false-self agenda of keeping the true self hidden?
For that matter, given that false-self establishment precedes any
opportunity for true-self liberation by centuries in the history
of Western civilization, how does a true self ever escape the
prison of its ideologically sanctioned and experientially verified
sense of unreality to establish a cooperative model of relationships among human agents believed to be "created equal" and
"endowed by their creator with certain inalienable rights?"

As Jean Delumeau asserts, in the early modern age, "there
existed a widespread belief in a mysterious force far stronger
than human liberty and more inclined to oppose than to favor
it."[84] The problem is not merely that "life, liberty, and the pursuit
of happiness" took centuries for Western "man" to articulate as
rights (and centuries more for other men and for women to
claim). It is that an experience of self *as* alive, as a potentially
free agent capable of fulfillment, had first to be retrieved from
rejected infantile selves whose emergence was never facilitated
by historical others.[85] How can the experience of aliveness be
wrung from a human existence characterized by misery and
self-abnegation?

A well-known scene in Shakespeare's *King Lear* offers one
possible answer. "Thy life's a miracle" says Edgar to his father
after foiling Gloucester's attempted suicide (IV.vi.55). Unlike the
character himself, the audience knows that Gloucester has not
truly leapt from Dover Cliff, spared only by the gods. But
Gloucester's resulting sense of life *as* miracle, his sense of *being
alive,* is a genuine wonder after all he has been through, even
though we recognize it as the explicable psychological consequence of his son's imaginative intervention. After all, that intervention is itself scripted by no less a mystery than
unconditional human love. One implication of the scene is that
the gods need not exist as ontological fact in order to perform
miracles. Faith is a sufficient cause for the human experience
of grace.

Something like grace is essential for the true self to emerge in human history. Not only historical but also psychological forces against the liberation of true selves render their historical emergence remarkable even as biological and psychological forces within human beings render the event inevitable. Winnicott points out that a sense of individuality feels dangerous to newly established selves. He explains this insight with reference to the ancient Hebrew name for God, Yahweh:

> Does not this name (I AM) given to God reflect the danger that the individual feels he or she is in on reaching the state of individual being? If I am, then I have gathered together this and that and have claimed it as me, and I have repudiated everything else; in repudiating the not-me I have, so to speak, insulted the world, and I must expect to be attacked. So when people first came to the concept of individuality, they quickly put it up in the sky and gave it a voice that only a Moses could hear.[86]

From this perspective, people first projected their sense of being onto an omnipotent God, who could defend the right. Later people began to view individual being as a right God had given to them. Historians often attribute this change in historical Western consciousness to the Reformation. They sometimes fail to note the degree of ambivalence with which the insight was greeted by some people of the day.[87]

The terror Winnicott describes may explain why a number of Renaissance texts subvert the notion of a true self even as they espouse it. One of the more outspoken advocates for the true self in Renaissance literature is Shakespeare's Polonius, who advises his son Laertes, "This above all: to thine own self be true, / And it shall follow as the night the day, / Thou canst not then be false to any man" (*Hamlet* I.iii.78–80).[88] The irony of the advice is readily apparent. Polonius is the epitome of a false self. His deferential attitude characterizes both his behavior and his perceptions, at least as he reports them. If the prince sees the image of a whale in a cloud, the cloud looks "Very like a whale," according to Polonius (III.ii.382). Thus Polonius' character undermines his claims. As an unselfconscious false self communicates the sincerest of aphorisms, the text registers profound skepticism about the true self.[89]

If Polonius' bluster is not enough to discredit the wisdom of being true, another notorious advocate for the true self in Renaissance literature is Milton's Satan, who, on finding himself in hell, meets his fate with bravado: "What matter where if I be still the same, / And what I should be, all but less than hee / Whom Thunder hath made greater?" (*Paradise Lost* I.256–58) Satan is the true self damned for narcissistic assertiveness against an authoritarian Other. Even after his fall, he remains self-satisfied, elated by the delusion of self-sufficiency: "The mind is its own place and in itself / Can make a Heav'n of Hell, a Hell of Heav'n" (I.254–55) Yet before long, Satan realizes the tragedy of being who he is:

> Which way I fly is Hell; myself am Hell;
> And in the lowest deep a lower deep
> Still threat'ning to devour me opens wide,
> To which the Hell I suffer seems a Heav'n.
>
> (IV.75–78)

While in *Hamlet,* Polonius' advocacy of the true self underscores his folly, in *Paradise Lost,* Satan's assertion of the true self epitomizes his evil.

As these examples illustrate, in Renaissance literature, "To be, or not to be" is a very big question (*Hamlet* III.i, 55). In asking it, Hamlet hedges on the verge of the only answer genuinely available to him. Unlike Ophelia, Hamlet has little hope for self-cancellation through suicide. Once he has been confronted by his father's ghost, Hamlet must face both the horror of Old Hamlet's death, which makes existence intolerable, and the specter of human immortality, which renders it inevitable: "For in that sleep of death what dreams may come, / When we have shuffled off this mortal coil, / Must give us pause" (III.i, 65–67). "To be, or not to be" is not merely a rhetorical question, however. It is the crux of Hamlet's dilemma, psychologically speaking. If only the apparition were *not* real, if only Hamlet *were* mad, if only Horatio and others were merely humoring him in claiming to share the perception, Hamlet could escape. But Hamlet's subsequent experiment of acting as if mad proves to be mere play, not the refuge of a true and stable identity which, though in itself undesirable, might be preferable to the certainty that things *are* as bad as they seem. In *Hamlet,* tragedy lurks where appearance and reality intersect. If the ghost is real, Hamlet must *be,* and if Hamlet *is,* Hamlet must act. Rather he must enact the tragic destiny of a true self doomed to emerge and take his stand in a dysfunctional milieu.[90]

In "Sinnes round," Herbert's I-speaker feels similarly trapped in the inescapable reality of his own being, though in his case the dilemma seems less tragic than absurd:

Sorrie I am, my God, sorrie I am,
That my offences course it in a ring.
My thoughts are working like a busie flame,
Untill their cockatrice they hatch and bring:
And when they once have perfected their draughts,
My words take fire from my inflamed thoughts.

My words take fire from my inflamed thoughts,
Which spit it forth like the Sicilian Hill.
They vent the wares, and passe them with their faults,
And by their breathing ventilate the ill.
But words suffice not, where are lewd intentions:
My hands do joyn to finish the inventions.

My hands do joyn to finish the inventions:
And so my sinnes ascend three stories high,
As Babel grew, before there were dissensions.
Yet ill deeds loyter not: for they supplie
New thoughts of sinning: wherefore, to my shame,
Sorrie I am, my God, sorrie I am.

The first line, repeated as the last line, frames the poem with
multiple possible meanings. Perhaps the speaker is saying "I am
sorry" twice to God for reasons not yet specified. Or maybe he
is saying "I am sorry [that] I am my God". Alternatively, he may
be apologizing (twice) to the God whose name means "I am."[91]
All of these readings may in fact be simultaneously operative.
Two other meanings seem equally compelling. First, the speaker
is apologizing for his very existence. ("My God, I am sorry—
sorry [that] I am.") Yet surely to apologize to one's creator for
one's existence is itself sinful. Thus, particularly the second time
the line comes round, the speaker is apologizing for the apology.
("My God, I am sorry [that] I am sorry.") The reader may arrive
at the same meaning by an alternative route. In the last two
lines of the poem, it is "to [the speaker's] shame" that he is sorry
(that he is), so he apologizes for it.

As the second line of the poem makes clear, the speaker is
sorry furthermore "That [his] offences course it"—both the fact
that he is and the fact that he is sorry—"in a ring." He is sorry
for the expression of himself. In subsequent lines, the speaker
represents himself as the passive witness of an uncontrollable
progression from internal to external manifestations of self:
thoughts, words, deeds. The "ill deeds" he renounces are not
ordinary deeds but "inventions"—poems, especially the one the
speaker's thoughts and words are now authoring against the

speaker's will. But the speaker is himself an invention in another sense.

The speaker is a false self first because he is self-repudiating and second because his will is the byproduct of his self-reflection on actions fueled by impulses which seem to originate in the "not-me" sector of the personality (that is, in the disavowed true self). The speaker's will is reactive rather than active. When the existence he is sorry for asserts itself in the apology, he reacts by apologizing further. Except for the apology, no sentence in the entire poem is predicated on "I," a subject which, if it were attached to a verb of doing rather than being, would assert personal agency.[92] This speaker does nothing; his actions do themselves to him. He watches in horror as his "offences course" (direct the course of and sing a chorus about) his being and his being sorry.[93] He stands helplessly by as his thoughts work "like a busie flame," and as his words take fire from them. Although the speaker claims the thoughts and words as "my thoughts" and "my words," he simultaneously disclaims them in relegating them to a realm outside his self-control. Even his hands join in the conspiracy against his impossible desire: to will himself out of existence, to be and not to be at the same time.

Ordinarily, the true self watches as the false self performs deeds which comply with the will of others. Here, the Other, if present, is devastatingly silent.[94] In the absence of externality, in the absence of anything to react to but the self, the false self projects himself into the site of the Other to watch and criticize the true self, who, temporarily split off from the false self, becomes extremely, almost irreverently, playful. The speaker's dire self-perpetuating attempt at symbolic self-cancellation, the blackest of unintended humor, gets driven by and parodied in the prosodic subject's round, a form as obsessively repetitious and circular as the speaker's irrationality warrants.[95]

True to the requirements of the form, the prosodic subject repeats the last line of each stanza in the first line of the next and the first line of the poem in the last line, thus folding the poem vertically into a circle. But in "Sinnes round," the circle also forms along the horizontal axis, as the first and last lines circle sideways back on themselves.[96] This circularity, paralleled at the discursive level by the cockatrice image, seems contradictory to the straight and upward image of erecting Babel. But perhaps not. As Janis Lull points out, Herbert's image of Babel may have been, like Brueghel's, an image of a tower which spirals upward.[97]

Other spatial effects in the poem are more disorienting, however. The speaker's "sinnes ascend three stories high" only as
the prosodic subject's round descends three stanzas down. The
idea of descent as well as dissent is evoked by the equivocal word
"dissensions" in line fifteen. Both "dissensions" and "ascend"
may also pun on the word *sin,* so that, somewhere amidst the
unending reverberations the poem insistently sets up, the
reader may mishear: "And so my sins have sinned three stories
high / As Babel grew, before there were de-sin-sions."[98] In either
case, one level of the text reverses the other; the tower is raised
and razed at once, though only so that the whole process can
recommence.[99] In the last line, the prosodic subject not only
ends the round but also, along with the speaker's "new thoughts
of sinning," teases the speaker-as-reader of this self/text back to
the beginning. How "new" the next round will seem is entirely
disputable.

A poem in many ways antithetical to "Sinnes round" is "Coloss
3.3," a poem which also explores a divided self:

> *My* words & thoughts do both expresse this notion,
> That *Life* hath with the sun a double motion.
> The first *Is* straight, and our diurnall friend,
> The   other   *Hid*   and   doth   obliquely   bend.
> One life is wrapt *In* flesh, and tends to earth:
> The other winds toward *Him,* whose happie birth
> Taught me to live here so, *That* still one eye
> Should aim and shoot at that which *Is* on high:
> Quitting   with   daily   labour   all   *My*   pleasure,
> To   gain   at   harvest   an   eternall   *Treasure.*

Here the speaker's "words & thoughts" comfort more than ter-
rify him, assuring him that while one life, one self—line seven
suggests one "I"—is merely flesh and destined for the grave, another "winds" upward toward the Divine Other.[100] The circle of
Being here is outwardly focused, revolving around the "Son"
(metaphorically, perhaps, the sun) rather than the self (earth).[101]
Thus the false self speaker repudiates not existence itself but
the life of flesh. As a false self, he continues to protect and hide
the self he perceives as true.

From the false self's point of view, true selfhood is possible
but deferred. Life in this world is false, unreal in that it leads
to death. The true self is disembodied potential which can be
actualized only "on high." But perhaps the poem as a whole
contradicts the speaker's claims, for, in it, the true self gains

material reality by being textualized. The true self's existence is encoded in the midst of the speaker's words. While the speaker's message, the poem *as* speech, is highly rhetorical—a careful deliberation on the two sides of his claim—the hidden message minces no words. It is singular and direct. As a message which no speaker enunciates, it is the unarticulated truth hidden in a body of words, one determined by the interplay of rhetoric and form.

One may argue that these hidden words have obviously been put carefully into place and the speaker's text has been written around them. Hence, the message I am calling "true" is produced within the text by a deliberate and artful contrivance. I concede the point. But the speaker's text, in relation to the encoded message, *is* that contrivance. In the same way that a false self is created around the true self, who is both protected and imprisoned by it, the speaker's text is created around the Bible verse. Thus the Bible verse is not only "the core or heart of the poem," as William B. Bache describes it; it is also the representation of the core or heart of the self.[102]

Other factors also suggest that the text/pretext relationship in this poem is the representational equivalent of a false self/true self relationship. Although in actuality the true self precedes the false, the false self appears first to an observer, and the true self, if it appears at all, must be discovered. Like the Bible verse, the true self is not self-invented, though the true self is individual as Herbert's changing *our* to *my* suggests.[103] The only real paradox here is that, in this context, the true self is truly the Other's creation. Hence, the "Word" of the Other, hidden in and explicated by the false self's words, genuinely articulates the true self's reality.[104]

In "Coloss 3.3," a true self is made to exist in words by the interplay of rhetoric and form. More often, the true self in Herbert's poems exists as form—shape, motion, affective resonance—rather than in words. One poem which can be read as dramatizing the true self / false self relationship in the interaction between form and content is "A Wreath," a poem in many ways comparable to "Coloss. 3.3" and "Sinnes round."[105] While in "Sinnes round" the false self turns inward, horrified at the life which erupts, like a volcano, at the core of his being, in "A Wreath," as in "Coloss. 3.3.," the false self turns outward, orienting himself in relation to the Other. But while in "Coloss 3.3," the circle of transcendent Being is positive in comparison to the time-bound (linear) life of flesh, in "A Wreath," as in "Sinnes

round," the speaker renounces the circle in which he finds himself. Like "Sinnes round," the poem circles back on itself formally as well as discursively. But in this case the circle is one of
doing rather than being, and therefore seems less vicious:

> A Wreathed garland of deserved praise,
> Of praise deserved, unto thee I give,
> I give to thee, who knowest all my wayes,
> My crooked winding wayes, wherein I live,
> Wherein I die, not live: for life is straight,
> Straight as a line, and ever tends to thee,
> To thee, who art more farre above deceit,
> Then deceit seems above simplicitie.
> Give me simplicitie, that I may live,
> So live and like, that I may know, thy wayes,
> Know them and practise them: then shall I give
> For this poore wreath, give thee a crown of praise.

The circle of doing differs from the circle of being in "Sinnes
round" in one very important respect. Although the speaker of
"A Wreath" renounces his "crooked, winding wayes," he also
feels himself to be the author of them, the "I" who gives, lives,
dies, knows, and so forth. But despite his sense of personal
agency, the speaker is not self-propelled. In Judy Z. Kronenfeld's
words, he is "more led than leading."[106] As the true self is the
source of a false self's energy, so here prosody is the prime mover
of the speaker's words. As prosodic motion winds and rewinds
the speaker's thoughts, sometimes untangling them in the process, the speaker is translated to himself.[107] Ultimately he is revealed as false, as not living but dying through his own agency.
"Life"—a disembodied abstraction—is "Straight as a line" and
aimed always toward the Other, who authors better ways. In the
second half of the poem, the speaker prays to know and practice
God's ways, to comply with his creator. Thus the speaker progresses from a sense of autonomous agency to a sense of absolute
dependence on God.[108]

Meanwhile, the prosodic subject completes the circle. As the
last half of each line is recapitulated in the first half of the next,
so the last line of the poem is recapitulated if the first line is
repeated; hence, form dictates that the poem recommence. Furthermore, the end words of the last four lines repeat in reverse
order the end words of the first four, forming a circle glued together by the repetition. The beginning and the end is "praise,"
praise of the Other. "My wayes" circle and merge with "thy wayes"

through rhyme.[109] Thus, through the workings of the prosodic subject, even "crooked winding wayes" are transformed.[110] While the false-self speaker renounces his deceitful acts in favor of simplicity, the prosodic subject's form as accomplished artifact exists in a state of perpetual motion, suggesting perhaps that unending doing in respect to the Other is a way of being eternally in relation to the Other. Being and doing, desire and capacity, merge as the prosodic subject prays without ceasing.

We may summarize and analyze the form/content relation in "A Wreath" as follows. Form as a teleological process, like a potential true self, is the source of the speaker's energy. Form as a product, like an emergent true self, becomes an agency (the prosodic subject) who exists and operates in his/her own right. As potential, form precedes; as product, it emerges from and goes on being after the speaker's enunciation. Both cause and effect, prosody exists in a doubly paradoxical relation to the speaker's words: it is manifested through them yet contradictory to them, circling back in a self-perpetuating motion as the speaker's voice dies on a note of self-cancellation.[111]

I am implying that in "A Wreath" the true self emerges *through* the false self's surrender to the Other. But how can a false self's compliance lead to a true self's liberation? If Herbert's God were an authoritarian Other—like Milton's, like Calvin's—it could not. The circle of form, if it were allowed to stand, would be sinful and idolatrous, a manifestation of a self who *should* be canceled. Many critics read "A Wreath" in this fashion, of course, and the poem does not shut out the possibility.[112] But neither does it preclude the alternative reading I am suggesting: the speaker is a false self, who, in compliance to the Other, seeks to renounce himself; he renounces himself as false; he renounces all actions of the self; he renounces the very renunciation. Meanwhile, the prosodic subject becomes an actualized true self who synthesizes being and doing in respect to the Other. The continuing existence of the artifact suggests that the false self is right in renouncing himself as false, but mistaken in renouncing the self altogether.

What does the emergence of this true self suggest about the psychological function of Christianity for some believers during the Reformation? Let me here suggest the answer I will develop further in pages to come. Psychoanalyst Erich Fromm points out that authoritarian religion—like Calvin's—completely devalues the human self, projecting all narcissistic libido onto the Other. This process leaves believers fixated, never transcending the nar-

cissistic position of passive adulation for an omnipotent Other.
As the Other arbitrarily and gratuitously confers value on the
self, his attentions make the self feel special in relation to most
other selves, who remain completely worthless and degraded.[113]
As I will argue, the self-Other relationship in *The Temple* is the
ground of a more constructive mode of being a self in relation
to others. Though the Herbertian subject regresses to a stage
prior to full blown secondary narcissism, to the stage of absolute
dependence or primary narcissism, the regression operates to
the end of growth rather than fixation. The empathic Other uses
the false self's submission as an opportunity to empower the
true self. Genuine compromise with and charity toward others
become possible precisely because the true self is not effaced.
The new Adam emerges as a socially responsible, true self. In
the words of Herbert's speaker, the Herbertian self becomes, "He
that doth still and strongly good pursue, / To God his neighbour
and himself most true." ("Constancie," 2–3, italics mine).

IV

Herbert's critics have traditionally claimed that Herbert's
speaker tends on the whole to isolate himself from the Baconian
marketplace. Although the speaker maps out a detailed social
agenda in "The Church-porch," makes multiple (often deroga-
tory) references to the ways of the world in "The Church," and
treats Christian history in "The Church Militant," the historical
context sometimes recedes for Herbert's readers as we journey
with the persona deeper and deeper into the recesses of the
heart.

But in spite of the speaker's isolation, Herbert's text is far
from being ahistorical. Object relations theory suggests that isolation does not ordinarily separate the individual from society
in an experiential sense. Psychologically speaking, others live
in each of us; history lives in each of us; we embody previous
experience not only in our interactions with each other but also
in our experience of ourselves. Thus, as several recent critics
have perceived, Herbert's speaker brings Renaissance social conventions to bear on his relationship to God.[114] I will add to their
insight my argument that the God of *The Temple* does not

merely participate in these conventions; Herbert's God rewrites the relationship in the service of the true self.

The process whereby Christ redeems the Herbertian subject parallels the clinical treatment of false self organization that Winnicott describes. At first, the false self attempts to conceal the true self. The therapist exposes the false self as false. Next, forming an alliance with the therapist, the false self reveals the true self. The therapist convinces the false self to relinquish its control and, to all effects and purposes, takes over the role of primary parent to the true self. Finally, the true self emerges in the holding environment which the clinical setting symbolically provides. The false self takes its place in the service of the true.[115]

These stages do not necessarily develop *as* stages in Herbert's poems, of course. Not only do we have no certainty which poems were written early and which late in Herbert's poetic development; the poems, as ordered in the Bodleian manuscript and the 1633 edition (the ordering followed by Hutchinson) do not always shape a consistent progression toward true-self discovery if we consider them as a sequence.[116] Furthermore, a single Herbert poem sometimes depicts more than one of the tendencies outlined in Winnicott's theory. But the muddling of a clinical model need not present a great obstacle. In spite of the fact that no consistent progression from being false to being true maintains in *The Temple,* one may look to "Perirrhanterium," near the beginning of the manuscript, to glimpse the false-self defense at its strongest. I will consider only a few poems here, ending with a discussion of "Love" (III), near the end of Herbert's manuscript. I will deal with other examples and further consider the social implications of this psychic rescripting in another chapter.

The speaker of "Perirrhanterium" is the false self par excellence in that he successfully conceals the true self from himself. Concerning himself with morals and manners alike, he implicitly assumes that all laws are equally binding.[117] His is a mindset governed by the imperative mode, enamored of sententiousness, and singlemindedly determined that all questions be framed rhetorically, leaving for an answer merely the obvious. His diagnosis of the human condition characterizes his approach to himself and others: "Man is a shop of rules, a well truss'd pack, / Whose every parcell under-writes a law" (141–42).

Like Polonius, this speaker preaches the text "Dare to be true" in the voice of a false self (77).[118] More specifically he preaches, "Lie not; but let thy heart be true to God, / Thy mouth to it, thy actions to them both" (73–74). He recommends the synthesis of being, speaking, and doing, of feeling, word, and action, which only a true self could manage. This message contradicts his other advice: to repress certain feelings (not only lust but also mirth), to prohibit some forms of speech (oaths, incautious witticisms), and to keep one's interactions with others inside very narrow confines.[119]

If the speaker were a conscious hypocrite, he would be far more sophisticated than Chaucer's Pardoner. But nothing at the discursive level indicates deliberate hypocrisy. Rather, the speaker is utterly sincere and absurdly oblivious of his own duplicity. Believing as he does in the rightness of his principles, he cares little whether they proceed from within or from without, even advising his protege—a young man whom he seeks to fashion falsely after himself—always to "Think the king sees thee still; for his King does"—always to act with reference to external authority, maintaining the sense of an other's surveillance to keep the self under control (122).[120]

Meanwhile, the prosodic subject alludes with the Venus and Adonis stanza to a less disciplined way of being, embodying the lustiness and mirth which the speaker has successfully repressed. Also, if construed in relation to the speaker as a true self in relation to a false self, prosody exists as evidence that the speaker cannot follow his own directives: "Lose not thy self, nor give thy humours way" (143). Prosody represents the self the speaker has all but lost, certainly one over whom he has lost control. As the false self focuses on another, he lets down his internal guard; the prosodic subject seizes the opportunity to "give . . . humours way." *Humours* refers to the passions, which, according to medieval physiology, arise from the composition of bodily fluids. As the self who expresses humours, the prosodic subject mediates between the body and the soul.

Many other poems in *The Temple* play on the subtleties of the false self's devices as he seeks to avoid self-disclosure before God. A particularly interesting example occurs in the final stanza of "Ungratefulnesse." Addressing a God who has graciously revealed himself through "two rare cabinets full of treasure, / The *Trinitie,* and *Incarnation*," the speaker evades the vulnerability self-revelation might entail by projecting his faults outside of himself onto generic man (7–8):

> But man is close, reserv'd, and dark to thee:
>> When thou demandest but a heart,
>> He cavils instantly.
>> In his poore cabinet of bone
>> Sinnes have their box apart,
> Defrauding thee, who gavest two for one.

>   (25–30)

In its purest manifestation, projection enables one to attribute to another that which one refuses to see in oneself; this defense parallels, in the intersubjective domain, the false self's intrapsychic tendency to repudiate part of the self as "not me." Here the speaker's paradoxical self-indictment is less mistakable than in typical cases.[121] But even so, his deflective, impersonal rhetoric obscures the reality he acknowledges elsewhere: "My God, I mean my self" ("Miserie," 78). By dwelling on moral proclamation rather than felt experience, the speaker refuses to reveal his own "heart" (metonymically the true self) to God. Hence he remains "close" (meaning closed) "reserved" and "dark," equivocating even as he discusses man's fraudulent tendencies. Revealing himself, he remains concealed; thus he enacts the very sin that he is deriding.

In "Dialogue," the speaker enacts the tendency to withhold himself from his "Sweetest Saviour" more directly, arguing with ironic politeness that his "soul" (the true self) is not "worth the having" (1, 2). The speaker is the aspect of the self who could "controll / Any thought of waving," if only he could be convinced of his worthiness (3). He is clearly a false self, who operates on the basis of intellect or understanding rather than desire. Addressing this persona as "Child," Christ assures him that his value (though not based on merit) is clear to God even if it cannot be made clear to the speaker himself (9).[122] The false self more complies with than concedes to the Other, resigning to a "reason" and a "way" he cannot understand (21, 22).[123] In the last few lines, Christ discusses all he has gone through to effect the self's salvation; the speaker interrupts Christ's recounting of how Christ once "Left all joyes to feel all smart" with the exclamation, "Ah! no more: thou break'st my heart" (31–32). Attending to the Other, the speaker feels empathy for the very sort of pain that a false self is designed to defend against. In "Dialogue," it is more than he can handle.

In the absence of an Other interested in calling forth the true self, the speaker of these poems might never overcome his own defenses. "Love" (III) depicts the way in which the Christ of *The Temple* gently pressures the Herbertian false self to recognize himself as false. The Christ of the poem is the good-enough mother of *The Temple*, a primary parent whose agenda is to facilitate the emergence of the true self:[124]

> L Ove bade me welcome: yet my soul drew back,
>   Guiltie of dust and sinne.
> But quick-ey'd Love, observing me grow slack
>   From my first entrance in,
> Drew nearer to me, sweetly questioning,
>   If I lack'd any thing.
>
> A guest, I answer'd, worthy to be here:
>   Love said, You shall be he.
> I the unkinde, ungratefull? Ah my deare,
>   I cannot look on thee.
> Love took my hand, and smiling did reply,
>   Who made the eyes but I?
>
> Truth Lord, but I have marr'd them: let my shame
>   Go where it doth deserve.
> And know you not, sayes Love, who bore the blame?
>   My deare, then I will serve.
> You must sit down, sayes Love, and taste my meat:
>   So I did sit and eat.

In the first stanza, as the speaking self makes his entrance, the soul withdraws. The spatial tension of this simultaneous approach and withdrawal reflects a degree of self-division.[125] Of course, the speaker (a false self) and his soul (a potential true self) are not fully separate. Although the soul is the one who feels "Guiltie of dust and sinne," and thus the one whose attitude determines bodily posture, the speaker himself "grow[s] slack." But although they share the same body, their roles do differ somewhat. The speaker shows the "respective boldnesse" toward a superior which he prescribes in "Perirrhanterium" (253). As the false self, he speaks on behalf of the true self, who is freed to shy away from the Other.

The prosodic subject more mimes than resolves the approach-withdrawal conflict in the poem. Line lengths alternate between pentameter and trimeter lines, perhaps to indicate the contrast between boldness and slackening. As the speaker mentions his soul's hesitancy at the end of line one, the final spondee ("drew back") suspends the rhythmic flow, necessitating a pronounced interlinear pause before the next stress falls at the onset of line two. The prosodic subject hesitates. But in line four, prosody also accentuates the speaker's eagerness to proceed. As the speaker refers to his "entrance in," the stresses fall enthusiastically on the side of moving "in" rather than back.

While in other poems, the prosodic subject agrees or disagrees with the speaker, in this poem, prosody confirms the split between the speaking "I" and the soul. Prosody mimes the ambivalence which cannot be resolved within the self. Only the Other can determine which of the competing desires holds sway. Love is "quick-eyed" enough to notice the bodily sign of hesitation and compassionate enough to settle the matter. Rather than telling the speaker what to do, Christ draws nearer, indicating through his own body language that the initial welcome was sincere.

In fact, throughout the poem, a maternal Christ communicates as much through the language of the body as through words. Christ not only observes and responds to the initial unarticulated quandary, himself taking action when the persona is paralyzed; his voice questions "sweetly," encouraging the speaker to let down his guard. When the speaker feels unable to maintain eye contact, Love takes his hand to reestablish a connection. At that point the speaker is freed to notice that the Other is smiling. Ultimately, Love concludes the physical transaction by feeding the self. This dumb show speaks to the inarticulate true self.[126]

If the physical transaction empathetically responds to the soul, the verbal transaction addresses the need of the false self to recognize himself as false and to relinquish his self-control. Christ's questioning whether the speaker lacks anything is precisely the right line of inquiry, therapeutically speaking.[127] According to Winnicott, the psychoanalyst in a similar dialogue must at some point indicate what the false self symbolically lacks (to quote Winnicott, "You have no mouth").[128] Here Love draws the answer out of the speaking self.

The speaker does not initially claim that he lacks a particular thing or part, but a whole identity; he lacks (because he *is* not) a worthy guest. Rather than arguing that the speaker *is* worthy, Christ indicates, "You shall be he." The future tense suggests that the actualization of the true (or worthy) self has yet to take place. Not getting the point, the false-self speaker continues to assert his (false-self) inadequacies. He lacks not only an "I," but "eyes" worthy to look on his Lord. Christ's response plays on the same words, since as creator he made human selves as well as human eyes.[129]

The speaker's request, "Let my shame go where it doth deserve" is pure false-self mannerism. Surely he does not mean, "Please let me go to hell."[130] Rather, deference has become so automatic that the speaker no longer processes the meaning of his words; he performs his lines on cue. The imperative to be polite completely undermines even unenlightened self-interest, constructing a verbal reflex that has no basis whatsoever in internal reality.[131]

Reminded that Love has already borne the blame, the speaker furthers his false-self agenda by offering to serve. This response, an inappropriate one under the circumstances, may also be automatic, especially since the false self has previously indicated that he is "ungratefull." On the other hand, the self-derogatory label may have been false in the first place. Or the speaker may be truly "ungratefull" but feel that he *should* be grateful. In any case, Love refuses the offer, preferring like the good-enough mother to serve rather than be served.

Stanley Fish objects that Love's "must" in the penultimate line, though on the surface "the politest of forms" is also the imperative *must,* the last of Love's strategies for undermining the speaker's right to make his own choices. If the speaker were a true self, this coercion might be as objectionable as Fish implies.[132] But Christ does not defeat the true self in this poem. Rather he triumphs over the false self's misguided efforts to protect his true self from being exposed, even to Love. *Must* as a command meets the need of the false self to be relieved of duty, while *must* as a polite form gently encourages the true self to enter into a relationship. Shorn of all lines of false-self defense, the false self ends where the true self begins, in the silent experience of being nurtured.

5

Counting One, Taking Part

LIKE WINNICOTTIAN CHILD DEVELOPMENT, THE HERBERTIAN REDEMP-
tive process begins in a context of relatedness, proceeds from
the foundation of the true self, and establishes a personality
capable of harmony with God, others, and the self. While more
frequently applied psychoanalytic theorists like Freud or Lacan
could be elicited to explain some aspects of fallen subjectivity,
Winnicott better accounts for the psychodynamics of redemption in *The Temple*. Since this assumption has guided me
throughout, it will be my thesis here. Approaching my conclusion from a theoretical angle will facilitate further discussion of
how redemption works and what it means in Herbert. This tack
will also place my work as a whole in theoretical perspective.

I begin with an overview. In a 1968 speech to math teachers,
Winnicott discusses the relationship between the self and society in terms of interpersonal mathematics, playfully exploiting
the coincidence between the Latin verb *sum,* meaning "I AM,"
and the English noun *sum*. For Winnicott, "mathematics is a
disembodied version of the human personality."[1] As the starting
point of arithmetic is the integer "1," the starting point of a
healthy personality is the integrated "I," a unit established with
"the arrival and secure maintenance of the stage of I AM."[2]

According to Winnicott, the capacity to count to one in this
way is a maturational achievement, "a state indeed that may
never be achieved."[3] We might say that *sum* (I am) is the sum
of innate potential and good–enough mothering.[4] A mother who
is not good enough may thwart the child's biological striving
toward growth so that the child remains an extension of the
primary caretaker or the environment. She (or he) divides the
child from the true self, leaving the child a fraction. Although a
self may be "part of society" in this too literal way, meaningful

social participation is the prerogative of whole persons, while compliance is the conditioned reflex of partial selves.[5] As we have seen, in Herbert's day typical child rearing practices fostered compliance at the expense of wholeness. The resulting self-organization was in keeping with Tudor ideology, which figured the property and person of every subject as an extension of the monarch's public body. Although Puritan ideology later transferred attributions of personal wholeness and the historically coinciding right to property (or material extensions of self) to male heads of households, the majority of English selves remained parts or property of others, and even "the people" derived their rights to being and having from Yahweh, of whom they were extensions.

The idea that each "member" of the church is part of the Body of Christ is not specific to Calvinism of course. But the way the idea works psychologically hinges on interpretation. Does God disdain depraved humanity and redeem by impoverishing the self? Or does God love his creation and redeem by empowering the self? Does Christ relate to the members of his church by appropriating them as his self-objects or by joining with them in a holding relationship which works to strengthen them?

Like Erich Fromm, Winnicott endorses the latter approach: "It seems to me that what is commonly called religion arises out of human nature," he states, "whereas there are some who think of human nature as rescued from savagery by a revelation from outside human nature."[6] In health, "the capacity to believe," emerges from experience. "The concept of, say, everlasting arms" is meaningful to a child because of "the preverbal expression of love in terms of holding and handling."[7] A parent who teaches about God by "inculcating morality" risks "robbing the growing child of the capacity *on his own* to come to a personal sense of right and wrong, to come to this out of his own development."[8]

In perceiving the self as essentially good though dependent on good-enough mothering to realize natural potential, Winnicott opposes Freud, who views the self as innately amoral and self-centered.[9] The Freudian baby is a solipsistic bundle of impulses exploiting others to attain pleasure. Eventually, the self must be subordinated to the operations of the "reality principle," forced to relinquish individual aims for the good of society. The father more than the mother is society's agent in civilizing a child, and he accomplishes his task through frustrating libidinal drives. Although the Freudian self begins and ends as a unit, the developmental equation which results in a mature self is paradoxically divisive: one (father/superego) over one (child/ego-id) equals one (the socially adaptive personality).[10]

If Lacan follows Freud in attributing the genesis of the social self ("Je") to the child's identification with the "Law of the Father" (the abstract principle which governs the Symbolic) Lacan is far more divisive than Freud in his approach to the mathematics of the self. The Lacanian self begins as a fraction. Imaginary wholeness is a delusion to which the self is predisposed, as evidenced by the infant's "jubilant assumption" of his or her mirror image during the mirror stage.[11] But as the child begins to interact with others, the delusion of wholeness is subverted from without by a failure of communication between self and Other just as it is subverted from within by intrapsychic discrepancies among the Real, the Imaginary, and in time the Symbolic, selves. Finally, the self is a set of loosely connected self–representations rather than a unit.[12]

Differences between Winnicott and Lacan begin with their assumptions about earliest life. While Lacan, like Freud, assumes that from the infant's perspective, there is no Other, Winnicott proclaims, "there is no such thing as a baby," no infant in isolation.[13] It follows that for Winnicott there is no Lacanian Real except as the result of trauma. The infant is unintegrated rather than disintegrated and comes to suffer the anxiety associated with disintegration only if maternal support fails after some integration has been achieved.[14]

Differences extend to the mirror stage as well. While for Winnicott, mirroring comes from a mother who recognizes the child's potential prior to the child's realization of it, for Lacan it comes from a literal mirror which distorts the truth of the child's inadequacy, offering false hope.[15] The Lacanian Other's (unconscious) role is to alienate the child from his or her self-image. As the toddler begins to interact with the Other, the child seeks to become what she desires. Inevitably the child fails since mothers desire the "phallus" (again a disembodied concept) which the child neither is nor has. Hence in Lacan, an early false self is normative.[16]

For Lacan, there is no true self.[17] The self's decentering is predetermined by the Symbolic realm to which a child must aspire in order to survive. As in Freud, so in Lacan socialization diminishes the self even if it guarantees the (diminished) self's survival. While in Freud, individual discontent is compensated for by the advantages of civilization, in Lacan, there is no payoff;

civilization itself is dehumanized, functioning not by bodily but by linguistic laws.[18]

For both Freud and Lacan, desire and illusion are at odds with social life and must be renounced. In Freud, infantile desires must be rooted out so that the self can become responsible; in Lacan they should be renounced because their objects are illusory and accepting this reality may ameliorate a person's inevitable discontent. For Winnicott, the good-enough mother must satisfy her baby's desires, supporting the illusion that the world is the infant's creation, if the child is to come to terms later with the reality principle. As the child grows, a gradual failure of adaptation is as appropriate as the mother's initial attempt at near perfect adaptation. But even in maturity the capacity to enjoy illusion (recognizing it as such) is the basis for creative living, for feeling real, for the capacity to operate within a less-than-perfect environment.[19]

Throughout my work, I have indicated ways that our understanding of the redemptive process represented by or enacted through the speaker and prosodic subject of *The Temple* as they relate to Christ may be enhanced with reference to Winnicott. In the sections to come I will reiterate the core concepts of previous chapters, in contrast to Freudian and Lacanian ideas, to show how Winnicott's model makes more sense of *The Temple* than these other theories do. Also, I will elaborate on these earlier ideas in the light of my work as a whole.

First, although Herbert's speaker often views fallen human beings as driven by desire for pleasure or narcissistic sustenance, the need for relatedness characterizes prelapsarian humankind and becomes the major motivator of the new Adam. By breaking through the speaker's false-self defense, Christ awakens primary attachment. This awakening marks a new beginning for the Herbertian self. Second, Herbert's poems do not always represent the self as a unit the way Freud does, but neither do they represent the self as irreparably divided the way Lacan does. While the speaker often represents himself as less than one, the prosodic subject enacts a unification of sensibility in response to Divine holding. In Christ's presence, the speaker and prosodic subject come together. Third, as Christ re-forms the human subject, illusion precedes disillusionment, deepening the self's capacity to love and cope in an imperfect world. Herbert's Christ fits the role of Winnicottian mother perfectly, albeit paradoxically, in being "good enough" but not too good at each stage of his child's development. Fourth, the determination of self by Other in *The Temple* is not always, as in Freud, a conflictual process, nor is it, as in Lacan, self-alienating. Rather Christ works through the true self, establishing the new Adam on the foundation of his potential. Converted *to* rather than *from* himself, the Herbertian self emerges more responsive, responsible, and spontaneous.

II

As Herbert's speaker represents the case of sinful "man," a definitive feature of fallen human nature is self-centered pleasure seeking. Variations on this theme are pervasive in *The Temple*. In "Vanitie" (II), the speaker warns a "poore silly soul" who seeks pleasure instead of heaven that "earthly joy / Is but a bubble, and makes thee a boy" (1, 17–18). In "Dotage," the speaker laments "the folly of distracted men" oriented toward "false glozing pleasures," which prove to be mere "womens and childrens wishes" or otherwise insubstantial (13, 1, 2). In both poems, the speaker's emphasis on human pleasure-seeking is commensurate with Freud's drive theory. So is his traditional Judeo-Christian renunciation of unchecked sensual satisfaction as an illusory wish fulfillment inappropriate to male-centered maturity.

In "Miserie" also, the speaker preaches against the "folly and sinne" of "man," who will not "temper his excesse" (3, 9). The speaker figures humanity as "a foolish thing" (2). Man drinks too much, and worse still "wed[s]" himself to "strange pollutions," an image which registers sexual revulsion on the speaker's part (13).[20] If in categorically repudiating pleasure the false-self speaker places himself at odds with his own body, he nevertheless supports Freud's contention that, regardless of one's attitude toward physical life, bodily pleasure is a primary human concern.

Characteristic of poems in which the speaker renounces fallen humanity's emphasis on pleasure is the subtle self-repudiation these poems logically entail. As the speaker objectifies "man," with whom he grudgingly identifies in the last line of "Miserie," he manifests an empathic failure toward others and himself.[21] Unavoidable in the Lacanian model of self-Other relations, lack of empathy is a sign of fallenness in *The Temple*, and it extends beyond one fallen human being's judgment of another. As the Christ of "The Sacrifice" diagnoses the situation, "If sinfull man could feel, / Or feel his part" of Christ's sorrow, "he would not cease to kneel, / Till all were melted, though he were all steel" (209–211).[22]

From a Winnicottian perspective, empathic failure is one possible outcome of self-repudiation. False selves do not merely lack access to feeling; they exist as a defense against suffering and vulnerability. The effectiveness of the false self as defense explains why the quickening of the true self or the speaker's heart is sometimes represented in *The Temple* as torture. In spite of the speaker's lack of insight into the matter, we may deduce that Christ's treatment of the speaker is contrived to revitalize the speaker's capacity for relationship.

"Love unknown" allegorizes the suffering a self must endure as the false self places the true self in the hands of an Other. Given that the poem is quite long, a brief summary will be more expedient than full quotation. The speaker tells his story to a friend. After offering his heart to his Lord, the speaker has seen it "washt, and wrung," and, in a second encounter, thrown it into "A boyling caldron, round about whose verge / Was in great letters set *AFFLICTION*" (17, 27–28). Finally, fleeing this "scalding pan," the speaker has arrived home only to find "that some had stuff'd the bed with thoughts" or rather "*thorns*" (35, 51–52). To the first incident, the friend responds, "*Your heart was foul, I fear*"; to the second, "*Your heart was hard, I fear*," and to the third "*Your heart was dull, I fear*" (18, 37, 56). In the end, the friend sums up phase one of the Herbertian redemptive process:

> The Font did onely, what was old, renew:
> The Caldron suppled, what was grown too hard:
> The Thorns did quicken, what was grown too dull:
> All did but strive to mend, what you had marr'd.
> Wherefore be cheer'd, and praise him to the full
> Each day, each houre, each moment of the week,
> Who fain would have you be new, tender, quick.
>
> (64–70)

If one were to view "Love unknown" as a manifestation of the author's psyche, the choice to communicate the pain of a true self's awakening through allegory seems an intriguing compromise between the vulnerability being depicted and the false self's need to distance himself. While the details of this particular allegory underscore the self's sense of torture, allegory as a narrative mode serves to ward off the pain, to de-realize it, configuring it in terms accessible to the split off intellect.[23]

Within the text, the persona seems false in that he remains fixated on the external details of his narrative, lacking insight altogether.[24] His quandary is extreme. The authority figure has not acted in a way which a false self could predict, in spite of the speaker's careful attention to good manners and social appropriateness. The speaker has decorously offered his heart in the middle of a dish of fruit; he has asked pardon when he committed "Many a fault more then [his] lease [would] bear"; he has even noticed and responded to class cues, specifically by noting the "greatnesse" of the cauldron's "owner" and offering a sacrifice which he deemed appropriate—not his heart again; instead he has offered a "sacrifice out of [his] fold" (20, 29, 30). From a false-self point of view, the speaker has done all the right things only to suffer further with each attempt.

Although the Lord's actions seem sadistic, the new self which the friend hypothesizes marks a definite improvement over the speaker, who himself shows no signs of being renewed. The speaker is incapable of genuinely relating to his friend, a fact his initial remarks reveal:

> DEare Friend, sit down, the tale is long and sad:
> And in my faintings I presume your love
> Will more complie then help. A Lord I had,
> And have, of whom some grounds, which may improve,
> I hold for two lives, and both lives in me.
> To him I brought a dish of fruit one day,
> And in the middle plac'd my heart. But he
> (I sigh to say)
> Lookt on a servant, who did know his eye
> Better then you know me, or (which is one)
> Then I my self.
>
> (1–11)

One form or another sort of profound relational failure is here obscured by a mystery. Who is this friend? If external, the friend is one whom the speaker perceives as a self-object. Thus, the speaker considers his friend's knowledge of him identical to his knowledge of himself and expects the friend "will more complie then help," mirroring his confusion without altering his perspective.[25] But the friend could also *be* some part of the speaker's self, specifically the new self the speaker obviously is not.[26] In this case, the speaker's problem is not that he perceives another person as part of himself, but rather that he perceives part of himself as other. Or perhaps the "friend" is the Lord, the second of the "two lives" within the speaker.[27] If so, the speaker's defensive splitting of the Lord positions the speaker, as do the other two scenarios, at a developmental stage where intersubjectivity remains problematic.

The speaker's initial diatribe is characteristic of the whole poem. The tale is indeed "long" if not as "sad" as the speaker claims.[28] Obsessed with himself yet completely unaware of himself, the speaker finds it impossible to get to the bottom of his own story. He frequently interrupts himself and sometimes even interrupts the interruptions, as when he tells his friend about offering an animal sacrifice to his Lord:

> But as my heart did tender it, the man,
> Who was to take it from me, slipt his hand,
> And threw my heart into the scalding pan;
> My heart, that brought it (do you understand?)
> The offerers heart. *Your heart was hard, I fear.*
>
> (33–37)

Contorted syntax and prosodic enjambment facilitate an infinitely regressive habit of speech. The speaker digresses from his story to underscore a detail he considers important, then digresses from the digression to make sure his mirror is being appropriately empathic. Although the friend's interruption stops the speaker on the word *heart,* in Lacanian terms punctuating a word the speaker has used four times in five lines, the speaker can no more hear himself than he can attend to his friend. In spite of the fact that the speaker and friend together refer to the speaker's heart eleven times in the poem, the speaker might say of his storytelling what he says of his prayers: "Though my lips went, my heart did stay behinde" (59). This speaker does not feel these matters which with himself he too much discusses; he thinks about them instead.

In the passage quoted, the word *heart* is twice subject and twice object in both grammatical and interpersonal terms; the Lord's treatment of the heart underscores its status as a thing, yet the Lord's actions work ultimately to repersonalize rather than to depersonalize the true self. Specifically, the Lord seeks to make tender, to tend and attend to the heart which seeks to "tender" (use for payment) a self-object (the scapegoat) rather than the self.[29]

In the same way that the Lord treats the speaker's heart as an old, hard, dull object, the prosodic subject mimes the speaker's rigidly defensive report in a relatively monotonous seventy-line strophe emblematic of the speaker's deadness. All lines are pentameter except when the speaker reports three times the one emotional expression which seems genuine: his sighs. These lines are dimeter. Signifying the prosodic subject's potential for quickness, they also divide the speaker's remarks into four discursive blocks, each longer than the one before it. The friend's occasional interruptions add further rhythmic variation to the poem, spelling the reader from what would otherwise constitute a dreary monologue.[30]

In "Love unknown," the prosodic subject objectifies the heart of an object self ("moi") rather than embodying the heart of a human subject. "Home" stands in direct contrast. Although "Home" is longer than "Love unknown" (seventy-eight lines as opposed to seventy) it is far more pointed and poignant. The poem is divided into thirteen sestets with varying line lengths. A pithy rather than digressive syntax communicates passion rather than dullness:

> COme Lord, my head doth burn, my heart is sick,
>   While thou dost ever, ever stay:
> Thy long deferrings wound me to the quick,
>   My spirit gaspeth night and day.
>   O show thy self to me,
>   Or take me up to thee!
>
> How canst thou stay, considering the pace
>   The bloud did make, which thou didst waste?
> When I behold it trickling down thy face,
>   I never saw thing make such haste.
>   O show thy self to me,
>   Or take me up to thee!
>
> When man was lost, thy pitie lookt about
>   To see what help in th' earth or skie:
> But there was none; at least no help without:
>   The help did in thy bosome lie.
>   O show thy self to me,
>   Or take me up to thee!
>
>   (1–18)

In these stanzas, the speaker and prosodic subject unite to feel and enact the longing caused by the Lord's absence. The speaker's focus moves from his own pain to the maternal Christ's Passion and compassion. He begs to see Christ's face, to be taken up, held in Christ's bosom. Meanwhile the prosodic subject images both the speaker's wound "to the quick" and the blood trickling down Christ's face. As the speaker plays on the idea of "quickness," a speeded visual and aural rhythm signifies suffering and aliveness in the body of Christ and in the speaker as member of that body. Through the me/thee rhyme of the poem's refrain, the prosodic subject enacts the merging of self and Other which the speaker desires.

Whereas the speaker of "Love unknown" is mystified by what the Lord does to start a relationship, the speaker of "Home" is mystified by what the Lord fails to do to consummate one. In this regard, "Home" seems reminiscent of Donne's "Elegie" (XIX), where what is deferred is a man's sexual encounter with his mistress: "Come, Madam, come, all rest my powers defie, / Until I labour, I in labour lie" (1–2). Like Donne's persona, Herbert's impatiently tries to hasten contact with another by complaining about how the wait is affecting him. But unlike Donne's, Herbert's speaker renounces libidinal satisfaction in favor of a more holistic form of relatedness. Rejecting "woman-kinde," as well as "meat and drink," and other trappings of a world which seems "Nothing but drought and dearth, but bush and brake," Herbert's speaker begs for a different sort of dying (39, 37, 49):

> What have I left, that I should stay and grone?
> The most of me to heav'n is fled:
> My thoughts and joyes are all packt up and gone,
> And for their old acquaintance plead.
> O show thy self to me,
> Or take me up to thee!
>
> (67–72)

Instead of preaching at depraved humanity as in "Vanitie" (II), "Dotage," and "Miserie," the speaker of "Home" undergoes the full experience of his own humanity. Although he here represents himself as divided from himself, the speaker is not as self-alienated as in other poems. His sense that most of him is elsewhere registers the way he experiences separation from the Other.[31] As subsequent stanzas make clear, even denouncing pleasure, the speaker cannot really divorce the self based in the body. He remains "pinion'd with mortalitie" and prays with "flesh and bones and joynts"—his whole body—"And ev'n [his] verse" for reunion with the holding mother (63, 74, 75).

If the speaker of "Home" is a false self, he is one acutely aware of his core. Unlike the self-obsessed false self of "Love unknown," he is Other-obsessed and speaks on behalf of a true self in the transitional phase. Able to recognize separation, he responds with deeply felt desire. Whereas the speaker of "Love unknown" remains fixated on a (secondary) narcissistic injury, the self of "Home" longs to regress to the infantile state which Freud terms "primary narcissism."

While for Freud regression is always negative, Winnicott views it as a potentially revitalizing experience, one which, handled well, may further the growth of a personality arrested by traumatic childhood experiences. One must "become as a little child" to enter the kingdom of health. As for the term *primary narcissism,* Michael Balint argues that it is nebulous, referring to a state which cannot be rigorously defined or clinically substantiated. What is it to love only the "self" before the ego exists? Balint claims that a primitive form of object love is more primary than narcissism.[32] Taking a different tack, Winnicott argues that the term *primary narcissism* "leaves out the tremendous differences that result from the general attitude and behaviour of the mother."[33] Whereas a good-enough mother orients herself to her baby so that the infant feels merged with her and experiences a sense of omnipotence, an unempathic primary caretaker subverts this experience, and the infant learns to comply with her at the expense of the true self. For Winnicott, then, primary narcissism is an optimal but contingent state rather than a negative and universal one. The incontrovertible fact of infancy is not narcissism but dependence.[34]

The contrast between "Love unknown" and "Home" shows that Herbert's speaker regresses toward a state of profound attachment to another, not toward a megalomaniacal archaic ego. Although the infant self remains partial, he is at last connected to the good-enough mother who can make him whole.

Like "Home," "The Pearl" shows that for the redeemed Herbertian self the Winnicottian need for relationship is more primary than the Freudian drive for pleasure or the Lacanian desire for confirmation from others, and illustrates how the speaker's renewed awareness of his need for the Other rehumanizes him. The speaker enthusiastically discusses "the wayes of

Learning," "the wayes of Honour," and "the wayes of Pleasure," all of which he claims to know (1, 11, 21). Implying that these objects are not as satisfactory as the Other, the speaker nevertheless approaches them from the standpoint of his own humanity:

> I know the wayes of Pleasure, the sweet strains,
> The lullings and the relishes of it;
> The propositions of hot bloud and brains;
> What mirth and musick mean; what love and wit
> Have done these twentie hundred yeares, and more:
> I know the projects of unbridled store:
> My stuffe is flesh, not brasse; my senses live,
> And grumble oft, that they have more in me
> Then he that curbs them, being but one to five:
>   Yet I love thee.
>
>   (21–30)

As the speaker talks of pleasure, the prosodic subject embodies the "the lullings and the relishes of it" in iambic pentameter lines speeded by a forceful rather than digressive syntactic pace. Frequent enjambment enacts a prosodic dance. Such "mirth and musick mean" that this speaker's "stuffe" is indeed "flesh, not brasse." The last dimeter line is the speaker's refrain, his answer to each of the world's offerings. As in "Home," this speaker does not approach God through renouncing other people, nor does he enter into relationship with God through death to his own desires; he enters into it fully alive. "With open eyes / I flie to thee," he claims (32–33). With his whole self, the speaker approaches Christ, desiring him more than any temporal object.[35]

The need for an Other, specifically God, is the cornerstone of the redeemed Herbertian subject. Although the need often manifests itself in infantile form, the speaker's renewed capacity to experience it marks progress toward a more fully realized self. Since Herbert's poems delve beyond the psychic to the mythic roots of subjectivity, the speaker's emphasis on relationship as a means to self realization has greater than personal implications. In *The Temple,* the speaker's reconnecting with primary need puts him in touch not only with his own potential but also with the potential of prelapsarian humankind.

"The Pulley" shows that need for the Other is indeed primary in *The Temple.* Herbert's speaker imagines God creating human nature just after God created humankind:

WHen God at first made man,
            Having a glasse of blessings standing by;
Let us (said he) poure on him all we can:
Let the worlds riches, which dispersed lie,
            Contract into a span.

            So strength first made a way;
Then beautie flow'd, then wisdome, honour, pleasure:
When almost all was out, God made a stay,
Perceiving that alone of all his treasure
            Rest in the bottome lay.

            For if I should (said he)
Bestow this jewell also on my creature,
He would adore my gifts in stead of me,
And rest in Nature, not the God of Nature:
            So both should losers be.

            Yet let him keep the rest,
But keep them with repining restlesnesse:
Let him be rich and wearie, that at least,
If goodnesse leade him not, yet wearinesse
            May tosse him to my breast.

Unlike many poems in *The Temple*, "The Pulley" does not represent any object of human desire as intrinsically bad. Following Augustine, the speaker distinguishes between enjoying God's gifts as manifestations of God's benevolence and treating them as ends in themselves.[36] Libidinal motivators (beauty and pleasure) and narcissistic motivators (beauty, strength, honor, and wisdom) are by no means off limits; the God of "The Pulley" wants people to have them. But Herbert's God means for himself to be humanity's primary object, and he deliberately renders all other objects secondary, seeing to it that longing for him characterizes even prelapsarian humankind.[37]

The prosodic subject of "The Pulley" embodies the story the speaker tells in a highly expressive stanza form. An initial trimeter line, three middle pentameter lines, and a closing trimeter line build a five-line stanza which expands and contracts to signify God's generosity and his withholding. This stanza form also signifies the way that God holds his creation. God separates from humankind to pour his blessings down and later draws human beings back to himself. He opens then closes interpersonal space. The *ababa* rhyme scheme adds a vertical dimension to this "give and take" relational rhythm. The ebb and flow of lines and the alternation of rhymes enact "repining restlesnesse" and involve the reader in the "wearinesse" which tosses people to God's "breast."[38] The obsessive repetition of various forms and meanings of the word "rest" intensifies this effect.[39]

Thus "The Pulley" ascribes mythic dimension to primary human need. In the poem's version of creation, the infancy of the human race is founded on a relational rather than a self-centered basis.[40] The poem implies that without God, human beings are dissatisfied, that even when people's desire for pleasure or self-advancement is satiated, people remain hungry for the Divine Other's holding.

III

The need for holding itself implies that without God, human selves are incomplete. Many Herbert poems develop the theme explicitly. The Freudian unit self would make little sense to the speaker of Herbert's "Trinity Sunday," for example. In this obscure poem not included in *The Temple,* the speaker exploits the metaphor of interpersonal mathematics in cryptic proverbial style:

> HE that is one,
>   Is none.
> Two reacheth thee
> In some degree.
> Nature & Grace
> With Glory may attaine thy Face.
>   Steele & a flint strike fire,
>   Witt & desire
> Never to thee aspire,
> Except life catch & hold those fast.
>   That which beleefe
> Did not confess in the first Theefe
>   His fall can tell,
>   ffrom Heaven, through Earth, to Hell.
>   Lett two of those alone
>   To them that fall,
> Who God & Saints and Angels loose at last.
>   Hee that has one,
>   Has all.

For this speaker, a self-enclosed self ("He that is one") is doomed to annihilation; a self joined to Christ is capable of fulfillment.

The speaker goes on to indicate that "Grace" must supplement "Nature" for a person to "attain [God's] face"—to see God and also to attain the self created in God's image. Neither "wit" nor "desire" suffice to actualize human potential. "Beleefe" is required (11). Possessing Christ, the self "Has all."

The poems of *The Temple* calculate self-Other relations similarly. Herbert's speaker repeatedly figures himself as less than one: as "all throat or eye," as having "no parts but those of grief," as a "pile of dust" with a heart so devastated "That ev'ry part / Hath got a tongue," as a self "Broken in pieces all asunder" whose "thoughts are all a case of knives" ("Complaining," 13, 15, "Longing," 41, 75–76, "Affliction" (IV), 1, 7). At times the pieces even talk to each other. A detached intelligence at war with introjects and self-fragments, the speaker addresses his thoughts and emotions as if they had lives of their own. In "The Glimpse," he quibbles with delight as it flees; in "The Bag," he bids despair to go away; in "Assurance" he upbraids a "Spitefull bitter thought" that tortures him, and in "Conscience" he talks back to an internal "pratler" unable to enjoy the pleasurable aspects of living ("Assurance," 1, "Conscience," 1). In "The Discharge," "The Size," and "The Method," he delivers sermons to his own wayward heart.

The lines of Herbertian self-division are multiple: the body fragmented, the heart broken, the speaking self at odds with himself. Lack of integration unsettles every layer of the speaker's being. Beyond intense personal suffering, self-fragmentation entails a lack of integrity which threatens social relations. So the speaker of "Giddinesse" implies:

> OH, what a thing is man! how farre from power,
>   From setled peace and rest!
> He is some twentie sev'rall men at least
>   Each sev'rall houre.
>
> One while he counts of heav'n, as of his treasure:
>   But then a thought creeps in,
> And calls him coward, who for fear of sinne
>   Will lose a pleasure.
>
> Now he will fight it out, and to the warres;
>   Now eat his bread in peace,
> And snudge in quiet: now he scorns increase;
>   Now all day spares.

He builds a house, which quickly down must go,
      As if a whirlwinde blew
And crusht the building: and it's partly true,
      His minde is so.

O what a sight were Man, if his attires
      Did alter with his minde;
And like a Dolphins skinne, his clothes combin'd
      With his desires!

Surely if each one saw anothers heart,
      There would be no commerce,
No sale or bargain passe: all would disperse,
      And live apart.

Lord, mend or rather make us: one creation
      Will not suffice our turn:
Except thou make us dayly, we shall spurn
      Our own salvation.

Herbert's speaker here pronounces yet another judgment on generic "man"—a powerless, unsettled, restless, and changeable "thing." Object constancy, (that is, belief in the permanence and reliability of others) is beyond the grasp of this speaker's projective understanding, at least in the realm of human affairs. Mutability seems to him to strike to the human core, producing Protean "man." The spiritual miser who "counts of heav'n, as of his treasure" is split off from a pleasure-oriented bodily self and is ridiculed for his self-denial by a "thought" which "creeps in" from parts unspecified. In other words, "man" is organized by false-self defenses; he lacks access to or control over all the pieces of himself. From an object-relations perspective, the speaker's subsequent description of "man" follows logically from the premise of a disempowered core self. "Man" vacillates impulsively between aggression and passivity. He is stingy one day and wasteful the next, particularly of time. Man builds, and he destroys, caught up in a whirlwind of mental activity.

In the last three stanzas, the speaker imagines that humanity as collective essence, if understood, would undermine humanity as a social body. Interpersonal "commerce" hinges on the invisibility of human hearts, the psychic barrier which isolates people from each other. Self-enclosure becomes a perverse remedy for an antisocial human community which might otherwise dissolve. If people recognized themselves in others, there would be no bond strong enough to hold society together. Lack of intimacy between selves is the tie which binds people together (in spite of their being all alike.)

Harold Toliver compares the fallen condition represented in "Giddinesse" to falls in Milton's texts and in Shakespeare's *King Lear*, arguing that Herbert's is "the least visualized and social, the most moralized fall . . . which concerns the dizzy inconsistency not of powerful men but simply of man."[41] In contrast, Marion White Singleton sees "Giddinesse" and other Herbert poems as fundamentally "social" in that the self represented in the poems embodies the dissolution of the Renaissance court and church:

> It is as if the voices of the disintegrating court world, the divided seat of ecclesiastical rule, and all the inhabitants of the brave palace of the world have been incorporated into his mind and cry out their agonies within that house.[42]

Although I do not disagree with Singleton, I think it is important to note that "Giddinesse" approaches the (reciprocal) relationship between self and society from a perspective opposite from hers. Reasoning from "man" in the singular to the world at large, from individual incoherence to the (global) social consequences of (universal) personal dissolution, the poem suggests not that societies constitute selves but that selves compose society. While Winnicott would posit an interpersonal origin for personal instability in the mother-child relationship (and perhaps indirectly a sociological origin in cultural child rearing practices), and while Singleton posits a sociological origin for the self's instability in a disintegrating culture, Herbert's speaker suggests a mythical origin for man's dissolution in the fall—hence his final appeal to the divine Other for re-creation. The poem is "social" nevertheless in that it addresses the impossibility of genuine interpersonal bonds in a world composed of false (in Herbert's terms, fallen) selves.

The speaker of "Giddinesse" seems indeed to "live apart," a detached intelligence capable of objectively assessing "man." Only in the last stanza does the speaker include himself among "us" as he addresses the Divine Other. The speaker's cynicism is extreme, and in the end his solution is radical. He tells God to start over and to keep starting over daily. If the speaker's emphasis on universal human depravity seems Calvinistic, he goes beyond even Calvin in prescribing the correction for it,

implying that by tomorrow, the "new Adam" will be in need of
further renewal. But unlike Calvin, the speaker universalizes the
possibility of human re-creation as well.[43]

Prosody in "Giddinesse" has complex, somewhat contradictory
effects. As a whole, the verse depicts a condition similar to the
one the speaker ascribes to human society. Lines glued together
by an *abba* rhyme scheme are held apart by varying line lengths.
In each stanza, a pentameter first line rhymes with a dimeter
fourth line, and a trimeter second line rhymes with a pentameter third line. At odds with itself, the stanzaic body awkwardly
coheres, its frame slanting far left, its middle slanting slightly
in the opposite direction. Although the stanza form remains the
same throughout the poem, a floating caesura in the pentameter
lines combined with varying sites and degrees of enjambment
in each verse produce seven distinctly cadenced stanzas. No two
run into each other. To the extent the form represents collective
"man," stanzaic segregation preserves a barrier between selves.
To the extent the stanza form represents a single subject, it
dramatizes changeability. But the prosodic subject also enacts—
once for each day of the week—a daily re-creation.[44]

For a poem which focuses on the possibility of a unified humanity we may look to "Man." The speaker represents humankind as God's dwelling place and as the height of God's creation.
"Man" is a well-integrated whole, mirrored by all things:

> Man is all symmetrie,
> Full of proportions, one limbe to another,
> And all to all the world besides:
> Each part may call the furthest, brother:
> For head with foot hath private amitie,
> And both with moons and tides.
>
> (13–18)

Looking to the whole poem, we may see how the prosodic
subject supports the stanza's image. Stanzas in "Man," like those
in "Giddinesse," are individuated in that no two merge through
enjambment. But in the discursive context of "Man," the separation of stanzas signifies more the bodily integrity of created man
than the psychic isolation of fallen man. There is much variation
among the stanzas of "Man" in that, with the exception of stanzas
two and eight, no two share the same rhyme scheme; furthermore, the poem's cadences change from one stanza to another.
But in "Man," variation signifies not man's inconstancy but the
infinite variety of creation. Finally, there is sameness in differ-

ence. Each six-line stanza has three rhymes, and lines of varying lengths shape a stanza form consistent throughout the poem—counting feet 354453. Whereas the unmatched dimeter and trimeter lines in each verse of "Giddinesse" contribute to a stanza form suggestive of tension and divisiveness, three paired line lengths in "Man" are arranged in symmetrical sequence to shape a picture of harmony and the organic relatedness of parts.[45]

One may construe the stanza form of "Man" as an abstract of the human body: head and feet at top and bottom are the smallest parts; shoulders and hips are the largest; the middle is of a size proportionate to the rest. As an architectonic construct, this stanza form depicts solidity and balance; it accords with the speaker's depiction of man as God's "stately habitation" (2). As an image of the human body, the form suggests idealized symmetry and proportion. It figures man in accordance with the speaker's sense of human wholeness. But a crucial question remains: does this image point to a megalomaniacal sense of imaginary sufficiency? Or does it rather imply a self-love based in love of an Other and productive of intersubjective harmony?

If we look to the text for answers, we are met with ambiguity. On the one hand, the speaker praises Man highly. In accordance with humanist premises, he transfers a narcissistic sense of "me" onto "us." Humanity is the center of the universe. Although "Man" is a thing so empty that God may "dwell in it," the human self as body is nevertheless "stately" and superior to the rest of creation (50, 4). The speaker vacillates between anthropomorphic pride (in Kohutian terms, mobilizing a species-based grandiose self) and adulation of God (in Kohutian terms, mobilizing the idealized Other position of the narcissist's relational repertoire). According to the speaker, "Man is ev'ry thing, / And more" (7–8). The whole world and even the angels exist to suit humankind. Humanity is superior, and other created beings should appreciate us: "Reason and speech we onely bring. / Parrats may thank us, if they are not mute" (10–11).

On the other hand, the speaker undercuts Man's self-esteem; with the parrot image he lapses into a self-parodying humor which registers the irony of praising fallen Man.[46] Is Man so full of himself that he would ask a parrot for thanks? Are we the "onely" ones who bring speech to the parrot, or do we "onely bring" it from another source? In other passages, the speaker criticizes humanity for the sort of self-satisfaction he is enacting. Man fails to realize his potential: "He is ... / A beast, yet is,

or should be more" (8–9).[47] Man makes the world his "prey,"
victimizing nature (20). He is self-involved, imperious, unappre-
ciative, and cruel: "More servants wait on Man, / Then he'l take
notice of: in ev'ry path / He treads down that which doth be-
friend him" (43–45). Although this speaker does not hedge on
idealizing the Other's handiwork, he is not oblivious to the flaws
of fallen "man."

From a theoretical perspective, we may perceive further cause
for ambivalence. On the one hand, Herbert's speaker, like most
people of Herbert's day, maintains a Neo-Platonic hierarchy
which posits clear lines of division and rank within the self and
among created beings: "All things unto our flesh are kinde / In
their descent and being; to our minde / In their ascent and
cause" (34–36). Mind is superior to matter; spirit is better than
body. And of course the Renaissance humanist body is mem-
bered, hence hierarchical. Although "head" and "foot" are interdependent, they are not created equal. To the extent that the
self is organized by the mind's dominance over the flesh, the
self remains organized by false-self defenses. To the extent that
the social body coheres through the subordination of one member to another, the speaker's world remains in a state of narcissistic arrest.

On the other hand, in poems like "Man" we see the embryonic
stirrings of intersubjectivity in Herbert's world. Christ is the
head of the body. God is the spirit who may "dwell in it" (50).
Each person is a self, not the self-object of others; yet, there is
potential accord among selves. Within the original body of Man
and created nature, members are related, "one limbe to another," as equals, and "all to all the world," as wholes (14–15).
Based on love of the Other, self-love becomes a passage to mutu-
ality among human selves.

In "Man," Herbert's speaker superimposes an awareness of
fallenness on an image of original human potential; humanity's
flaws are accentuated with reference to prelapsarian unity. In
other poems, the contradiction between humanity's potential
and the actuality of human life is resolved as the speaker imagines the day of general resurrection. While divine rebuke for
"sinne" makes human hearts "Pine, and decay, / And drop away, /
And carrie with them th' other parts," divine love "wilt sinne
and grief destroy; / That so the broken bones may joy, / And tune
together in a well-set song" ("Repentance," 25, 28–30, 31–33).
Resurrection in Herbert's poems entails not only reunification

of decomposed body parts and of the dead body with the living soul, but also the reunification of the self with others. In "Dooms-day," stanza one, these events occur synchronously:

> Come away,
> Make no delay.
> Summon all the dust to rise,
> Till it stirre, and rubbe the eyes;
> While this member jogs the other,
> Each one whispring, *Live you brother?*
>
> (1–6)

The body rises from the ground until the eyes—and I's—become visible. The "members" are first body parts and then individuals as part of the Body of Christ.[48] Here each whole self comes together in relation to other whole selves.

In Herbert's poems, as in Christian belief more broadly, the day of general resurrection promises ultimate restoration of the self in relation to a transcendent community. The implications of this forward looking mode of faith are more idealistic than practical. But the psychological birth of a whole self in relation to Christ also occurs here and now in Herbert's poems. Faith is not merely hope for future transformation; "faith is the *substance* of things hoped for," the realization of personal transformation in the material world (Heb. 11:1 AV, italics mine).

If the God of *The Temple* were narcissistic, he might desecrate his creation to preserve humanity's dependence on him. A continual emptying out of the self would elevate the Other; connection to the Other would elevate the self, and the whole process would be repeated in a psycho-cosmic seesaw which could never come to rest. While some of Herbert's poems imply this dynamic—as when the speaker of "The Crosse" accuses God of "Taking me up to throw me down"—others show that the Christ of *The Temple* is not interested in lording his superiority over human bits and pieces (22). The Herbertian self is afforded the opportunity to merge with and be part of Christ's body, but when "wearinesse" at last tosses him to God's "breast," he finds a resting place from which he may emerge a stable self ("The Pulley," 19–20).

The transformation of the Herbertian self comes through close connection to the Other and brings with it playful confidence as in "Clasping of hands":

LOrd, thou art mine, and I am thine,
    If mine I am: and thine much more,
Then I or ought, or can be mine.
Yet to be thine, doth me restore;
So that again I now am mine,
And with advantage mine the more,
Since this being mine, brings with it thine,
And thou with me dost thee restore.
    If I without thee would be mine,
    I neither should be mine nor thine.

Lord, I am thine, and thou art mine:
So mine thou art, that something more
I may presume thee mine, then thine.
For thou didst suffer to restore
Not thee, but me, and to be mine,
And with advantage mine the more,
Since thou in death wast none of thine,
Yet then as mine didst me restore.
    O be mine still! still make me thine!
    Or rather make no Thine and Mine!

The playfulness of rhetoric and prosody combine to figure a unified self in relation to the Other. Two rhymes—mine/thine and more/restore—carry the speaker through twenty lines which probe all the ways that the self is connected to Christ. The words *mine* and *thine* and other cases of the first and second person pronouns occur not only as rhyme words but throughout the poem. As A. L. Clements notes, "At least one and often both of these words occur in eighteen of the poem's twenty lines."[49] The image of hands holding each other is expressed in tangible terms through the intermingling of these pronouns and through the ten line stanzas figuring the intertwined fingers of self and Other.[50]

Whereas a speaking infant might say, "thou art I, and I am thou," in "Clasping of hands" self and Other are not identified but are interrelated by reciprocal possession. The speaker cannot have himself unless Christ first owns him, and Christ, having given himself up to restore the speaker, can restore himself only in the speaker. There are two bodies here—two interdependent wholes.[51] Although the speaker's self-possession still entails possessing and being possessed by the Other, intersubjectivity is possible. The last lines of the poem suggest that the speaker longs to regress further back to the point of merger rather than dyadic relatedness.[52] The desire suggests that he is in the transi-

tional phase. The persona's playfulness is a sign that the potential space between self and Other is a healthy one which can
foster growth.

IV

For both Winnicott and Herbert, the true self begins *in* an
Other. The Other identifies closely with the self in the beginning
but gradually requires the child to deal with psychological or
actual separations from the Other. Over time, this process works
to strengthen the self. Through this process, the Other molds
the child's experience of self and others by bringing the child
into being as a true self in relation to the Other rather than as
a potential self embedded in the self-Other matrix.

At first, the Christ of *The Temple* meets human needs with
perfect empathy, rendering superfluous the speaker's attempts
to fend for himself. We see this dynamic in "Redemption," a
sonnet in which Herbert's speaker is an Everyman figure first
discovering the meaning of Christ's New Covenant:

> H Aving been tenant long to a rich Lord,
>   Not thriving, I resolved to be bold,
>   And make a suit unto him, to afford
> A new small-rented lease, and cancell th' old.
> In heaven at his manour I him sought:
>   They told me there, that he was lately gone
>   About some land, which he had dearly bought
> Long since on earth, to take possession.
> I straight return'd, and knowing his great birth,
>   Sought him accordingly in great resorts;
>   In cities, theatres, gardens, parks, and courts:
> At length I heard a ragged noise and mirth
>   Of theeves and murderers: there I him espied,
>   Who straight, *Your suit is granted,* said, & died.

From the start, the speaker realizes that he cannot meet the
terms of his former contract with his Lord (the Old Covenant),
but he continues to assume that he must take some action. Specifically, he believes that he has a responsibility to negotiate with
the Lord for a new contract. Mustering courage to make the
request, the speaker moves in circles, to the Lord's manor and
back, through "cities, theaters, gardens, parks, and courts," looking everywhere for the Lord who has come to him. The prosodic

subject's sonnet form supports the effect of futile effort.[53] Three quatrains build the stages of Everyman's convoluted journey, yet by the end of twelve and a half lines the speaker is still at point zero. The couplet punctures the speaker's narrative of self-initiative as Christ's responsiveness renders his efforts superfluous.[54] Given the sonnet form's traditional use, the form here also conveys an intimacy between self and Other of which the speaker, who defines his connection to his Lord in pragmatic, impersonal terms, is paradoxically unaware. The prosodic subject understands the self-Other relationship better than the speaker does.[55]

Although Christ is explicitly figured as a masculine feudal Lord, his behavior is analogous to that of a Winnicottian mother. Just as a mother identifies with her infant, imagining life from the baby's point of view, the Lord understands his dependent's need prior to its being articulated and assumes the dependent's place in order to meet the need. Christ does not defer gratification but meets the speaker's need performatively at the same time that he answers the request verbally.[56] The last line's inversion of syntax underscores the near simultaneity of the Lord's words ("*Your suit is granted*") and the deed which realizes those words. Like a good-enough mother, Christ does what is necessary when it is needed. He does so even though the act requires self-sacrifice, even though it cannot be reciprocated, and even though the speaker, up until the end, is utterly oblivious to how much he is asking. As William Flesch writes, "the Lord's generosity, which the speaker expects will not be a very great drain on his resources, requires all he has."[57]

Other poems also focus on Christ's perfect empathy and availability. For instance, the speaker of "Mattens" asserts, "I cannot ope mine eyes, / But thou art ready there to catch / My morning-soul and sacrifice" (1–3). The speaker of "Prayer" (II) begins, "Of what an easie quick accesse, / My blessed Lord, art thou!" (1–2). Later in the poem he claims that "We cannot ask the thing, which is not there, / Blaming the shallownesse of our request" (11–12). Like the mother of an infant, the Christ of these poems responds immediately and accurately to the speaker's needs and desires. But of course, the Other of *The Temple* does not always attune himself perfectly to the speaker. The speaker must suffer intense frustration and separation anxiety because of the Other's absence in poems like "Longing," "Home," "The Search," and "Deniall." From a Winnicottian perspective, since optimal frustration is prerequisite to growth, we may hypothesize that the maternal Christ of Herbert's poems operates to the speaker's ultimate advantage in being good enough, but not too good, at each phase of his child's development.

"Affliction" (I) offers the most extensive picture of the way that the self-Other relationship in Herbert's poems develops over time. The poem shows that the believer's ongoing life with Christ progresses gradually from the speaker's experience of a totalizing relationship to his disillusionment. It also shows how, for Herbert's speaker as for a small child, painful disappointment leads to personal growth.

The first four stanzas deal with the beginnings of the relationship:

> WHen first thou didst entice to thee my heart,
>   I thought the service brave:
> So many joyes I writ down for my part,
>   Besides what I might have
> Out of my stock of naturall delights,
> Augmented with thy gracious benefits.
>
> I looked on thy furniture so fine,
>   And made it fine to me:
> Thy glorious houshold-stuffe did me entwine,
>   And 'tice me unto thee.
> Such starres I counted mine: both heav'n and earth
> Payd me my wages in a world of mirth.
>
> What pleasures could I want, whose King I served,
>   Where joyes my fellows were?
> Thus argu'd into hopes, my thoughts reserved
>   No place for grief or fear.
> Therefore my sudden soul caught at the place,
> And made her youth and fiercenesse seek thy face.
>
> At first thou gav'st me milk and sweetnesses;
>   I had my wish and way:
> My dayes were straw'd with flow'rs and happinesse;
>   There was no moneth but May.
> But with my yeares sorrow did twist and grow,
> And made a partie unawares for wo.

                                            (1–24)

In these and subsequent stanzas, several levels of analogy operate simultaneously. God is a master, the speaker his servant. God is a king, the speaker his subject. God is a lover who entices the speaker, the bridegroom to a feminized believer. Finally God is the mother who feeds and nurtures the infant soul. Other aspects of the poem reinforce the developmental dimension on which I will focus. According to many critics, the poem is autobiographical and the first stanzas focus on Herbert's literal youth.[58] More importantly, as I will argue, even the stanzas on Herbert's adulthood show the speaker grappling with an existential dilemma analogous to that of a small child whose primary parent has disappointed him.

At first the Other holds and supports the true self. The speaker's "stock of naturall delights" is "Augmented" rather than diminished through connection to the Other. The persona takes great pleasure in counting the Other's possessions as his own. God's "furniture," which *is* fine, becomes "fine to me," meaning that the natural world becomes intersubjective, a holding environment rather than an objective space. As extensions of the Other, even the Other's possessions "entwine" or hold the speaker. God gives the child persona "milk and sweetnesses;" the speaker has his "wish and way;" he is completely satisfied. This childhood sense of Edenic bliss is precisely the "illusion" which Winnicott believes good mothers support.

Prosody in these stanzas functions to reinforce the speaker's Edenic sense of holding. Through couplet rhyme, lines five and six add to the speaker's "naturall delights" God's "gracious benefits," signifying the idea of augmentation. The curling enjambment of lines nine and ten mirrors the speaker's sense that God's possessions "entwine" him. The me/thee rhyme of lines eight and ten conveys the speaker's sense that he is being enticed, drawn to the Other through the "glorious houshold-stuffe" which, in the interceding line, entwines him. The sense of being encircled by the Other's comforting presence gives way at the end of these stanzas to the "twist" of sorrow, however, a motion which prosody embodies as a trochee substitutes for an expected iamb in the third foot of line twenty-three: "But with my yeares sorrow did twist and grow." As the reversal twists the line, the falling rhythm introduces a downward change of course.

Subsequent stanzas show the speaker discovering the limits of the self-Other relationship. In spite of his connection to the

Other, the speaker must cope with the pain and frustration inherent in a fallen world:

> My flesh began unto my soul in pain,
>   Sicknesses cleave my bones;
> Consuming agues dwell in ev'ry vein,
>   And tune my breath to grones.
> Sorrow was all my soul; I scarce beleeved,
> Till grief did tell me roundly, that I lived.
>
> When I got health, thou took'st away my life,
>   And more; for my friends die:
> My mirth and edge was lost; a blunted knife
>   Was of more use then I.
> Thus thinne and lean without a fence or friend,
> I was blown through with ev'ry storm and winde.
>
>   (25–36)

Confronted by sickness, sorrow, and loss, the speaker complains to an Other who no longer meets his needs or satisfies his desires as before. Prosody deepens but does not contradict the speaker's assertions. Frequent enjambment and the scattering of the second and fourth lines of each stanza away from the left margin convey an image of writhing. Thus the lines "roundly" indicate the self's bodily and affective aliveness and existential suffering. The prosodic subject's line break after "I scarce beleeved" in line twenty-nine momentarily suggests that the speaker loses faith in the Other as a consequence of his sickness. Line thirty clarifies that the speaker's suffering causes him to lose faith not in the Other but in his own existence. Since the Other is the ground of that existence, the reversal does not cancel our sense of the speaker's anger, however, which becomes considerably less subtle by lines thirty-one and thirty-two, where the speaker overtly blames God for the deaths of human others on whom he depends.

The speaker further indicates that, because of these losses, he does not feel held. He is "without a fence"—both without a protective physical enclosure and without *defense*.[59] Just as a child experiences a loss of self in the absence of maternal holding, the speaker loses his "mirth and edge"—elements of his personality—and by becoming "thinne and lean," loses bodily substance as well.

In subsequent stanzas, the speaker's confrontation of the Other continues:

> Whereas my birth and spirit rather took
> > The way that takes the town;
> Thou didst betray me to a lingring book,
> > And wrap me in a gown.
> I was entangled in the world of strife,
> Before I had the power to change my life.
>
> Yet, for I threatned oft the siege to raise,
> > Not simpring all mine age,
> Thou often didst with Academick praise
> > Melt and dissolve my rage.
> I took thy sweetned pill, till I came where
> I could not go away, nor persevere.
>
> Yet lest perchance I should too happie be
> > In my unhappinesse,
> Turning my purge to food, thou throwest me
> > Into more sicknesses.
> Thus doth thy power crosse-bias me, not making
> Thine own gift good, yet me from my wayes taking.
>
> > > > > (37–54)

The speaker feels that God ignores his natural predisposition (his "birth") and personal inclinations (his "spirit") and thus "betray[s]" him. The child wants to play, but the parent says to study, even choosing the child's course of study and vocation. If the conflict over vocation occurred in the human realm (as it often did in Renaissance parent-child relationships), the Other would be imposing an identity on the child rather than helping him realize his own identity. But, of course, having created the speaker, the Other of Herbert's poems knows the child's identity as no human parent can. Historically, the Reformation idea that a person's vocation is for God rather than a (human) parent to choose liberated young people to discover their own paths. And at any rate, the poem goes on to indicate that the speaker begins to take pleasure in the "Academick praise" which rewards his study. Although the speaker represents this praise as a "sweetned pill" which the Other uses to quiet his desire to rebel, the speaker's enjoyment of the academic life suggests that the Other has chosen a place for the speaker which fits his potential.

The speaker's ambivalence is quite important, however, since it is affectively and rhetorically the deep structure of the poem. At the discursive level, the poem builds ambivalence through a dialectical progress. In lines one through twenty-two, the speaker's life in relation to the Other feels all good; in lines twenty-three through forty-two, it feels all bad; in lines forty-three through sixty-six, the speaker's black and white sense of life turns gray, "cross-bias[ing]" perceptions he has previously registered of good and ill.[60] That which seems good (or pleasurable) is undermined by negative coincidences or effects. That which seems bad (or unpleasurable) comes to seem good.

A "sweetned pill" is nice, for instance, but the sweetening does not cancel underlying bitterness, and if the pill is a "purge," the sweetening does not negate its (short term) sickening effects. Squinting modification makes it unclear whether the speaker turns his purge (perceived ill) to food (perceived good) by making himself happy in his unhappiness (coming to enjoy his study) or whether the Other turns the purge to food and then (or *thereby*) throws the speaker into more sicknesses. In any case, pleasure and displeasure—the speaker's subjective good and ill—become so closely linked that at times they are indistinguishable.

Throughout the poem the prosodic level mirrors the speaker's ambivalence. When read in conjunction with the discursive text, twisting lines which at first mean entwining, enticing, or holding later come to mean mental anguish and bodily contortion and by line forty-one, they begin to suggest the speaker's entanglement in a world of strife. Regarded in this manner, prosody is not so much a separate self as the embodiment (hence the unification) of a deeply divided self.

Ambivalence toward the Other and toward life itself culminates in the final stanzas:

> Now I am here, what thou wilt do with me
>   None of my books will show:
> I reade, and sigh, and wish I were a tree;
>   For sure then I should grow
> To fruit or shade: at least some bird would trust
> Her houshold to me, and I should be just.
>
> Yet, though thou troublest me, I must be meek;
>   In weaknesse must be stout.
> Well, I will change the service, and go seek
>   Some other master out.
> Ah my deare God! though I am clean forgot,
> Let me not love thee, if I love thee not.

                                             (55–66)

In the penultimate stanza the speaker's wish to be a tree initially seems whimsical (even an accident of rhyme) but the wish is not without symbolic significance. Perhaps the image alludes to Ovid's Myrrha, doomed to a state in between life and death because she committed incest with her father, or to Dante's suicides, turned into trees because they rejected their own bodies. Herbert's speaker reverses the notion which these stories share that a tree is neither fully alive nor dead. The speaker explains that a tree grows either to fruit (life) or to shade (death). A tree is *not* in between—he is.[61] Furthermore, the tree's body is "just," straight, not contorted by physical, emotional, and spiritual affliction.[62]

In the first two lines of the last stanza, the speaker tries to bring himself around to the Other's point of view, telling himself that he must persevere in spite of pain. This attempted resolution does not satisfy him; rather it precipitates a rapid mood swing, a sudden shift to the notion that he can flee the Other rather than remain miserable in the Other's service. The thought of escape is itself rapidly overturned, perhaps as the thought of seeking "some other master out" summons the thought of who the other master is (Satan).[63] In the end, the speaker remains tied to an Other whom he passionately loves and hates, one whose point of view he cannot embrace yet whose loss he cannot abide.

The last lines preserve and resolve both sides of the speaker's ambivalence. It is possible to understand the verb *let* as equivalent to the optative *may* (May I not love you if I do not love you). Understood in this way, the line avows the strength of the persona's love by vowing the love's negation as the hypothetical consequence for its not existing. The vow is tautological but not meaningless, suggesting that the most damning consequence of not loving God is not loving God.[64] This reading of the line as asserting love is supported by the speaker's apostrophe to it— "Ah my deare God!"—and by the extreme condition he places on it, "though I am clean forgot."[65] The speaker loves the Other regardless of what the Other does.

On the other hand, the last line does not close off the possibility that the speaker remains ambivalent, even hateful, toward the Other. If the verb *let* is understood to mean *allow* in the imperative mode, the speaker may be asking for permission to hate the Other (Allow me not to love you, if I do not love you).[66]

As Schoenfeldt discerns, the line thus understood is richly paradoxical: "The if-clause posits a human ontology separate from divine will, while the let-clause entails an ontology of total dependence. Syntactically and politically, the line vibrates between autonomy and contingency."[67] From a Winnicottian perspective, the line vibrates with all the contradictory resonances of the transitional phase. The mother's granting her child the right to hate her is what characterizes her as good enough during this stage, since the child's being allowed to hate the Other (internally to destroy her) is prerequisite to the child's later ability to find and love her as a separate person. And of course, the request for permission itself implies a continuing sense of relatedness in spite of anger. Hence, even if it asserts hate, the line implies continuing love.

My reading attributes to the implied audience of "Affliction" (I) (the God whom Herbert's speaker addresses so freely) a capacity for maternal tolerance which many readers will find incompatible with Reformation views. Most critics share the position articulated by Chana Bloch that "Affliction" (I) "is, finally, an indictment" of the speaker.[68] Eugene Veith suggests that "the poem maintains an undercurrent of ironic self-criticism."[69] John R. Mulder argues that the speaker's "tribulations" amount to the "inevitable consequences of his ignorance that insisted on having 'my wish and way.'"[70] James Boyd White argues that the speaker's initial claim of absolute gratification seems by the end "an expression not of bliss but of moral ignorance and worse, an instinctive selfishness that has, through these very afflictions, been ground away."[71] According to Louis Martz, the poem presents "a blasphemous grumbling against God's justice, stemming from a desire for personal, worldly glory," and according to Marion White Singleton, "by blaming God for his mistaken optimism, [the speaker] essentially denies his own responsibility in the matter."[72] Rodney Edgecombe bluntly asserts that the first stanza reveals a "wrong" attitude, the last stanza a "right" attitude toward God.[73]

These and other readings suggest that Anne C. Fowler is on the right track when she claims that "Affliction" (I) offers "insights into the vagaries of the immature psyche that we simultaneously sympathize with and deplore, as we feel the poet does also."[74] There is only one problem: the poet's disdain for "the immature psyche" is nowhere on the page. Debora Shuger gets to the heart of the matter when she challenges conventional critical response to poems like "Affliction" (I):

> Critics of Herbert generally seem rather too eager to fault the speaker of the poems for their demands and complaints, as if human pain were somehow evitable and to feel it sinful. While there is certainly precedent in Calvinism for equating murmuring with infidelity, Herbert generally displays only sympathy—and identification—with his personae.[75]

"Affliction" (I) is commensurate with Winnicott's ideas because it typologically translates the myth of Eden and its loss into individual terms without explicit recourse to the doctrine of original sin. The speaker speaks unabashedly from his own perspective, without attempting to justify the Other's actions. He catalogs the limits on his happiness mysteriously imposed by an Other who *is* perfect (according to Herbert's belief system) yet chooses to be merely good enough (as Winnicott defines the term). When a mother lets a child down, she typically does so by accident or necessity; since Christ cannot make mistakes and does not *have* to do anything, the question of *why* he lets the speaker down (why God permits evil, why believers suffer, how religion absorbs and explains the reality principle) is troubling. It is, as Shuger asserts, "*the* question of the Bible."[76] In "Affliction" (I) Herbert does not foreclose the problem through appeal to a theocentric system. Instead, undergoing the inexplicable reality of suffering, he is transformed by the experience.

The poem finally suggests more about the effects than the causes of Christ's refusal. First, throughout the poem, the speaker trusts the Other enough that he feels free to express his anger within the context of the relationship rather than to bear it alone, attempting to belie it, hide it, or turn it on himself. Such deep-lying trust is the basis for the capacity to grow through disillusionment instead of being rendered false by it. Second, in the end, the speaker discovers the nature of intersubjective love by either of two routes. He discovers that the worst consequence the Other could tie to his not loving the Other would be that he would lose the joys inherent in loving. This realization enables him to love the Other in spite of what the Other does. Alternatively, the speaker discovers that even if he hates the Other, he hates in a relational context secured by the Other's love. He discovers that the Other can love him in spite of his anger. In either case, the speaker learns that separateness—even when it entails disagreement—and love are not mutually exclusive.

V

The idea that the self-Other relationship in *The Temple* as it is represented in poems like "Affliction" (I) proceeds along Winnicottian lines from merger to separation (or from illusion to disillusionment) implies that Christ's mothering of the speaker works ultimately to increase the speaker's autonomy. This idea is not unproblematic from a Reformation point of view. Central to Reformation Christianity—and to Herbert's—is the recognition that Christ's love, not the believer's, initiates a relationship to which the believer brings nothing and in which the believer can invest only those capacities which the Other gives. In "The Holdfast," Herbert's speaker finds that he cannot obey "the strict decree" of God's law, that he cannot have faith in God, nor even confess his inadequacy without God's help (1). "To have nought is ours" (9). Similarly, in "The Thanksgiving" and "The Reprisall," the speaker attempts to match Christ's gifts to him with equivalent gifts to Christ. In the course of the poems, the speaker abandons the contest, realizing that "There is no dealing with [Christ's] mighty passion," that he cannot repay the Other's love ("The Reprisall," 2). From a Freudian standpoint the autonomous Herbertian self is completely undermined by grace. The speaker loses separateness and independent initiative.[77] From a Winnicottian standpoint, as I will argue presently, a more genuine sense of personal agency emerges through Christ's grace, which is analogous to the grace of the good-enough mother.

Nancy Chodorow defines the difference between Freud's notion of individualism and Winnicott's:

Object-relations theory does not need to idealize a hyperindividualism; it assumes a fundamental internal as well as external relatedness to the other.... The relational individual is not reconstructed in terms of his or her drives and defenses but in terms of the greater or lesser fragmentation of his or her inner world and the extent to which the core self feels spontaneous and whole within, rather than driven by, this world. Even the sense of agency and autonomy remain relational in the object-relations model, because agency develops in the context of the early relationship with the mother and bears the meaning of her collaboration in and response to it.[78]

Poems like "Assurance," "Conscience," and "The Quip" show how the Other becomes useful to the speaker as a psychological object capable of transforming the speaker's relationship to himself and to his internal world. They demonstrate that the self-Other relationship of *The Temple* works ultimately to reduce internal fragmentation rather than to alienate the believer from himself. The relationship works by replacing the pseudoautonomy of the Herbertian false self with a more genuine sense of agency—one established on a relational foundation. These poems also illustrate that the speaker grows in relation to the Other, in some poems manifesting the "relational individualism" which Chodorow discusses. Moreover, as even a cursory look at a number of other poems will show, the implications of this transformation are interpersonal as well as personal.

In "Assurance," the Other's presence is internal, but in the poem's terms it is also actual. Direct appeal to the Other affords the speaker increased control over intrapsychic conflict. The true–self speaker (a child self in relation to God) begins by addressing a "spitefull bitter thought" which threatens to "raise devils," to create an intrapsychic hell, by raising doubts about the quality of the speaker's relationship to God (1, 17).[79] In the middle, like a small child threatening to tattle on a bully, the speaker warns this alien thought, "I will to my Father, / Who heard thee say it" (19–20). Finally, the speaker addresses the Father directly, enlisting the Other in the service of silencing the persecutory thought. The speaker's prayer indicates his complete lack of autonomy, even in the Winnicottian sense:

> O most gracious Lord,
> If all the hope and comfort that I gather,
> Were from my self, I had not half a word,
>   Not half a letter to oppose
>   What is objected by my foes.
>
> (20–24)

In "Assurance," absolute dependence on an Other who is actually present is the speaker's sole means of quieting internal chaos. In himself, the speaker lacks even self-control.

While in "Assurance" the usefulness of the object as mediator between warring factions of the self is contingent on the Other's actual presence, in "Conscience" the speaker evokes the absent Other through transitional objects. The Other, thus evoked, functions as antidote to the self-alienating power of an internal prattler constructed out of prohibitions against all that might give the speaker pleasure or comfort:

> PEace pratler, do not lowre:
>   Not a fair look, but thou dost call it foul:
> Not a sweet dish, but thou dost call it sowre:
>   Musick to thee doth howl.
> By listning to thy chatting fears
> I have both lost mine eyes and eares.
>
>   Pratler, no more, I say:
> My thoughts must work, but like a noiselesse sphere;
> Harmonious peace must rock them all the day:
>   No room for pratlers there.
> If thou persistest, I will tell thee,
> That I have physick to expell thee.
>
>   And the receit shall be
> My Saviours bloud: when ever at his board
> I do but taste it, straight it cleanseth me,
>   And leaves thee not a word;
> No, not a tooth or nail to scratch,
> And at my actions carp, or catch.
>
>   Yet if thou talkest still,
> Besides my physick, know there's some for thee:
> Some wood and nails to make a staffe or bill
>   For those that trouble me:
> The bloudie crosse of my deare Lord
> Is both my physick and my sword.

In Freudian terms the internal prattler is the speaker's super-ego, so the speaker's alienation from this voice must be construed as negative. In Winnicottian terms, however, the prattler may be construed as a false self. This understanding seems closer to the poem's meaning. Having gained the upper hand, a true self speaker (a self redeemed by love) talks back to a false self (a self enslaved by the law) that has previously alienated him from bodily life, from his eyes and ears.[80] The speaker seeks a more seamless relationship to his thoughts, which should emanate from him (circling around him like planets) and work noiselessly in his service rather than prattling against him. Since false-self organization begins when the mind separates to form a self distinct from the true (or bodily based) self, Herbert's speaker images the very realignment of true and false self that Winnicott theorizes as healthful.

Because the speaker of "Conscience" occupies the site of the true self, the poem's prosody merely reinforces his statements. In each stanza, a trimeter first line rhymes with a pentameter third line, crossing left to right at the same time that a pentameter second line rhymes with a trimeter fourth line, crossing right to left. A final heroic couplet closes each six line stanza. Chiasmic form registers both the speaker's feeling at cross purposes with himself and the antidote to that condition: the evocation of Christ's cross in the final sestet.

In "Conscience," the Other's relationship to the true self begins to gain potency. Not only is the self undergoing reorganization; that reorganization is beginning to occur at the self's initiative through indirect evocation of the Other rather than through the Other's direct actions. The speaker evokes the Other's presence by using the Other's blood, which the speaker may taste eucharistically, and "the bloudie crosse" as "physick" to soothe the self and as weapons against the conscience which divides the self; thus, the speaker has advanced to a stage where transitional objects can be used to perform the Other's role if the Other is temporarily absent.

While for a child in the transitional phase the Other is not yet real enough internally to seem useful when his or her actual presence is deferred too long, a child further along developmentally is able to evoke the imago of the parent as a response to internal or external threats. In "The Quip," we see a child's experience of a persecutory world transformed through his self-assured reliance on a powerful protective parent imago:

> The merrie world did on a day
> With his train-bands and mates agree
> To meet together, where I lay,
> And all in sport to geere at me.
>
> First, Beautie crept into a rose,
> Which when I pluckt not, Sir, said she,
> Tell me, I pray, Whose hands are those?
> *But thou shalt answer, Lord, for me.*
>
> Then Money came, and chinking still,
> What tune is this, poore man? said he:
> I heard in Musick you had skill.
> *But thou shalt answer, Lord, for me.*

Then came brave Glorie puffing by
In silks that whistled, who but he?
He scarce allow'd me half an eie.
But thou shalt answer, Lord, for me.

Then came quick Wit and Conversation,
And he would needs a comfort be,
And, to be short, make an Oration.
But thou shalt answer, Lord, for me.

Yet when the houre of thy designe
To answer these fine things shall come;
Speak not at large; say, I am thine:
And then they have their answer home.

In spite of the speaker's assertion in stanza one that the world jeers only "in sport," and is, after all, "merrie," a sense of real threat comes through as "train-bands" or trained soldiers meet together with "mates" (shipmates, playmates) and all together conspire against an isolate "me." These others, the speaker claims, have intruded "where I lay," so the speaker is not in a position to fight or flee but is taken off guard, vulnerable, lying down. Probably the intruders come in dreams. The dream allegory mechanism scripts the poem's transformations: actual others out of Renaissance court life are abstracted into types (the beautiful, the rich, the vain, and the witty), named as essences or as things (Beautie, Money, Glorie, quick Wit and Conversation) then repersonified. Since the dreamer remakes as persons in their own right those attributes of others which most threaten his sense of self, the boundary between human and non-human impingements on the self is compromised along with the boundary between reality and the dream.[81]

Thus, in stanza two, Beautie is a form which creeps into a rose (a particular instance of the Beautiful) but may symbolize a woman or women in general.[82] The speaker leaves unresolved whether the threat is sexual temptation from a human Other symbolized by the rose, temptation to overvalue the natural world metonymically represented by the rose, or temptation to embrace philosophic absolutes (the Platonic form, Beauty) as ultimate Reality. The speaker's refusal applies equally to all three temptations. Whatever Beautie represents, she challenges the speaker's refusal, mocking his seeming lack of self-possession, insinuating that if his hands were his, he would pluck the rose to possess her. But self-possession is as much

preserved through chaste refusal as it is lost through apparent
self-denial. The speaker chooses one Other (God) over another
(Beautie); he chooses the Other who preserves rather than the
Other who (in his subjective experience) accosts the self.

One might argue that the speaker's various refusals in this
poem depict in sum a false self denying his own body, material
life, and the social world. But we may as easily construe this
poem as depicting a whole (true) self denying objects which
would render him partial—a type rather than a self in relation
to a holding Other. "Glorie," for example, "scarce allow[s]" the
speaker "half an eie." The line means not only that Glorie
scarcely glances at the speaker, that Glorie winks at the speaker
or perhaps that Glorie scarcely says hello, but also that Glorie
scarcely gives to or recognizes in the speaker half an "I." The
self in relation to Glorie is merely a self-fragment.

The Lord, in contrast, allows the speaker a whole self. Though
the speaker comes across as a still dependent child not yet able
to talk back to his persecutors on his own recognizance, in this
poem the child is autonomous enough to anticipate the parent's
future answer to the world, even when the parent is not immediately available.[83] The Other is audience of the speaker's retrospective communication, but he is not actually present in the
narrative the speaker recounts to him. Within the narrative, the
speaker is self-sufficient; he is capable of saying no, of not complying because he has transformed his dependence on the actual
Other to reliance on an internalized representation of the Other.
The self in relation to God has emerged as an autonomous
true self.

If the singsong tetrameter embodies the mocking tones of the
"merrie world," it also turns those tones back on their source,
defusing the terrors of an environment where others, in succes-
sion, tempt, ridicule, ignore, or relate falsely to the speaking
self. Prosody also embodies playful energy, affectively conveying
a sense of safety, of trust in the Other the speaker is addressing;
children rarely singsong or otherwise play in the presence of
untrustworthy others.[84]

The childlike quality of the poem emerges despite the
speaker's apparent chronological maturity. Beautie calls the
speaker "Sir"; Money addresses him as "poore man," and the
temptations the speaker faces are not the temptations of a child
(though of course Freud would argue that all adult temptations
have infantile correlatives in which their meaning lies). In spite
of the disparity between prosodic playfulness and the seri-

ousness of the dramatic situation (since temptation, we may assume, is a serious matter for a Reformation Christian) the prosodic subject is more the psychic ground of the speaking self than an other in contradiction to him. After all, the speaker himself confronts temptation through childlike psychological dependence on God. In "The Quip," the Herbertian self is transparently multilayered but not really split. Simultaneously, the prosodic subject plays; the speaker as God's child leans on an internal Other's strength, and the speaker facing outward to the world says no to the world's temptations. Three self ideas (true self, Other's child, adult in the world) work as a unity.

Although "The Quip" compromises the distinction between inside and outside, showing how the external world impinges on the true self in dreams, it also establishes an internal boundary between self and other selves. Relatedness to the Other who builds and supports the self enables the speaker to stand apart from social pressures. Since the poem's dream mode places events inside the speaker, we may assume that the line between "me" and "them" established in the dream represents an emerging ego boundary rather than actual social detachment.

The speaker of "The Quip" has reached the stage of "I am," which begins with a self's narcissistic opposition to all that seems outside the self/self-object continuum. That which is "me" or "mine" is good, while that which is "not me" is bad. "The Quip" shows the negative side of this dynamic quite clearly. That the Lord will answer for the speaker means not only that the Lord will respond on his child's behalf to the bullying world, but also that the Lord will stand with the speaker to answer the Father on Judgment day.[85] The implication that the Lord may not stand with the "merrie world" is ominous, especially given the prosodic subject's playfulness. Does the pleasure derive from the speaker's overt meaning, "Lord, you will take care of me," or from his covert meaning, "They're going to get it"?[86] Both understandings are true to this phase. But as Winnicott emphasizes, the picture is not all bad, because once the line between self and others becomes clear, a person moves one crucial step closer to the capacity to contribute to society.

One way that the self-Other relationship of *The Temple* positively transforms the speaker's relationship to his environment is by enhancing his capacity for creative living. For Winnicott, creative living is not finally about Edenic bliss or narcissistic self-gratification. Rather, it means the capacity to deal with life on life's terms without being essentially compromised. Emerging from the true self's sense of ongoing relatedness to the Other, the capacity for creative living means not only personal agency but also social accountability. We see this capacity at work in "The Elixir," a poem in which the speaker's relationship to the Other becomes the foundation for his capacity to bring a responsive self to worldly obligations. In the first two stanzas, the speaker prays:

> TEach me, my God and King,
>   In all things thee to see,
> And what I do in any thing,
>   To do it as for thee:
>
> Not rudely, as a beast,
>   To runne into an action;
> But still to make thee prepossest,
>   And give it his perfection.
>
> (1–8)

Just as a child internalizes the mother-child relationship and afterwards does everything in relation to the maternal imago, the speaker of "The Elixir" prays to make the Other "prepossest," an internalized object to whom all his efforts may refer.[87] Like an introjected mother, the indwelling Other is to humanize the speaker, enhancing his capacity to approach all tasks with dignity. Prosody adds an upbeat rhythm to the speaker's words, indicating the speaker's ability in the Other's presence to approach his responsibilities playfully as well.[88]

Later in the poem, the speaker claims that even the most menial tasks can be rendered "bright and clean" if they are carried out "for thy sake" (15–16). "A servant with this clause / Makes drudgerie divine" (17–18). Relationship to God transforms the believer's experience of and attitude toward mundane responsibilities. As "the famous stone / That turneth all to gold," an attitude of continual reference to the Other also confers value on the self who performs "mean" tasks: "For that which God doth touch and own / Cannot for lesse be told" (21–22, 15, 14, 23–24).[89]

While a child's submission to the Freudian father/superego results in narcissistic injury, and a child's incapacity to communicate with the Lacanian Other results in irremediable lack, a child's relation to the Winnicottian mother gives the child narcissistic sustenance; furthermore, whereas the Freudian father/ superego prohibits the self from doing evil, and the Lacanian Law of the Father ensures the child's observance of social codes which symbolically castrate (disempower) every subject, the Winnicottian mother/object empowers the child to do good. The God of "The Elixir" is a source of power, not prohibition; the believer's sense of the Other's worth fosters a relational sense of self-worth and contributes to the believer's capacity to be worthwhile in the social realm.

Although the poems of *The Temple* are only infrequently set in the social world, other poems also imply that through relationship to an empowering Other, the speaker's relationship to society is transformed. In "Trinitie Sunday," for example, the speaker attributes his capacity "to do good" to God's sanctification of him and prays that the Other will enrich not only his "heart" but also his "mouth" and "hands" (3, 7). That is, he asks that the Other transform not only what he is or feels (the true self) but also what he says and does. He prays for "charitie," a social virtue, as well as for the internal virtues of "faith [and] hope."[90] As Herbert discusses Charity in *The Country Parson,* it entails not merely a loving attitude toward others but socially responsible acts: "When he riseth in the morning, he bethinketh himselfe what good deeds he can do that day, and presently doth them; counting that day lost, wherein he hath not exercised his Charity."[91] Similarly, for the speaker of "Divinitie," the fundamental imperative for Christian life concerns not doctrine but attitude and action: *"Love God, and love your neighbour. Watch and pray. / Do as ye would be done unto"* (17–18).

"Constancie" also develops the theme of the true self's social accountability. The "honest man" is one "that doth still and strongly good pursue, / To God, his neighbour, and himself most true" (1–3). "Honestie" implies that the man "abhorres deceit" and is a virtue that extends to his "works and fashion" as well as to his "words" (6, 18, 19). The honest man is one "Whom others faults do not defeat; / But though men fail him, yet his part doth play" (29–30). He is capable of serving his role in the world even "When the wide world runnes bias from his will" (32). The honest man has negotiated the terms of the "reality principle" so successfully that he can be socially responsible even when others let him down. As the last line of the poem makes clear, his capacities are grounded in relationship to God, to whom he prays for the virtue he manifests.

Even though Herbert does not often deal with social life, instead focusing on the transformation of the self in relation to God, those poems in which he does address social action suggest that in Herbert, grace theology does not mean the abolition of an ethical imperative. Instead, it means the establishment of that imperative on a relational foundation. Christ's mothering of the believer alters the believer's relationships not only to God and himself but also, at least potentially, to others.

The implications are historical as much as individual. If the self often represented by Herbert's speaker is a culturally determined self deeply at odds with the bodily and existential life residing in the true self and expressed by form, genuine life is aborted for the sake of appearances. History shows that such a condition was by no means aberrant in the Renaissance. What is striking is that the Herbertian true self remains viable in spite of the conflict and in some poems comes to dominate even the speaking sensibility. In these poems, the Herbertian self is converted *to* rather than *from* himself. Through faith, "Herbert" intuits the path of relational individualism, the middle way between subjection and unenlightened self-interest.

Notes

Introduction

1. William Pahlka, *Saint Augustine's Meter and George Herbert's Will* (Kent, Ohio: Kent State University Press, 1987), 131–72. I should acknowledge here that, while I challenge some of Pahlka's conclusions in regard to Herbert's form, I share many of his interests and ways of reading, and I have found his book quite beneficial not only as a source that sent my own thinking in new directions but also as a source to which I have referred numerous times.

2. Richard E. Hughes, "George Herbert and the Incarnation," in *Essential Articles for the Study of George Herbert's Poetry (Essential Articles)* ed. John R. Roberts (Hamden, Conn.: Archon, 1979), 52–62, passim. Heather A. R. Asals, *Equivocal Predication: George Herbert's Way to God* (Toronto: University of Toronto Press), 70–72.

3. Eliot refers to "a new unity" that the metaphysical poets forged, but also discusses the unity/unification of sensibility in process terms: "When a poet's mind is perfectly equipped for its work, it is constantly amalgamating disparate experience." T. S. Eliot, "The Metaphysical Poets," in *Selected Essays* (San Diego: Harcourt & Brace Jovanovich, 1950), 245, 247.

4. For a good sense of Crews' critiques of psychoanalysis, see Frederick Crews, *Skeptical Engagements* (New York: Oxford University Press, 1986), e.g. 18–42 and 75–111; for his debate with a number of advocates of Freudianism and some contemporary applications of Freudian ideas see also Crews' *The Memory Wars: Freud's Legacy in Dispute* (New York: The New York Review of Books, 1995), passim. In regard to Crews' debate with theoretically minded trends in literary criticism, see especially *Skeptical Engagements,* 115–78.

5. Crews, *Skeptical Engagements,* 173.

6. Ibid., 21, 30–31, and 159–78.

7. William Empson, *Seven Types of Ambiguity* (London: Chatto and Windus, 1930), 286–95.

8. Rosemond Tuve, "On Herbert's Sacrifice," in Roberts, *Essential Articles,* 434–52. Cf. Tuve, *A Reading of George Herbert* (Chicago: University of Chicago Press, 1952), esp. 19–99.

9. Eugene Veith makes this point in the opening chapter of *Reformation Spirituality: The Religion of George Herbert* (Lewisburg, Pa.: Bucknell University Press; London and Toronto: Associated University Presses, 1985), esp. 12–13.

10. Brooke Hopkins, "Jesus and Object Use: A Winnicottian Account of the Resurrection Myth," in *Transitional Objects and Potential Spaces: Literary Uses of D. W. Winnicott,* ed. Peter L. Rudnytsky (New York: Columbia University Press, 1993), 250.

11. Donald W. Winnicott, *Playing and Reality* (London: Tavistock Publications, 1982), xi.

12. Peter L. Rudnytsky, *The Psychoanalytic Vocation: Rank, Winnicott and the Legacy of Freud* (New Haven: Yale University Press, 1991), esp. 155 and 166–67.

Chapter 1. Notes Toward Another Music

1. Albert McHarg Hayes, "Counterpoint in Herbert," 283–97; and Alicia Ostriker, "Song and Speech in the Metrics of George Herbert," 298–310, both in *Essential Articles;* Louise Schleiner, "Jacobean Song and Herbert's Metrics," *SEL* 19 (1979): 109–26; Coburn Freer, *Music For a King: George Herbert's Style and the Metrical Psalms* (Baltimore: Johns Hopkins University Press, 1972); and Helen Wilcox, "Herbert's Musical Contexts: Countrey Aires To Angels Musick," in *Like Seasoned Timber: New Essays on George Herbert,* ed. Edmund Miller and Robert DiYanni (New York: Peter Lang, 1987). For an intriguing discussion of the idea of harmony in the English poetry tradition, including some discussion of Herbert, see John Hollander, *The Untuning of the Sky: Ideas of Music in English Poetry 1500–1700* (New York: Norton, 1970).

2. Although prosody is often not the primary focus, it is an integral component of critical work focusing on the visual dimension of Herbert's poems. See Bart Westerweel, *Patterns and Patterning: A Study of Four Poems by George Herbert* (Amsterdam: Rodophi, 1984); Elizabeth Cook, *Seeing Through Words: The Scope of Late Renaissance Poetry* (New Haven: Yale University Press, 1986), 40–44, 48–71; Charles A. Huttar, "Herbert and the Emblem: Herbert and Emblematic Tradition," in Miller, *Like Seasoned Timber;* and Martin Elsky, *Authorizing Words: Speech, Writing and Print in the English Renaissance* (Ithaca: Cornell University Press, 1989), 147–83. For two good sources on the visual dimension of Renaissance British literature more generally (each making brief reference to Herbert) see Ernest B. Gilman, *The Curious Perspective: Literary and Pictorial Wit in the Seventeenth Century* (New Haven: Yale University Press, 1978); and Murray Roston, *Renaissance Perspectives in Literature and the Visual Arts* (Princeton: Princeton University Press, 1987).

3. Richard Todd, *The Opacity of Signs: Acts of Interpretation in George Herbert's The Temple* (Columbia, Mo.: University of Missouri Press, 1986), 156–198; Veith, *Reformation Spirituality,* 107–116; Pahlka, *Saint Augustine's Meter;* David Ormerod, "Number Theory in George Herbert's 'Trinity Sunday'," *George Herbert Journal* 12 (1989): 27–36; Sybil-Lutz Severance, "Numerological Structures in *The Temple,*" in *Too Rich to Clothe the Sunne: Essays on George Herbert,* ed. Claude J. Summers and Ted-Larry Pebworth (Pittsburgh: University of Pittsburgh Press, 1980); and Susanne Woods, "The Unhewn Stones of Herbert's Verse," *George Herbert Journal* 4 (1981). See also Hughes, "Herbert and the Incarnation," and Philip Harlan Christensen, "The Sonnets from Walton's Life: Sonnets of the Sonne," in Miller, *Like Seasoned Timber.*

4. Arnold Stein, *George Herbert's Lyrics* (Baltimore: Johns Hopkins University Press, 1968); and Rodney Edgecombe, *"Sweetnesse Readie Penn'd": Imagery, Syntax, and Metrics in the Poetry of George Herbert,* James Hogg, ed. (Salzburg: Salzburg Studies in English Literature, Elizabethan and Renaissance Studies, 84.2, 1980).

5. Joseph H. Summers, *George Herbert: His Religion and Art* (London: Chatto and Windus, 1954), 73–94; and Stanley Fish, *Self-Consuming Artifacts: The Experience of Seventeenth-Century Literature* (Berkeley and Los Angeles: University of California Press, 1972).

6. According to Scarry, "What matters (what signifies, what has standing, what counts) has substance." Elaine Scarry, ed., *Literature and the Body: Essays on Populations and Persons* (Baltimore: Johns Hopkins University Press, 1988). xxii.

7. Summers, *Herbert: His Religion and Art*, 73–77; Pahlka, *Saint Augustine's Meter*, e.g., 147.

8. Asals, *Equivocal Predication*, 70–72.

9. Hughes, "Herbert and The Incarnation," esp. 54.

10. Asals, *Equivocal Predication*, 71.

11. Freer, *Music For a King*, 194–95.

12. For a fuller sense of the possible irony, compare Lodge's use of the stanza to Herbert's:

> Lord how her lippes doo dwell vpon his cheekes;
> And how she lookes for babies in his eies:
> And how she sighes, and sweares shee loues and leekes,
> And how she vowes, and he her vowes enuies.
>   Trust me, the enuious Nimphs in looking on,
>   Were forst with teares for to assist her mone.
>
> ("Glaucus and Silla," 619–24)

See Thomas Lodge, *The Complete Works of Thomas Lodge,* ed. Edmund W. Gosse, 1883 (New York: Russell and Russell, 1963), vol 1: n.p..

13. Writing on Spenser, Richard Helgerson makes my point:

> Discursive forms matter. . . . They have a meaning and effect that can sometimes complement but that can also contradict the manifest content of any particular work. Forms in this view are as much agents as they are structures. They make things happen. (*Forms of Nationhood,* p. 6)

14. My way of reading here parallels that of Pahlka, though I will argue for a more personalized, embodied sense of unity than he argues for in interpreting similar data. See Pahlka's *Saint Augustine's Meter,* e.g. 86–99.

15. On form in "The Collar," see Summers, *Herbert: His Religion and Art,* 92.

16. For the pun on "re-forming" in regard to "The Altar," see M. Thomas Hester, "Altering the Text of the Self: The Shapes of 'The Altar,'" in *A Fine Tuning: Studies of the Religious Poetry of Herbert and Milton,* Mary Maleski, ed. (Binghamton, N.Y.: Medieval and Renaissance Texts and Studies, 1989), 95.

17. Martin Luther, *Luther's Works,* 55 vols., ed. Jaroslav Pelikan and Helmut T. Lehmann (St. Louis: Concordia Publishing House, 1955), vol. 25, 313.

18. Philipp Melanchthon, *On Christian Doctrine,* ed., trans. Clyde L. Manshrek (New York: Oxford University Press, 1965), 314; Luther, *Works,* vol. 25, 309–12.

19. cf. vol. 35, 356.

20. The phrase "two Herberts" is, of course, not original. Douglas Bush discusses how in *The Temple* "the Anglican parish priest merges with the larger poet, with the very human saint who gives fresh and moving utterance to the

aspirations and failures of the spiritual life." Douglas Bush, *English Literature in the Earlier Seventeenth Century, 1600–1660* (London: Oxford University Press, 1945; reprint 1946), 138. Stanley Fish discusses two critical views of Herbert: on the one hand, Herbert is an artist who crafts "a structure that is firm, secure, and complete," but on the other hand, Herbert is a speaker who articulates his experience in terms of "a structure (if structure is the word) that is precarious, shifting, and unfinished." Stanley Fish, *The Living Temple: George Herbert and Catechizing* (Berkeley and Los Angeles: University of California Press, 1978), 1–11, esp. 11.

While Fish seeks to move beyond this dialectic, I seek a synthesis of the two opposing positions. If we may construe stable form as a persona distinguishable from, yet through divine intervention emerging out of, an unstable speaker, then both Herberts may be *in* the text (as well as in history if we wish to seek them there) and their difference may be construed as part of the text's meaning.

21. Robert W. Halli Jr., "The Double Hieroglyph in George Herbert's 'Easter Wings,'" *Philological Quarterly* 63 (1984).

22. Cf. Hunter, who claims that Herbert often uses imagery of rising to represent the soul's ascent toward God during the eucharist. Hunter interprets this imagery with reference to Calvin's assumption that God's Real Presence is not in the bread or wine but rather in heaven, and those who observe the eucharist in faith are lifted up spiritually to him ("'With Winges of Faith.'") As will become clear in due course, I do not view Herbert's theology as essentially Calvinist; especially in regard to his attitudes toward physical life, Herbert shares more with Luther than Calvin, I believe.

23. All quotations of Donne's poems will come from *Complete English Poems of John Donne*, ed. C. A. Patrides (London: Dart, 1985).

24. Halli, "Double Hieroglyph," 268–69.

25. John Donne, *The Sermons of John Donne*, vol. 4, ed. George R. Potter and Evelyn M. Simpson (Berkeley and Los Angeles: University of California Press, 1959), 56–57.

26. On how early editions were printed—the stanzas arranged on separate, facing pages to represent two angels' wings, the "upper edges of the wings . . . less steeply inclined than the lower edges"—see C. C. Brown and W. P. Ingoldsby, "George Herbert's 'Easter-Wings,'" in Roberts, *Essential Articles,* esp. 465–66.

27. Elsky, *Authorizing Words,* 156.

28. Sidney, *A Defense of Poetry,* 77. Of course, the Greek word, ποίειν, from which we derive *poet,* is related to the Latin verb *facere* only through their English translations. Nevertheless, once Sidney anglicizes the notion of poet as maker, the pun on the etymological roots of *mortification* becomes available to Herbert.

29. Philip Sidney, "A Defence of Poetry,"in *Miscellaneous Prose of Sir Philip Sidney,* Katherine Duncan-Jones and Jan Van Dorsten, eds. (Oxford: Clarendon Press, 1973), 79.

30. Ibid., 78.

31. Ibid., 79. On the Humanist equation between Eden and the Golden Age and on the poet's function as spiritual alchemist, see also Hiram Collins Haydn, *The Counter-Renaissance* (New York: Charles Scribner's Sons, 1950), 514–15.

32. Sherwood offers a good discussion of the theme of quickening in *The Temple,* but he interprets *quickness* in terms of the spirit rather than the

body and focuses on the way that *The Temple* develops this theme discursively rather than formally. Terry G. Sherwood, *Herbert's Prayerful Art* (Toronto: University of Toronto Press, 1989), 121–43. In the fullest sense of the word, *quickening* refers to the inspiration of the body or to the union of pneuma (breath, life, soul) and soma.

33. A number of assumptions will inform my treatment of meter throughout my work. I would like to explain them here.

Some prosodic theorists insist that only two degrees of syllabic stress (stress/nonstress) inhere in the English language and that the contrast between the two is heightened in English prosody; others contend that at least four levels of stress variation are audible in English poetic lines (primary, secondary, and tertiary stress and nonstress); hypothetically scientific instruments should be able to register ten variations on stress in most iambic pentameter lines. Finally, my ear can count to about three: stress (/), non-stress (˘), and something in between (\ ).

1) A seemingly insignificant word or syllable (e.g., a preposition, a conjunction, an article, an empty suffix) falls in a stress position,
and
2) the other syllable in the foot seems equally insignificant;
especially if
3) more substantive words or syllables in the line fall in non-stress positions,
and
4) these more substantive words or syllables occur in feet where alternate words or syllables have primary stress;
therefore,
5) these more important words or syllables in non-stress positions also merit intermediate (secondary) stress.

My scansion of the opening of Milton's *Paradise Lost* will illustrate:

> ˘ / \ / ˘ / ˘ \ /
> Of Man's First Disobedience, and the Fruit
> ˘ / \ / ˘ / ˘ / ˘
> Of that Forbidden Tree, whose mortal taste
> \ / ˘\ ˘ / ˘ / ˘ /
> Brought Death into the World, and all our woe,
> / / ˘ \ \ ˘ / ˘ /
> With loss of *Eden,* till one greater Man
> ˘ / \ \ ˘ / ˘ / ˘ /
> Restore us, and regain the blissful Seat,
> \ / ˘ / ˘ \ ˘ / ˘ /
> Sing Heav'nly Muse, that on the secret top
> ˘ / \ ˘ / \ ˘ /
> Of *Oreb,* or of *Sinai,* didst inspire
> \ / ˘ \ \ / ˘ / ˘ /
> That Shepherd, who first taught the chosen Seed
> \ ˘ ˘ / ˘ / ˘ / ˘ /
> In the Beginning how the Heav'ns and Earth
> / ˘ ˘ /
> Rose out of *Chaos.* (PL 1–10)

One of the best prosodists in the language, Milton typically puts insignificant words or syllables in stress positions only in lines where other feet seem hyperstressed. Rhythm is enriched because there is as much tension between as within feet and the places within lines where feet exist in tension to each other vary from line to line. Furthermore, through placing seemingly empty words or syllables in stress positions, Milton (even more than other poets) raises them to a level of heightened importance; words like *and* in lines one and five, *till* in line four, *on* in line six, and *or* in line seven signal grammatical relationships imperative to our understanding of Milton's Logocentric rhetoric.

In the marked passage, other secondary stresses may be possible, especially in the first and second feet of line two (Should *that* receive more emphasis than the first syllable of *forbidden?*). But as my scansion of the first foot of line ten suggests, it is not necessary to mark all insignificant words in stressed positions with secondary stresses. "On" in line six and "or" in line seven receive secondary stresses because both fall in stress positions and are juxtaposed with equally insignificant words in their respective feet; "or" in line seven warrants a secondary stress also because, like "in" in line nine, it sounds an internal rhyme with a strongly stressed syllable in an adjacent foot. On the other hand, "out" in line ten need not receive a secondary stress (though some readers might mark one) because within the foot, *rose,* a strong verb, warrants a primary stress in spite of its position; hence, line ten may be said to exemplify principles of metric substitution more than it illustrates principles of secondary stress.

As a rule of thumb, I tend to hear, in accordance with formalist habits of hearing, a five-beat line when there is an underlying pentameter pattern, a four-beat line when there is an underlying tetrameter pattern and so on. As poems like "Deniall" and "The Collar" make clear, such patterns may arise in Herbert's poems even out of apparent chaos. To some degree, these patterns are projected, to some degree discovered. Of course, there are instances (rare in Herbert) when poetic lines cannot (or for mimetic/dramatic reasons should not) be neatly resolved to approximate a base measure.

In using a three-value stress system, I am assuming that the ear and mind register the binary value of a secondary stress relative to its prosodic environment. Within a duple foot, if a secondary stress precedes a full stress or follows a non-stress, one may hear an iamb, as in the second and third feet of Shakespeare's line:

$$\smallsmile \quad / \quad \backslash \quad / \quad \smallsmile \quad \backslash \quad \smallsmile \quad / \quad \smallsmile \quad /$$
"And tell sad stories of the death of kings."

Thus, following a binary system, some readers would mark the line as regular:

$$\smallsmile \quad / \quad \smallsmile \quad / \quad \smallsmile \quad / \quad \smallsmile \quad / \quad \smallsmile \quad /$$
"And tell sad stories of the death of kings."

However, within the line as a whole, the perceived value of a secondary stress may be increased or decreased relative to other secondary stresses. Thus other readers using a binary system might mark the same Shakespeare line as having two substitutions:

$$\smallsmile \quad / \quad / \quad / \quad \smallsmile \quad \smallsmile \quad \smallsmile \quad / \quad \smallsmile \quad /$$
"And tell sad stories of the death of kings."

Here, the spondaic substitution in the second foot balances a pyrrhic substitution in the third foot.

In short, binary scansion can attend only to one or the other of two competing phenomena: the syllable's value within the foot or the syllable's value within the line. A three-value accounting of stress leaves open the possibility that a syllable may be construed once within the foot and a second time within the line; a foot may seem iambic in itself yet pyrrhic or spondaic in relation to another foot. Thus, as I use a secondary stress mark, it represents not an absolute determination of a syllable's stress value but rather a variable in a complex metric equation. I assume that a good listener may entertain more than one sense of a syllable's relative stress value, just as a good reader may entertain more than one sense of a word's (or a line's or a text's) meaning. In its very failure to specify how to resolve metric ambiguities which some readers hear with reference to the foot, others hear with reference to the line, and still others hear as metric paradoxes, a three-level stress system seems preferable to the more sophisticated four-level system. By measuring intermediate stress itself in binary terms (secondary, tertiary), the four-level system quantifies the relative tension between syllables in the foot and among syllables or feet within the line which the written product embodies; in doing so, it negates the experience of ambiguity in regard to the stress value of a single syllable which the reading process negotiates.

An assumption implicit in much of what I have said thus far is that with some lines, multiple scansions may be equally plausible. The first line of "Love" (III) provides a good example. The line is clearly iambic pentameter, but how are we to scan it?:

> / \ \ / ‿ \ ‿ / \ /
> Love bade me welcome: yet my soul drew back.
>   / ‿ / ‿ / ‿ / ‿ /
> Love bade me welcome: yet my soul drew back.
> / ‿ ‿ / ‿ / ‿ / \ /
> Love bade me welcome: yet my soul drew back.

Given that the line is built primarily around strong monosyllables, all three of these (and several other) scansions are possible. Much depends on a reader's sense of verse and of how versification rules may be modified to fit with the discursive level of a text; the rest depends on more specific points of interpretation. We may even theorize about what set of prosodic rules and exceptions and what sense of the line's meaning might determine each of these scansions.

The first scansion is attuned to the dramatic situation. A reader offering this scansion might reason that *Love* is the name and nature of the speaker's God, so it is one of the more emphasized (hence stressed) words in the line; the words *bade* and *me* are less important, but since both have long vowels, since "bade" falls in a stress position, and since "me," the object of "Love," denotes the second party in the self-Other relationship and furthermore may register the speaker's surprise that Love would bid *him* welcome (Who? me?), both words may receive secondary stresses; the first syllable of *welcome* is the high point (and loudest syllable) of the first clause; *yet*, though in a stress position, should receive only a secondary stress because it is only a conjunction; *soul* is an important word in a stress position, and the soul's drawing back is made more vivid if prosody is understood to mime the soul's shuddering withdrawal with three stressed syllables in a row. But since *drew* falls in a non-stress position, it should receive only a secondary stress.

The second scansion (the least appealing from my own point of view) respects the iambic pentameter base measure of the line more than the line's dramatic possibilities. A reader offering this scansion might argue that, in the absence of pronounced substitutions, we can assume that a line is regular. Most monosyllabic lines can be scanned in accordance with a metronome.

The third scansion interprets the drama of the line somewhat differently than the first does; also, it is more attuned to the line's base meter than the first scansion is, but at the same time it allows for more rhythmic play in the line than the second scansion does. In contrast to the first scansion, the third de-emphasizes *bade* and *me*. A reader marking the line this third way might contend that most alternate syllables in a pentameter line should remain unstressed in order to render exceptions to the rule more rhythmically and dramatically compelling; this reader might then reason that since the speaker portrays himself throughout the poem as insignificant relative to the Other, *me* should be unstressed and *Love* stressed; furthermore, the transitive verb which indicates that Love uttered (*bade*) pales in comparison to the object of the verb which indicates what Love uttered (*welcome*). The third reader might also assert that a caesura (a silence roughly a foot long in duration) corresponds with the line's colon. The caesura emphasizes the competition between the line's two independent clauses which the contrasting connector *yet* announces: such competition makes sense rhetorically, since the first five-word clause describes Love's action, while the second five-word clause describes the soul's equal and opposite reaction. The line splits in two. In addition, by strongly emphasizing *yet,* this third marking of the line allows for a possible pun. The soul, "guiltie of dust and sinne" resists God *yet*—that is, even after arriving in heaven ("Love" (III), 2).

One of the more provocative writers on Herbert's form, William Pahlka, writes that meter is "mathematics, not dramatics" (*Saint Augustine's Meter,* xi). I view prosodic interpretation, like all interpretation, as somewhat subjective, though not entirely so. It is at the very least more like geometric proof than arithmetical calculation. My scansion throughout will reflect readerly prosodic performance in relation to sensed meaning, affect, or emphasis, as much as it registers the (often indeterminate or competing) objective properties of language (e.g. accent, loudness, vowel length, syllable duration) in tension with the exigencies of a set form. Finally, even though I find it useful to articulate the principles underlying my scansion habits in systematic terms, I view all of these principles as more descriptive than prescriptive. As with most things that matter, in regard to poetic form there is ample room for debate.

For alternative approaches to scanning Herbertian metrics, see Pahlka, *Saint Augustine's Meter,* esp. xvi–xxi; and Stein, *George Herbert's Lyrics,* esp. 45–84; in relation to Stein's method, cf. Freer, *Music For a King,* e.g., 229ff. In regard to the subjective component of scansion, note esp. Stein, 46; and see Susanne Woods, *Natural Emphasis: English Versification from Chaucer to Dryden* (San Marino, Calif: Huntington Library, 1984), 10–14. For theory about how metric substitutions in one foot pressure other feet within a line and about how metrical substitutions relate to discursive meaning, see Paul Fussell, *Poetic Meter and Poetic Form,* rev. ed. (New York: Random House, 1979). For a prosodic theorist who advocates abandoning the concept of poetic feet in favor of line-based scansion, see Derek Attridge, *The Rhythms of English Poetry* (London: Longmans, 1982). For further general information on poetic form, see James McAuley, *Versification: A Short Introduction* (Detroit: Michigan State University Press, 1966).

34. I should note that Woods is discussing another poem in this context— not "The Altar." But see her "Unhewn Stones," 36.

35. In regard to the noun, the *OED* indicates, "The pronunciation 'cement is found from 14thC., but is now almost superseded by ce'ment after the vb"— a statement from which I deduce that the verb *was* accented on the second syllable in the speech of the Middle Ages and the Renaissance. Donka Minkova

of the UCLA English department confirms this assumption, explaining that "Generally, homophonous disyllabic verbs and nouns of French/Latin origin allow stress on the first syllable for the noun, but rarely, if ever, for the verb." (E-mail to the author, 10 February, 1997).

Another interesting point about the word *cement* is its derivation from Latin words meaning "rough stone" (*caementum*) and "to cut" (*caedere*). As many critics point out, Herbert's poem alludes to Bible passages (esp. Exodus 20:25; and Deuteronomy 27:2–5) in which God tells the Israelites to make his altar of unhewn stones and not to use any tools in constructing it; the altar—a type of the human heart, as Summers points out—is not to be polluted by human construction. So the etymological roots of "cemented" ironically mediate between what God asks for ("rough stone") and what he forbids ("to cut"). Of course, Herbert's altar, untouched by "workmans tool," is "cemented"—that is held together—"with teares," and "nothing but / [God's] pow'r doth cut"—or shape—it.

On Biblical references in "The Altar," see esp. Summers, *Herbert: His Religion and Art,* 140–42; and Barbara K. Lewalski, *Protestant Poetics and the Seventeenth-Century Religious Lyric* (Princeton: Princeton University Press, 1979), e.g., 312. On the paradox of agency in "The Altar," see Fish, *Self-Consuming Artifacts,* 207–15; Richard Strier, *Love Known: Theology and Experience in George Herbert's Poetry* (Chicago: University of Chicago Press, 1983), 191–95; and Michael C. Schoenfeldt, *Prayer and Power: George Herbert and Renaissance Courtship* (Chicago: University of Chicago Press, 1991), 166–67.

36. On the Donne echo, see Herbert, *George Herbert The Complete English Poems,* ed. Tobin.

37. If the stress mark on the first syllable of *cemented* in some editions accurately represents Herbert's intentions, then the line calls attention to itself as paradoxically artificial by departing from speech stress. Otherwise, as Minkova explains, the whole line may be understood as a substitution, one purpose of which may be to "draw attention to the content of the line." Minkova scans the line as "headless" and "not pure iambic" since "it contains four triples, feet of the type : x x X—trisyllabic feet rather than disyllabic, but still not real anapests, because the line is embedded in pure iambic" measure. Although as she points out, even by this scansion the line is "not without precedent" and is consistent with expectations in regard to its syllable count, I continue to believe that the line—scanned either way—is somewhat awkward, and appropriately so if we are to view the form as mimetic. (Minkova, e-mails to the author 12, 13 February 1997).

38. James Boyd White, *"This Book of Starres": Learning to Read George Herbert* (Ann Arbor, Mich.: University of Michigan Press, 1994), 86–87.

39. Ibid., 79.

40. Summers, *Herbert: His Religion and Art,* 141–43; cf. *Works of George Herbert,* F. E. Hutchinson, ed. (London: Penguin, 1991), 484–85.

41. Strier, *Love Known,* 1–28; Veith, *Reformation Spirituality,* 43–48, 150–51.

42. William V. Nestrick, "'Mine' and 'Thine' in *The Temple,*" in Summers, *Too Rich,* esp. 115 and 127.

43. Stanley Fish, "Letting Go: The Reader in Herbert's Poetry," *ELH* 37 (1970): 475–94; Cf. *Self-Consuming Artifacts,* 207–15.

44. Barbara Leah Harman, *Costly Monuments: Representations of the Self in George Herbert's Poetry* (Cambridge: Harvard University Press, 1982), 188.

45. T. S. Eliot, *T. S. Eliot: The Complete Poems and Plays 1909–1950* (San Diego: Harcourt Brace Jovanovich, 1971), 5.

46. Jacques Lacan, *The Seminar of Jacques Lacan: Bk I, Freud's Papers on Technique, 1953–54,* ed. Jacques-Allain Miller, trans. John Forrester (New York: Norton, 1988), 215.

47. White, *"This Book of Starres",* 81.

48. Winnicott, *Playing and Reality,* 111–18.

49. To elaborate on "mirroring," an infant is born without a sense of separateness from others or the environment. This "oceanic" sense of self continues for some months. But in the second stage of development—labeled by Lacan "the mirror stage"—the infant begins to understand that the self is distinct from others. In Lacan's model, a fundamental conflict to be resolved at this stage is the tension between the baby's sense of the "Real" (which entails an awareness of her or his body as helpless, flailing, fragmented) and the baby's "imaginary" sense of wholeness—a self-image which originates in the infant's joyful recognition (or misrecognition) of self in the mirror. In Winnicott's model, the mirror stage self-image is not illusory at all; it comes to the child from the mother, who perceives the child's potential wholeness and communicates it to the child: "The precursor of the mirror is the mother's face" (*Playing and Reality,* 111). For Winnicott, the Real does not exist unless the mother as mirror fails. See Sigmund Freud, *Civilization and Its Discontents,* vol. 21 of *The Standard Edition of the Complete Psychological Works of Sigmund Freud,* ed. & trans. James Strachey, et. al. (London: Hogarth Press, 1927–31), 64–73; Jacques Lacan, *Ecrits: A Selection,* trans. Alan Sheridan (New York: Norton, 1977), 1–7; and Winnicott, *Playing and Reality,* 111–118.

50. For Winnicott, either a mother mirrors the child so that when the baby looks into the mother's face, "what the baby sees is himself or herself"—and this is always a positive experience—or the mother fails to mirror the child by not responding or by projecting her own mood onto the child (*Playing and Reality,* 122). In a sense, then, to argue that form registers the Real (which by Winnicottian logic would not exist if the mother-child relationship were good enough) is to argue that the Other does not "mirror" the speaker at all; rather, prosody reflects a self-alienation born in the absence of mirroring.

An alternative Winnicottian reading is possible, however. I will argue in chapter 4 that, from a Winnicottian standpoint, the speaker may be understood as a false self. Here prosody reflects the truth about the false self—that he is fragmentary, and, from a psychoanalytic standpoint, too brittle. As the last section of chapter 4 will make clear, the proper mirror for a false self *is* a negative mirror: an Other who recognizes the false self (definable as such by its incompleteness) as inadequate.

For Lacanian theory regarding the mirror stage dimension of poetic expression, see Julia Kristeva, *Revolution in Poetic Language,* trans. Margaret Walker (New York: Columbia University Press, 1984).

51. Hester, "Altering the Text," 111.

52. Two of the critics who have discussed the "I" shape of the altar, Donald R. Dickson and M. Thomas Hester, disagree on this point. Dickson argues that the classical altar shape "suspiciously resembles the pronominal 'I'," implying that the self signified by this pronoun is the same fallen self who has tried to erase himself in the course of the poem. For Dickson the "I" hieroglyph is part

of the speaker's missing the point, as is the physicality of the classical altar shape. Donald R. Dickson, *The Fountain of Living Waters: The Typology of the Waters of Life in the Poetry of Herbert, Vaughan and Traherne* (Columbia, Mo.: University Press of Missouri, 1987), (93) In contrast, Hester argues that "'The Altar' is centrally concerned with a re-forming, reframing, or re-creating of the self (or the various 'parts' of the self)." Thus, as Hester reads the poem, it "is as much self-creating as self-consuming," the speaker's re-formation being signified by the prosodic "I." ("Altering the Text," esp. 95 and 111).

53. Those familiar with Winnicottian ideas will recognize that I am gesturing here toward a reading of prosody as the "true self" of *The Temple,* in contrast to the speaker as a false self; a full development of the idea will come in Chapter 4. In very general terms, I am implying throughout this essay that like a true self, the prosodic subject is a psychosomatic unity "based in the body," while the speaker is a fragmentary self based in the mind; that the prosodic subject is a self born through Christ's good-enough mothering, while the speaker's symptoms of personality disorder suggest that his mothering was not good enough; that form becomes an agency empowered through the grace of the good-enough mother (Christ) while the speaker manifests the sense of lack and inadequacy that characterizes a false self. See Donald W. Winnicott, *The Maturational Processes and the Facilitating Environment: Studies in the Theory of Emotional Development* (New York: International Universities Press, 1965), esp 140–52.

54. Strier, *Love Known,* 195.

55. Ibid., xiii–xiv.

56. Luther, *Works,* vol. 37, 99.

57. Strier, *Love Known,* 217.

58. Dickson, *Fountain of Living Waters,* 107–8, 101–2.

59. Ellie Ragland-Sullivan, "Seeking the Third Term," in *Femininism and Psychoanalysis,* ed. Richard Feldstein and Judith Roof (Ithaca: Cornell University Press, 1989), 62.

60. Winnicott, *Maturational Processes,* 37–55.

61. Norman Holland, *Poems in Persons: An Introduction to the Psychoanalysis of Literature* (New York: Norton, 1973), 84; see also his *5 Readers Reading* (New Haven: Yale University Press, 1975), 86–87; or for more recent developments in Holland's theory, see his *The Brain of Robert Frost* (New York: Routledge, 1988).

62. Chana Bloch, *Spelling the Word: George Herbert and the Bible* (Berkeley and Los Angeles: University of California Press, 1985), 171–72.

63. For an account of Herbert as a reader of natural signs, see Todd, *Opacity of Signs.*

Chapter 2. On Herbert's Feminine Form

1. E. Pearlman, "George Herbert's God," *ELR* 13 (1983): 88–112, esp. 95.

2. For two critics who do mention the possibility that God is maternal in Herbert's poems, see Helen Vendler, *The Poetry of George Herbert* (Cambridge: Harvard University Press, 1975), 55; and John N. Wall, *Transformations of the World: Spencer, Herbert, Vaughan* (Athens: University of Georgia Press, 1988), 236. For a critic who pursues the implication that Christ is feminine, see Schoenfeldt, *Prayer and Power,* 249 and 265.

3. Summers, *Herbert: His Religion and Art,* 89.

4. Pearlman, "George Herbert's God," 97.

5. Fish, *Living Temple,* 54–89.

6. On the fluidity of gender boundaries in the Renaissance and on the relationship between gender and social position, see Thomas Walter Laqueur, *Making Sex: Body and Gender from the Greeks to Freud* (Cambridge: Harvard University Press, 1990), esp. 122–42.

7. See for instance Theodora A. Jankowski, "As I Am Egypt's Queen: Cleopatra, Elizabeth I and the Female Body Politic," *Assays* 5 (1989): passim.

8. Count Baldesar Castiglione, *The Book of The Courtier,* trans. Leonard Eckstein Opdycke (New York: Horace Liveright, 1929), 28–29.

9. Stephen Greenblatt, *Shakespearean Negotiations: The Circulation of Social Energy in Renaissance England* (Berkeley and Los Angeles: University of California Press, 1988), 92; see also Thomas Elyot, *A Critical Edition of Sir Thomas Elyot's the Boke Named the Governour,* ed. Donald W. Rude (New York: Garland Publishing, 1992), 33.

10. On the feminization of mankind and Christ in relation to God in medieval thought, see Caroline Walker Bynum, *Jesus as Mother: Studies in the Spirituality of the High Middle Ages* (Berkeley and Los Angeles: University of California Press, 1982), 110–69. For an extension of these ideas to the early-modern period, see Gail Kern Paster, " 'In the Spirit of Men There is No Blood': Blood as Trope of Gender in *Julius Caesar,*" *Shakespeare Quarterly* 40 (1989): passim.

11. Bynum, *Jesus as Mother,* 110–69; also see her "The Body of Christ in the Later Middle Ages: A Reply to Leo Steinberg," *Renaissance Quarterly* 39 (1986); and her *Holy Feast and Holy Fast: The Significance of Food to Medieval Women* (Berkeley and Los Angeles: University of California Press, 1987), 260–76.

12. Bynum, *Jesus as Mother,* 132; and *Holy Feast,* 65. Cf. Leah Sinanoglou Marcus, *Childhood and Cultural Despair: A Theme and Variations in Seventeenth-Century Literature* (Pittsburgh: University of Pittsburgh Press, 1978), 146.

13. Laqueur might phrase the point differently. In fact, he argues that gender was more "real" and primary than sex to people in the Renaissance; although they recognized vast differences between males and females in a legal sense, they believed both were variations on a single sex. See Laqueur, *Making Sex,* e.g., 8.

14. Laqueur, *Making Sex,* 106 and 123–25.

15. On James' reference to himself as nursing mother, see for instance Paster, "In the Spirit of Men," 295; Coppelia Kahn, "The Absent Mother in *King Lear,*" in *Rewriting the Renaissance: The Discourses of Sexual Difference in Early Modern Europe,* ed. Margaret W. Ferguson, Maureen Quilligan, and Nancy J. Vickers (Chicago: University of Chicago Press, 1986), 59; and Debora Kuller Shuger, *Habits of Thought in the English Renaissance: Religion, Politics and the Dominant Culture* (Berkeley and Los Angeles: University of California Press, 1990), 239.

16. For this point and for an extensive discussion of mothering in the Renaissance, see Margaret L. King, *Women of the Renaissance* (Chicago: University of Chicago Press, 1991), 1–24.

17. On psychoanalytic implications of the virgin mother from a Lacanian point of view, see Julia Kristeva, *Tales of Love,* trans. Leon S. Roudiez (New

York: Columbia University Press, 1987), 234–63. For the contrast between Eve and Mary, see esp. 239.

18. Aristotle, "Generation of Animals," in vol. 1 of *The Complete Works of Aristotle: The Revised Oxford Translation,* ed. Jonathan Barnes (Princeton: Princeton University Press, 1984), 1146 (738b: 25–26). For discussion of how Aristotle's ideas influence Renaissance thinking about women, see Ian Maclean, *The Renaissance Notion of Woman: A Study in the Fortunes of Scholasticism and Medical Science in European Intellectual Life* (Cambridge: Cambridge University Press, 1980), 2–10. Cf. Laqueur, *Making Sex,* 28–32.

19. On patriarchal defensiveness against the powers of maternity, see Kahn "The Absent Mother in *King Lear*", 44; Louis Adrian Montrose, "*A Midsummer Night's Dream* and the Shaping Fantasies of Elizabethan Culture: Gender, Power, Form," in *Rewriting the Renaissance,* 71–76; and Laqueur, *Making Sex,* 57–58.

20. King, *Women in the Renaissance,* 1–24; cf. Steven Ozment, *When Fathers Ruled: Family Life in Reformation Europe* (Cambridge: Harvard University Press, 1983), 119–21; and Elizabeth Wirth Marvick, "Nature versus Nurture: Patterns and Trends in Seventeenth-Century Child-Rearing," in *The History of Childhood,* ed. Lloyd deMause (New York: Psychohistory Press, 1974), 308–11.

21. Greenblatt, *Shakespearean Negotiations,* 78–92.

22. John N. Wall, *Transformations of the Word: Spenser, Herbert, Vaughan* (Athens: University of Georgia Press, 1988), 236.

23. Ibid., 236.

24. On form in poetry (and art) as performing a maternal handling function, see Christopher Bollas, "The Aesthetic Moment and the Search for Transformation," in *Transitional Objects.*

25. Donald W. Winnicott, *The Child and the Outside World: Studies in Developing Relationships,* ed. Janet Hardenberg (New York: Basic Books, 1957), 137; and his *Maturational Processes,* 37–55.

26. Donald W. Winnicott, *Psycho-Analytic Explorations,* ed. Clare Winnicott, Ray Shepherd, Madeleine Davis (Cambridge: Harvard University Press, 1989), 44; and his *Home Is Where We Start From: Essays by a Psychoanalyst,* ed. Clare Winnicott, Ray Shepherd, Madeleine David (New York: Norton, 1986), 144–45.

27. Donald W. Winnicott, *Babies and Their Mothers,* ed. Clare Winnicott, Ray Shepherd, Madeleine Davis (Reading, Mass.: Addison-Wesley Publishing Company, 1986), 94–95; and his *Psycho-Analytic Explorations,* 102.

28. Winnicott, *Maturational Processes,* 43–63.

29. Ibid., 47.

30. King, *Women of the Renaissance,* 18.

31. Robert Greene, *Menaphon,* in vol. 6 of *The Life and Complete Works in Prose and Verse of Robert Greene, M.A.,* ed. Alexander B. Grosart (New York: Russell & Russell, 1964).

32. Ibid., 43–44.

33. Ibid., 42–43.

34. George Gascoigne, "Gascoignes Lullabie," in *A Hundredth Sundry Flowers,* ed. C. T. Prouty, *The University of Missouri Studies* 17 (142): 150–51.

35. Schoenfeldt, *Prayer and Power,* 248.

36. Nancy Chodorow, *The Reproduction of Mothering: Psychoanalysis and the Sociology of Gender* (Berkeley and Los Angeles: University of California

Press, 1978), 164–70. Cf. Coppelia Kahn, "The Hand That Rocks the Cradle: Recent Gender Theories and Their Implications," in *The (M)other Tongue: Essays in Feminist Psychoanalytic Interpretation,* ed. Shirley Nelson Garner, Claire Kahane, Madelon Sprengnether (Ithaca: Cornell University Press, 1985), 76–77; and Jim Swan, "Difference and Silence: John Milton and the Question of Gender," in Garner, *The (M)other Tongue,* 160–62.

37. George Herbert, *The Works of George Herbert,* ed. F. E. Hutchinson, corrected ed. (Oxford: Oxford University Press, 1945), 275.

38. Ibid., 239.

39. On the importance of the Logos doctrine in Herbert's poetry, see Hughes, "Herbert and the Incarnation," esp. 55–56.

40. Most readings of the pruning conceit emphasize growth, protection, playfulness, or personal unification and thus support the idea that God is "holding" the speaker. See Lewalski, *Protestant Poetics,* 200; Stanley Stewart, *The Enclosed Garden: The Tradition and the Image in Seventeenth-Century Poetry* (Madison: University of Wisconsin Press, 1966), 102–3; Anna K. Nardo, *The Ludic Self in Seventeenth-Century English Literature* (New York: State University of New York Press, 1991), 98–99; Marcus, *Childhood and Cultural Despair,* 110; and Marion White Singleton, *God's Courtier: Configuring a Different Grace in George Herbert's Temple* (Cambridge: Cambridge University Press, 1987), 100.

41. Aristotle, "Generation of Animals," 1133 (730a: 24–30). For a reference to Aquinas's effect on Renaissance thinking about generation, see Charles H. George and Katherine George, *The Protestant Mind of the English Reformation, 1570–1640* (Princeton: Princeton University Press, 1961), 263.

42. Aristotle, "Generation of Animals," 1134 (730b: 1–30).

43. Ibid., 1146 (738b: 25–26).

44. On sexual resonances in the last lines of "Jordan II," see Janis Lull, *The Poem in Time: Reading George Herbert's Revisions of "The Church"* (Newark, Del.: University of Delaware Press; London and Toronto: Associated University Presses, 1990), 45–46; and Tuve, *Reading of George Herbert,* 189.

45. For information on Aristotle's possible borrowing of Pythagorean polarities, see Maclean, *Renaissance Notion of Woman,* 2–3.

46. In this and the preceding paragraph, I am summarizing and analyzing Augustine's *On Music* as a whole. Augustine, *On Music,* trans. Robert Catesby Taliaferro, in vol. 2 of *The Fathers of the Church,* ed. Ludwig Schopp et. al. (New York: Cima Pub., 1947). Pahlka in *Saint Augustine's Meter* relies heavily on this source to offer a comprehensive theological account of meter in *The Temple.*

47. Pahlka, *Saint Augustine's Meter;* Ormerod, "Number Theory,"; and Louis Martin, "The Trinitarian Unity of *The Temple:* Herbert's Augustinian Aesthetic," *George Herbert Journal,* 13 (1989–90).

48. Asals, *Equivocal Predication,* 63.

49. For a discussion of "Easter" which comprehends a far more pervasive tradition behind Herbert's text than Augustinian theory alone, see Diane McColley, "The Poem as Hierophon: Musical Configuration in George Herbert's 'The Church,'" in *A Fine Tuning: Studies of the Religious Poetry of Herbert and Milton,* ed. Mary Maleski (Binghamton, N.Y.: Medieval and Renaissance Texts and Studies, 1989), esp. 128–35.

50. Edmund Spenser, *Spenser's Poetical Works,* ed. J. C. Smith and E. De Selincourt (London: Oxford University Press, 1912), 174–76.

51. Ibid., 611.

52. Richard Helgerson, *Forms of Nationhood: The Elizabethan Writing of England* (Chicago: University of Chicago Press, 1992), 30; see more broadly 1–61 for Helgerson's detailed discussion of political motives for formal choices in the Elizabethan era.

53. The Harvey quotation may be found in Spenser, *Poetical Works*, 623–24.

54. Thomas Nashe, "A Reply to Harvey," in vol. 2 of *Elizabethan Critical Essays*, edited with an introduction by G. Gregory Smith (Oxford: Clarendon, 1904), esp. 240.

55. See Milton's headnote on "The Verse" of *Paradise Lost*, in John Milton, *Complete Poems and Major Prose*, ed. Merritt Y. Hughes (New York: Macmillan, 1957), 210.

56. Luther, *Works*, 35:164.

57. Ibid., 36:98.

58. Robert Higbie, "Images of Enclosure in George Herbert's *The Temple*," in Roberts, *Essential Articles*, 269.

59. Ibid., 269.

60. Ibid., 270.

61. On God's punitive role in this poem, see Lewalski, *Protestant Poetics*, 307.

62. Fish, *Self Consuming Artifacts*, 163.

63. Chodorow, *Reproduction of Mothering*, 43.

64. Dickson argues that the bubbles refer to a hardness of heart so severe that the speaker's "soul has dissipated"—evidence that the "spirits" of the heart have been affected" (*Fountain of Living Waters*, 99). Given that "diet" is one of the things that "do end in bubbles," I think indigestion is a simpler explanation, if not a more poetic one. See Schoenfeldt, *Prayer and Power* 259–60

65. See Patrides, *English Poems of George Herbert* (London: Dart, 1974), 81–82.

66. Pahlka points out that prosodic enclosures are established in three ways in "Even-song": through the envelope rhymes, through the way that stanzas one and three enclose two, and two and four enclose three, and through the way that each stanza forms a box after the first line (*Saint Augustine's Meter*, 93).

67. Winnicott, *Babies and Their Mothers*, 98–99.

68. On prosody in "Longing," see Veith, *Reformation Spirituality*, 159; Freer, *Music For a King*, 210; and Diana Benet, *Secretary of Praise: The Poetic Vocation of George Herbert* (Columbia: University of Missouri Press, 1984), 56.

69. See Benet, *Secretary of Praise*, 57; and Singleton, *God's Courtier*, 94–95.

70. On the feminization of Christ here, see Schoenfeldt, *Prayer and Power*, 249.

71. Veith, *Reformation Spirituality*, 224.

72. White asserts without qualification that "The four lines that rhyme regularly—*abab*—are respectively of four, two, five, and three iambic feet" (*"This Book of Starres"*, 59).

73. Ibid., 58; on this device in the first stanza, see also John Hollander, *Vision and Resonance: Two Senses of Poetic Form* (New York: Oxford University Press, 1975), 131.

74. Given that Renaissance printing and punctuation practices were haphazard at best, I make this point with qualification. However, I will note that

lack of capitalization is not all that blurs sentence boundaries here. The line's meter contributes to the effect because the new sentence begins on a strongly stressed syllable (all) which completes the fourth foot of a strongly iambic line; thus meter ties the phrase "all day long" to the preceding predicate "And then not hear it crying" which it could logically modify. The result is a triple meaning: not only is the speaker's heart in his knee all day long; God does not hear all day long, and the dust cries all day long.

75. In separating the speaker's awareness from the prosodic subject's awareness, I am conceding that, as Strier says, "there is something odd about a prayer which implies that it has already received what it is requesting" (*Love Known*, 190). But at the same time, I am contending that the poem's closure is God's answer to the speaker's prayer. The speaker makes the request; the prosodic subject hears, even in the request, God's answer. If in *The Temple* prayer is "something understood"—that is apprehended in an unmediated, immediate way—Herbert's God needs no time to think about the speaker's request ("Prayer" (I), 14). As the prosodic subject realizes, the answer is already there. Only the speaker needs time to get the punch line.

For debate on whether the poem's closure indicates that the speaker has been healed, see Strier, *Love Known*, 190–91; Summers, *Herbert: His Religion and Art*, 136; Fish, *Living Temple*, 161; Benet, *Secretary of Praise*, 51; Stein, *George Herbert's Lyrics*, 16; and Singleton, *God's Courtier*, 84.

76. Fish argues that it is Christ who is "graved" (*Living Temple*, 34).

77. Asals argues that the middle of *Jesu* is close to *esse*, a form of "be" and linking verb. Christ means "I am you" (*Equivocal Predication*, 54–55).

Chapter 3. "Between this world and that of grace"

1. On the "nightmarish" quality of the speaker's "deanimation and fragmentation of the self," see Anne C. Fowler, "'With Care and Courage': Herbert's 'Affliction Poems,'" in Summers, *Too Rich*, 136.

2. As Schoenfeldt phrases a similar point, "The speaker is not sure whether he is 'a thing forgot' or an object of intense and frightening attention" (*Prayer and Power*, 128). Smithson, not perceiving a disparity, reconciles the two images thus: "'Broken in pieces' and 'tortur'd,' Herbert asks that he not be 'forgot' or lost, that he not become something for which the Lord must 'hunt.'" Bill Smithson, "Herbert's 'Affliction' Poems," *SEL* 15 (1975): 135.

3. "Interpersonal space" is often discussed under the rubric of "personal space," though some theorists do use the language I have chosen—the terminology most true to an object-relations psychoanalytic perspective. For an overview of ideas about interpersonal space, see Donelson R. Forsyth, *An Introduction to Group Dynamics* (Monterey, Calif.: Brooks/Cole Publishing Co., 1983), 286–97. On the cultural specificity of human use of space, see Edward T. Hall, *The Silent Language* (New York: Doubleday, 1959), esp. 187–209.

4. On the "bounded body ego" and "ego boundaries" as two origins of the "self," see Chodorow, *Reproduction of Mothering*, 67–68.

5. As Fish points out, this stanza constitutes "a thinly disguised accusation of God" (*Self-Consuming Artifacts*, 160).

6. Also, as Skulsky observes, the speaker softens the accusation by claiming that such measurement does not do *God* justice rather than arguing that

it is unfair to the speaker. Harold Skulsky, *Language Recreated: Seventeenth-Century Metaphorists and the Act of Metaphor* (Athens: University of Georgia Press, 1992), 193.

7. On "contrapuntal stanzas," see Hayes, "Counterpoint in Herbert," esp. 291.

8. Nardo, *Ludic Self,* 95.

9. Nuttall takes the image of "[falling] with dust" as indicative of the possibility that the speaker will be literally damned, "falling from grace." Aside from the fact that Nuttall is arguing for a Calvinist Herbert and the doctrine of "falling from grace" is contradictory to Calvin's idea of the perseverance of the saints, it seems untenable to imagine that the speaker "in an agony of generous love" could resign himself to eternal separation from his love object. A. D. Nuttall, *Overheard by God: Fiction and Prayer in Herbert and Milton, Dante and St. John* (London: Methuen, 1980), 35. Surely resignation to the possibility of being damned would be a sign of reprobation.

10. Stein, *George Herbert's Lyrics,* 29.

11. Strier, *Love Known,* 232–33.

12. On "The Agonie" as anti-rational, see Strier, *Love Known,* 43; and Dickson, *Fountain of Living Waters,* 95.

13. On Herbert's pun on *measure* throughout *The Temple,* see Kathleen J. Weatherford, "Sacred Measures: Herbert's Divine Wordplay," *George Herbert Journal* 15.1 (Fall 1991): esp. 24.

14. On the distancing effect of rhetoric in "The Agonie," see Richard E. Hughes, "George Herbert's Rhetorical World," in Roberts, *Essential Articles,* 109. Hughes' understanding of this effect is quite different from mine. On the relationship between "The Agonie" and Renaissance literature on meditation, see Louis Martz, *The Poetry of Meditation: A Study in English Religious Literature of the Seventeenth-Century* (New Haven: Yale University Press, 1954), 84–86.

15. For the background story of Gethsemane as it relates to "The Agonie," see John R. Mulder, *The Temple of the Mind: Education and Literary Tastes in Seventeenth-Century England* (New York: Pegasus, 1969), 73–74. On Herbert's use of the iconographical tradition in the poem, see Tuve, *Reading of George Herbert,* 118–31.

16. Cook, *Seeing Through Words,* 60.

17. The difference I am perceiving between the speaker's position and the prosodic subject's is in essence the difference between rational and participatory consciousness discussed by Debora K. Shuger (*Habits of Thought,* esp. 63–64). Shuger elsewhere offers an intriguing discussion of various subject positions available to readers of Calvinist Passion narratives; the split sensibility I attribute to two Herberts in "The Agonie" is in some ways similar to the divided subjectivity Shuger attributes to readers of these narratives. Debora Kuller Shuger, *The Renaissance Bible: Scholarship, Sacrifice, and Subjectivity* (Berkeley and Los Angeles: University of California Press, 1994), 89–127, esp. 98–104.

18. On the way that the stanza shape represents the Presse (the instrument of torture), see John Max Patrick, "Critical Problems in Editing George Herbert's *The Temple,*" in *The Editor as Critic and The Critic as Editor,* by John Max Patrick and Alan Roper (Los Angeles: William Andrews Clark Memorial Library, University of California, 1973), 17–18. Cf. Edmund Miller, *Drudgerie Divine: The Rhetoric of God and Man in George Herbert* (Salzburg: Salzburg

Studies in English Literature: Elizabethan and Renaissance Studies 84, 1979), 92–93.

19. Seelig argues that the reader *must* participate in this as in other stanzas:

> We are drawn deeply into the *agon* of the poem; its symmetry allows no returning to the objective stance of the opening, no easy way out; one must go through its process, one must experience forcefully, though vicariously, Christ's agony in order to read the poem.

Sharon Cadman Seelig, *The Shadow of Eternity: Belief and Structure in Herbert, Vaughan and Traherne* (Lexington: University Press of Kentucky, 1981), 25. Vendler, on the other hand, argues that a participatory involvement in the third stanza should contrast a merely visual involvement in the second, since "naturally Herbert does not want his bystander to 'know' sin experientially" (*Poetry of George Herbert,* 74). I am arguing that to "know" Christ in the second stanza—in all his agony—is to be already in a relationship of love; the reader knows sin experientially precisely by remaining distanced—a typical, though perhaps fallen, human response to another's pain.

20. Vendler even calls the two emblems "identical" (*Poetry of George Herbert,* 73).

21. E.g., Winnicott, *Playing and Reality,* 41, 64, 100, and 107–110; and *Psychoanalytic Explorations,* 57–58. For critical discussions of potential space in other Renaissance texts, see David Willbern, "Phantasmagoric Macbeth," in *Transitional Objects;* Antoinette B. Dauber, "Thomas Traherne and The Poetics of Object Relations," in *Transitional Objects;* and (on John Donne), Nardo, *The Ludic Self,* 49–77, esp. 53.

22. Winnicott, *Playing and Reality,* 1–25 and 96–97; and Winnicott, *Mother and Child: A Primer of First Relationships* (New York: Basic Books, 1957), 182–190.

23. Winnicott, *Playing and Reality,* 80; cf. 96–97.

24. Winnicott, e.g., *Playing and Reality,* 38–64, 96–100, and 108–109; *Psycho-Analytic Explorations,* 59–61; and *Home,* 36–59. See also Chodorow, *Reproduction of Mothering,* e.g., 67–84.

25. Winnicott, *Maturational Processes,* 184–85; and *Playing and Reality,* 14.

26. Winnicott, *Playing and Reality,* 90–94; and Chodorow, *Reproduction of Mothering,* 73.

27. For fuller development of the relationship between Winnicott's ideas and Christian belief see Hopkins' essay, "Jesus and Object Use."

28. Shuger, *Habits of Thought,* 113–14.

29. Bynum, *Jesus as Mother,* esp. 110–69.

30. Wall, *Transformations of the Word,* 250.

31. Cf. Harman, *Costly Monuments,* 183; and Veith, *Reformation Spirituality,* 192.

32. On the various possible meanings of *collar* in the poem, see Dale B. J. Randall, "The Ironing of George Herbert's 'Collar,'" *SP* 81 (1984): passim. Cf. Mary Ellen Rickey, *Utmost Art: Complexity in the Verse of George Herbert* (Lexington: University Press of Kentucky, 1966), 99–101.

33. For this argument see Jeffrey Hart's article, "Herbert's *The Collar* Reread," in Roberts, *Essential Articles.*

34. Schoenfeldt, *Prayer and Power,* 108.

35. For an overview on the concept of the false self, see Winnicott, *Maturational Processes*, 240–52. For the connection between a false self and a premature attempt to be autonomous, see John Bowlby, *Separation Anxiety and Anger*, vol. 2 of *Separation and Loss* (New York: Basic Books, 1973), 252–53. I will be addressing the idea of the speaker as a false self at length in chapter 4.

36. My reading of prosody here follows Joseph Summers' reading (*Herbert: His Religion and Art*, 92). See also Freer, *Music for a King*, 196–97; and Ilona Bell, "The Double Pleasures of Herbert's Collar," in Summers, *Too Rich*, esp. 86–87. For a comparison of Herbert's poem to Wesley's common measure version, see Vendler, *Poetry of George Herbert*, 131–36.

37. Schoenfeldt, *Prayer and Power*, 108.

38. Strier, *Love Known*, 226.

39. Veith argues that "The Collar" is "the classic example of the collision between the human will's desire for autonomy and the intervening grace of God" (*Reformation Spirituality*, 52). Clearly this is so. But the poem is also a classic example of the collision between a child's desire for autonomy and the same child's desire for absolute dependence. Divine intervention here works through human nature, not against it.

40. Roger B. Rollin, "Self-Created Artifact: The Speaker and the Reader in *The Temple*," in Summers, *Too Rich*, 153.

41. Thus, as Vendler points out, the speaker's final submission constitutes "a return to Herbert's own nature" (*Poetry of George Herbert*, 135).

42. Harman, *Costly Monuments*, 65–90.

43. On these points see, e.g., George and George, *Protestant Mind*, 348ff. and 360–62. Cf. J. J. Scarisbrick, *The Reformation and the English People* (Oxford: Blackwell, 1984), 162–165.

44. See, e.g., George and George, *Protestant Mind*, 140 ff.; and Christopher Hill, *Society and Puritanism in Pre-Revolutionary England* (New York: Schocken Books, 1964), 183–202.

45. Ozment, *When Fathers Ruled*, 141.

46. Hill, *Society and Puritanism*, 30–78; and George and George, *Protestant Mind*, 334–41.

47. Greenblatt illustrates the interplay between theatrical illusion and the practice of exorcism in his essay "Shakespeare and the Exorcists" (*Shakespearean Negotiations*, 94–128). Shuger also notes the coexistence of "irrational" with "skeptical, scientific, and rationalized attitudes" during the Renaissance and before (*Habits of Thought*, 21).

48. On this point see Paster, "In the Spirit of Men," 295; Kahn, "Absent Mother," 59; and Shuger, *Habits of Thought*, 239.

49. On whether the last lines of "Jordan" (I) substitute God for the king or place God first, the king second, see Singleton, *God's Courtier*, 70; Schoenfeldt, *Prayer and Power*, 59; and Anthony Low, "Herbert's 'Jordan (I)' and the Court Masque," *Criticism* 14 (1972).

50. Both the infantile state of merger and the toddler's separation from the mother—the two poles of the transitional phase—contribute to the individual's later capacity to love. See Martin S. Bergmann, "Psychoanalytic Observations on the Capacity to Love," in *Separation-Individuation: Essays in Honor of Margaret S. Mahler*, ed. John B. McDevitt and Calvin F. Settlage (New York: International Universities Press, 1971), esp. 32.

51. Winnicott states that, for an artist seeking a self through art, "The finished creation never heals [an] underlying lack of sense of self" (*Playing and*

Reality, 55). One might argue that in Herbert the speaker's continual breaking, despite God's healing of him in poem after poem, is the consequence of the failure of art to heal him in any permanent way. I tend to think otherwise, however, attributing these repetitive breakdowns to the nature of childhood rather than to the nature of art. As I will argue, Herbert's art facilitates genuine growth because in Herbert the potential space of art overlaps with the potential space of religion and of a child persona who relates to God as a primary parent. The best analogy is the potential space of therapy, which Winnicott believes to be efficacious in healing formative wounds (*Playing and Reality,* 38).

52. Joost Daalder, "Herbert's Poetic Theory," *George Herbert Journal* 9 (1986).

53. Low points out that the "painted chair" is as much the king's throne as Plato's chair ("Herbert's 'Jordan (I)'" 112).

54. Much debate centers on whether "Jordan" (I) advocates substituting religious for amorous poetry (or, as Low argues in "Herbert's 'Jordan (I),'" for the court masque) or whether it advocates abandoning poetry altogether. E.g., Tuve, *Reading of George Herbert,* 187; Nuttall, *Overheard by God,* 15; Stein, *George Herbert's Lyrics,* 12; and Michael P. Gallagher, "Rhetoric, Style and George Herbert," *ELH* 37 (1970), 506. For discussion not only of this topic but also of Platonic allusions in the poem, see D. M. Hill, "Allusion and Meaning in Herbert's 'Jordon (I),'" *Neophilologus* 56 (1972).

55. Skulsky, *Language Recreated,* 137; and Hill, "Allusion and Meaning," 349.

56. The point is made by many, e.g., Strier, *Love Known,* 39; Schoenfeldt, *Prayer and Power,* 168; Gallagher, "Rhetoric, Style and George Herbert," 507; Stanley Stewart, *George Herbert* (Boston: Twayne, 1986), 127; Tuve, *Reading of George Herbert,* 188; Fish, *Self-Consuming Artifacts,* 189 and 197; and Leah Sinanoglou Marcus, "George Herbert and the Anglican Plain Style," in *Too Rich,* 187.

57. Schoenfeldt, *Prayer and Power,* 168.

58. Schoenfeldt points out that the persona's desire to "clothe the sunne" is misguided in that it "inverts the hierarchy between God and mortal" (*Prayer and Power,* 170).

59. Here as with "The Collar," Schoenfeldt argues that the poem does not completely overcome solipsism since the speaker's assertion about the friend's voice does not definitively assert the Other's objective presence (*Prayer and Power,* 170). Again, I see this phenomenon as transitional and therefore decidedly unsolipsistic.

60. I am here disagreeing with critics who argue that at the end of the poem the friend advises that the author-persona cease to write his own verse and instead copy out words "already" written. I take the penultimate line to mean that in love there is a sweetness "readily" penned (because love is an inspiring relationship). As Skulsky argues, the poet will still be writing "about his own love of God, and hence . . . about himself," but he will cease "self promotion," instead "bearing witness" (Skulsky, *Language Recreated,* 139). For arguments to the contrary, see Stewart, *George Herbert,* 128; Harman, *Costly Monuments,* 47; and Fish, *Self-Consuming Artifacts,* 197.

61. As Gallagher argues, "What is central" here "is an eloquence that comes from within" ("Rhetoric, Style and George Herbert," 508). Strier, on the other hand, argues that the poem seeks to divorce religious art from all aesthetic standards (*Love Known,* 202).

62. Although Fish argues that the *He* who "craves all the mind," etc. is ambiguous in reference, Strier argues that the pronoun refers to God, and Bloch recognizes the Biblical allusion (*Self-Consuming Artifacts,* 201; *Love Known,* 203; and *Spelling the Word,* 60).

63. McColley, "The Poem as Hierophon," 127.

64. On whether, in the poem's terms, God actually writes *Loved,* see, e.g., Strier, *Love Known,* 205; Stein, *George Herbert's Lyrics,* 8; Singleton, *God's Courtier,* 71; Fish, *Self-Consuming Artifacts,* 202; and Todd, *Opacity of Signs,* 183.

65. Of course, as others have pointed out, the primary meaning of the first two stanzas is the rejection of a set of images relating verse to the world of the court and the world of trade. See, e.g., Malcolm MacKenzie Ross, *Poetry and Dogma: The Transfiguration of Eucharistic Symbols in Seventeenth-Century English Poetry* (New Brunswick, N.J.: Rutgers University Press, 1954), 145; Gallagher, "Rhetoric, Style and George Herbert," 505; and Singleton, *God's Courtier,* 103.

66. Freer, *Music For a King,* 230.

67. For critics who agree that Herbert's verse serves to bring the self into contact with God, see Asals, *Equivocal Predication,* 57; Gallagher, "Rhetoric, Style and George Herbert," 506; and Veith, *Reformation Spirituality,* 72–73; for dissent, see Vendler, *Poetry of George Herbert,* 183.

68. Schoenfeldt, *Prayer and Power,* 102; Todd, *Opacity of Signs,* 174; and Fish, *Self-Consuming Artifacts,* 218. For further information on Herbert's use of this rhyme, see Freer, *Music For a King,* 216.

69. Schoenfeldt, *Prayer and Power,* 102; and Fish, *Self-Consuming Artifacts,* 218.

70. Most children cast transitional objects as soothers, but some use babbling or singing instead of objects; hence, a child may play the parent's role to soothe the self (Winnicott, *Playing and Reality,* 2). Also relevant is that a transitional object evolves from being "both part of the infant and part of the mother" to being a "possession," more objectively perceived, hence treated as Other (Winnicott, *Psycho-Analytic Explorations,* 55).

71. Winnicott, *Playing and Reality,* 15 and 96–98; and *Mother and Child,* 187.

72. On the poems as a sequence, see Martz, *Poetry of Meditation,* 309–312.

73. On the arrow emblem as derived from the emblem tradition, see Lewalski, *Protestant Poetics,* 198.

74. Strier argues that spatial terms are replaced by relational ones, here as in "The Temper" (I) (*Love Known,* 238). Singleton stresses that physical space is a metaphor meant "to signify man's infinite spiritual distance from God" (*God's Courtier,* 185). Again, I would argue that Herbert's representation of interpersonal (or specifically transitional) space is not entirely metaphorical, though certainly any space between the believer and God would be more sensed than perceived.

75. On the end of this poem, see Elsky, *Authorizing Words,* 162–63; Stein, *George Herbert's Lyrics,* 15; Edmund Miller, *"Drudgerie Divine",* 20; Strier, *Love Known,* 196; and Vendler, *Poetry of George Herbert,* 269.

76. Fish, *Self-Consuming Artifacts,* 186.

77. On another's words as a type of transitional phenomenon, see Daniel N. Stern, *The Interpersonal World of the Infant: A View from Psychoanalysis and Developmental Psychology* (New York: Basic Books, 1984), 173. For a critic

who argues that the speaker loses himself in appropriating the Other's words, see Fish, *Self-Consuming Artifacts,* 187–88. For argument, see Stein, *George Herbert's Lyrics,* 123; Singleton, *God's Courtier,* 153; Bloch, *Spelling the Word,* 43–44; and Nardo, *Ludic Self,* 89. If the words are a transitional phenomenon, then Fish is not wrong that they represent a self-Other merger, but as Winnicott points out, transitional phenomena emerge only as the child separates from the Other: "The use of an object symbolizes the union of two now separate things, baby and mother, *at the point in time and space of the initiation of their state of separateness*" (*Playing and Reality,* 96–97).

78. Other critics who note the resurrection imagery include Vendler, *Poetry of George Herbert,* 53; and Freer, *Music For a King,* 224.

79. Fish, *Self-Consuming Artifacts,* 156. For a differing viewpoint, see Skulsky, *Language Recreated,* 82.

80. As Strier claims, "The difference between being in hell and heaven seems to be entirely a matter of perception" (*Love Known,* 247).

Chapter 4. "To God, His Neighbour, and Himself Most True"

1. Macbeth is, of course, very active, but he rarely feels himself to be the author of his actions. Even when his deeds originate inside himself, Macbeth feels himself to be acting out rather than enacting his thoughts. See Willbern, "Phantasmagoric Macbeth," esp. 113ff.

2. Jean Delumeau, *Sin and Fear: The Emergence of a Western Guilt Culture, 13th–18th Centuries,* trans. Erick Nicholson (New York: St. Martin's Press, 1990), 177.

3. Winnicott, *Home,* 28.

4. Lawrence Stone, *The Family, Sex and Marriage In England 1500–1800* (New York: Harper and Rowe, 1977), 4–6 and 253.

5. Natalie Zemon Davis, "Boundaries and the Sense of Self in Sixteenth-Century France," in *Reconstructing Individualism: Autonomy, Individuality, and the Self in Western Thought,* ed. Thomas C. Heller, Morton Sosna, and David E. Wellbery (Stanford: Stanford University Press, 1986), 59–60. The new sense of self Zemon Davis attributes to some young men in sixteenth-century France marks, as I will argue, a progression toward Winnicottian selfhood, but as Zemon Davis points out, this sense of self did not pertain to women in the same culture—or to young men of the lower classes.

6. Particulars will follow. See Stone, *Family, Sex and Marriage,* esp. 99–102; contrast Linda Pollock, *Forgotten Children: Parent-Child Relations from 1500 to 1900* (Cambridge: Cambridge University Press, 1983), e.g. 58–59 and 263–64. Pollock argues against many of Stone's conclusions and, as I will discuss, makes some good points, but I tend to agree with Stone that the Renaissance majority probably suffered one form or another of early childhood trauma, however inadvertent it may have been on their parents' part.

7. Christopher Hill, *Society and Puritanism,* 474.

8. Greenblatt, *Renaissance Self-Fashioning,* esp. 1–10.

9. As Jane Flax observes, "From the perspective of Winnicott's theories, almost all postmodernist critiques of the self would in fact describe and target a false one." Jane Flax, *Thinking Fragments: Psychoanalysis, Feminism, and*

Postmodernism in the Contemporary West (Berkeley and Los Angeles: University of California Press, 1990), 110.

10. For a good overview of the ideas of false and true selves, see Winnicott, *Maturational Processes*, 140–52. I will deal more with the particulars of Winnicott's theory in a later section. For confirmation of the relevance of false-self tendencies (the sense that life is unreal, the sense that the self is powerless, etc) to a Renaissance historical context, see Jean Delumeau, *Sin and Fear*, 145–85, esp. 177.

11. Winnicott describes this process in *Maturational Processes*, 95–96, though he does not refer specifically to the true self in this passage. Cf. *Maturational Processes*, 140–52 and 46.

12. Ibid., 148–49.

13. Ibid., 149.

14. Ibid., 148. For Greenblatt, "autonomy is an issue but not the sole or even the central issue: the power to impose a shape upon oneself is an aspect of the more general power to control identity—that of others at least as often as the self" (*Renaissance Self-Fashioning*, 1). My point will be that the power to "impose a shape upon oneself" or others is the power to fashion false selves, as Winnicott defines the term. Through "self-fashioning," as Greenblatt implies, absolutist power perpetuates its own interests.

Since I wish to consider how the self in history becomes empowered in spite of the forces at work against it, autonomy or the lack of autonomy will be an issue. However, by *autonomy,* I mean a sense of personal agency in the context of relationships rather than a sense of pristine individualism, which, as Norbert Elias implies, involves less the empowerment than the containment of what Winnicott calls the true self. Elias argues that, beginning in the Renaissance, the Western self internalized "civilizational self-controls," creating a wall between self and world, but at the same time permanently subordinating self to social structures; this version of the individual, as chapter 5 will make clear, is more Freud's than Winnicott's; Winnicott would call an individual defined solely by internalized control a variety of false self.

For a good discussion of the Winnicottian sense of *autonomy* and the *individual,* see Nancy Chodorow, "Toward a Relational Individualism," in Heller, *Reconstructing Individualism*. On the Western "individual" as a socialized isolate, see Norbert Elias, *The History of Manners*, vol. 1 of *The Civilizing Process*, trans. Edmund Jephcott (New York: Urizen Books, 1978), 252–63; on civilization's constitution of the individual, see also Freud, *Civilization and Its Discontents*.

15. E.g. Greenblatt, *Renaissance Self-Fashioning*, 127. Greenblatt probably means to imply by the quotation marks that the true self is not a biological but a cultural construct. I am aware that, to poststructuralist thinkers, Winnicott's idea of a true self will seem naive, especially since his starting point is the common literary and philosophical notion of a "real me" (for Winnicott a self based in the body) as opposed to a set of roles or behaviors determined by environment (*Home*, 65–66; *Maturational Processes*, 44–45). Nature versus nurture is an issue even people of Herbert's day argued over, of course. Winnicott's theory seems useful not because it is new or intellectually complex but because it offers a means of understanding (empathetically as well as theoretically) the profound experiential complications of being a self in Renaissance society.

16. Delumeau, *Sin and Fear*, 189.

17. Braden concurs that although Reformation emphasis on the utter depravity of humankind undermines the self as moral agent, Protestant inwardness creates a paradoxical form of individualism: "The gesture of attacking the self on one level quietly reaffirms the self on another; and that is ultimately not a problem but the point" Gordon Braden, "Unspeakable Love: Petrarch to Herbert," in *Soliciting Interpretation: Literary Theory and Seventeenth-Century English Poetry,* ed. Elizabeth D. Harvey and Katherine Eisaman Maus (Chicago: University of Chicago Press, 1990), 265–69, esp. 267.

18. But see George and George, who point out that "the autonomy of the individual in Protestantism, even in religious matters, is wholly relative," inasmuch as Protestants belong to churches, listen to ministers, and profess creeds; and furthermore, "each creed in its turn can become an intellectual strait-jacket for its adherents" (*Protestant Mind,* 86–87).

19. Zemon Davis, "Boundaries," 59–60.

20. Jacob Burckhardt, *The Civilization of the Renaissance in Italy,* trans. S. G. C. Middlemore, 5th ed. (New York: Macmillan, 1904), 129; Zemon Davis, "Boundaries."

21. On *naturel,* see Zemon Davis, "Boundaries," 59.

22. Qualification is essential here. The self defined as *naturel* was disentangled from patriarchal structure *in theory*—and therefore, *potentially,* in fact. But even if a few Renaissance selves matched the signifier, *naturel,* to actual true-self potential or predisposition, most—even young men of the middle or upper classes to whom the concepts of *personal nature* and *calling* were most available as warrants for self-discovery and limited self-assertion—probably lacked the ego strength to override prior conditioning. As the section which follows will imply, the mere concept of personal nature would not be sufficient to point a person back to a true self undermined early enough in life or with sufficient force; in such a case, the instilled qualities of the dominant false self (a clone of patriarchy situated in the mind) would seem, even to the person him or herself, constitutive of personal character, predisposition, or talent.

23. Stephen Greenblatt, "Fiction and Friction," in Heller, *Reconstructing Individualism.* esp. 35. Cf. Greenblatt's longer version of the essay in *Shakespearean Negotiations,* 66–93, esp. 75–76.

24. Greenblatt, "Fiction and Friction," 36ff.

25. Winnicott, *Maturational Processes,* 148.

26. Ibid., 148

27. Heinz Kohut, *The Search For the Self: Selected Writings of Heinz Kohut: 1950–1978,* 2 vols., ed. Paul Ornstein (New York: International Universities Press, 1978), vol. 1: 233–253, esp. 240.

28. Jonathan Dollimore critiques all essentialist models of subjectivity, arguing that such idealism "denies or at least seeks to minimise the importance of material conditions of human existence for the forms which that existence takes." Jonathan Dollimore, *Radical Tragedy: Religion, Ideology and Power in the Drama of Shakespeare and his Contemporaries* (Chicago: University of Chicago Press, 1984), 253. Dollimore argues furthermore that "essentialist theories of human nature, though not intrinsically racist, have contributed powerfully to the ideological conditions which made racism possible" (*Radical Tragedy,* 256). Dollimore's first argument creates a false dilemma, I believe, and his second puts the cart before the horse. Winnicott's model of subjectivity, positing both a core potential and a socially constructed self, accounts as well as materialist models of the human subject for the historicity of selves. At the

same time, Winnicott's model better explains how selves in history move beyond social conditions to become agents of change. As for Dollimore's equation between racism and essentialism, I would argue that while a pseudo-essentialism (a tendency to universalize the false self) has provided nebulous grounds for racist misconstructions of the subjectivities and bodies of others, the historical foundation for belief in, and activism on behalf of, human rights is also essentialist, as evidenced by the civil rights movement of the sixties in the U.S. and its roots in the idealism of Martin Luther King Jr. Faith in the ideal of universal humanity (and in the healthy social potential of each true self) may seem to many misguided, but clearly it is not the same as self-righteous convictions regarding universal standards for morality or civility (convictions held by the false self within each personality and held all the more tenaciously the more dominant the false self is).

For a Winnicottian argument against poststructuralist critiques of essentialism, see Rudnytsky, *Psychoanalytic Vocation,* 149–69. For an argument that Winnicott is more commensurate with poststructuralism than Freud or Lacan, see Flax, *Thinking Fragments,* e.g., 108–10. I tend to agree with Rudnytsky that Flax plays fast and lose with the term "human nature" when she argues that, by Winnicottian logic, it changes along with historical changes in social relations and family structures; I agree, however, with what I take to be her underlying idea: human personality, inasmuch as it is a composite of sociological (false self) and essential (true self) factors, changes shape in accordance with history. As best I can discern, in Winnicottian terms, "human nature" refers first and foremost to the infant's absolute dependence on the primary caretaker (here is the one universal fact of human life), and second to a drive toward the realization of individual potential if good-enough conditions exist. Culture affects personality in two ways: first, collective child rearing practices may determine whether or not the majority of people in a given culture realize true-self potential; second, a culture's social norms will determine the shape or character of the typical false selves within that culture.

29. Michel Foucault, *Discipline and Punish: The Birth of The Prison,* trans. Alan Sheridan (New York: Pantheon Books, 1977), 29–30.

30. Winnicott, *Psycho-Analytic Explorations,* 43.

31. Winnicott, *Maturational Processes,* 140–52, esp. 142–43. Although Winnicott capitalizes *True Self* and *False Self* in this essay and in some other passages, I will use the lower case throughout my discussion.

32. Ibid., 145.

33. Ibid., 145.

34. Ibid., 145.

35. Ibid., 147.

36. Ibid., 149.

37. Winnicott, *Home,* 65–70.

38. Bowlby, *Separation Anxiety and Anger,* 252–53.

39. Ibid., 253.

40. Stern, *Interpersonal World of the Infant,* 227.

41. Ibid., 227.

42. For a clearer sense of what Miller comes to stand for, see also, e.g., Alice Miller, *For Your Own Good: Hidden Cruelty in Child-Rearing and the Roots of Violence,* trans. Hildegarde and Hunter Hannum (New York: Farrer, Straus and Giroux, 1983); and her *Thou Shalt Not Be Aware: Society's Betrayal of*

the Child, trans. Hildegarde and Hunter Hannum (New York: Farrar, Straus and Giroux, 1984).

43. Esp. Kohut, *Search for the Self,* vol. 1, 427–75.

44. Here I restate the central premise of Alice Miller's *Prisoners of Childhood,* trans. Ruth Ward (New York: Basic Books, 1981).

45. Winnicott, *Psycho-Analytic Explorations,* 213–14.

46. This theme is prevalent in Alice Miller's books, for instance, *For Your Own Good;* and *Thou Shalt Not Be Aware.* Cf. deMause, "Evolution of Childhood."

47. Stone, *Family, Sex and Marriage,* 99–100. Cf. deMause, "Evolution of Childhood," esp. 34–35; Marvick, "Nature Versus Nurture," 264–69; Illick, "Child-Rearing," 308–311; and Nardo, *Ludic Self,* 38–39.

48. Stone, *Family, Sex and Marriage,* 101.

49. Ibid., 101 and 161–62. Cf. DeMause, "Evolution of Childhood," 37–38; M. J. Tucker, "Child as Beginning and End," in De Mause, *History of Childhood,* 242; Marvick, "Nature Versus Nurture," 269–71; Joseph E. Illick, "Child-Rearing in Seventeenth Century England," in DeMause, History of Childhood, 307; and Nardo, *Ludic Self,* 38–40.

50. Stone, *Family, Sex and Marriage,* 101–2 and 174–78. Cf. Illick, "Child-Rearing," 316–17 and 327; Philippe Aries, *Centuries of Childhood: A Social History of Family Life,* trans. Robert Baldick (New York: Knopf, 1962), 130–32; and Nardo, *Ludic Self,* 39.

51. Pollock, *Forgotten Children,* esp. 90 and 96–103

52. Ibid., 87.

53. Ibid., esp. 43–65.

54. Ibid., 50.

55. Alan Macfarlane, *The Family Life of Ralph Josselin, a Seventeenth-Century Clergyman: An Essay in Historical Anthropology* (Cambridge: Cambridge University Press, 1970), esp. 202.

56. Pollock, *Forgotten Children,* 217.

57. See Pollock, *Forgotten Children,* 235–36.

58. Ibid., 50–51.

59. Sherrin Marshall, "Childhood in Early Modern Europe," in *Childhood in Historical and Comparative Perspective: An International Handbook and Research Guide,* ed. Joseph M. Hawes and N. Ray Hiner (New York: Greenwood Press, 1991), 59; and Nardo, *Ludic Self,* 38–40.

60. Marshall, "Childhood in Early Modern Europe," 59.

61. Stone, *Family, Sex and Marriage,* 161–62. Nardo argues for some positive effects of swaddling, "security and warmth," but also discusses its hampering of the infant's discovery of self-boundaries and its negative effects on emergent self-assertion (Nardo, *Ludic Self,* 38–40).

62. Stone, *Family, Sex and Marriage,* 163–67 and 177. See also deMause, "Evolution of Childhood," 40–41; Illick, "Child-Rearing," 312; Tucker, "Child as Beginning and End," 246–48; and Nardo, *Ludic Self,* 40.

63. For Pollock's arguments on this point, see *Forgotten Children,* e.g. 151 and 154–56.

64. Ibid., 148–49.

65. Ibid., 189–91.

66. Ozment, *When Fathers Ruled,* 132–77, esp. 149.

67. Ibid., 133 and 150–51.

68. Delumeau, *Sin and Fear,* 268.

69. See, for example, Macfarlane, *Family Life of Ralph Josselin,* 91.

70. Stone, *Family, Sex and Marriage,* 167–71.

71. Tucker, "Child as Beginning and End," 246; and Stone, *Family, Sex and Marriage,* 95 and 117.

72. Foucault demonstrates that torture was a common form of "justice" in Europe until the eighteenth century (*Discipline and Punish,* 3–69).

73. Delumeau, *Sin and Fear,* 107.

74. As I argue in chapter 2, the prosodic subject of "Longing" indicates that Christ has not truly abandoned the speaker; thus, we may interpret the speaker's negative experience of Christ's mothering as transferential. The speaker's splitting of Christ into both the good-enough mother and a neglectful mother may result from the speaker's (or Herbert's) deep memory of a mother or mother substitute who failed the child on an occasional basis. The splitting could also result from the difference between Christ, the good-enough mother, and a human mothering figure (projected in the transference) who was not good-enough.

Although I prefer to make assertions about the speaker rather than the author, I should note that the facts of Herbert's early life are indeterminate. William Kerrigan reasons that Magdelen Herbert may have had to send George Herbert away while she tended a dying husband when the poet was quite young. We know that the adult Herbert was very close to his mother, but from that, we can deduce little about her mothering skills. Herbert's closeness to his mother may signify that she was a good mother, but such attachment could also result from infantile fears of abandonment because of the (ostensible) separation or from excessive maternal control of or need for the child.

For a psychoanalytic account of Herbert's early life, see William Kerrigan, "Ritual Man: On the Outside of Herbert's Poetry," *Psychiatry* 48 (1985). For a biography of Herbert, see Amy M. Charles, *A Life of George Herbert* (Ithaca: Cornell University Press, 1977). For parallels between the God of Herbert's *Temple* and the mother of his *Memoriae Matris Sacrum,* see Pearlman, "George Herbert's God."

75. Vendler, *Poetry of George Herbert,* 168–69.

76. On the author's early life, see Kerrigan, "Ritual Man."

77. Strier notes that contrasts between the speaker and God are drawn "on the basis of power" throughout the poem (*Love Known,* 8).

78. Marcus, *Childhood and Cultural Despair,* 42–93. Cf. Tucker, "Child as Beginning and End," 231; Aries, *Centuries of Childhood,* 111–14; and deMause, "Evolution of Childhood," 47.

79. On the way enjambment in the poem works "to emphasize the speaker's desire to be pliable to God," see Woods, "Unhewn Stones," 42.

80. Veith, *Reformation Spirituality,* 138.

81. According to some critics, what the speaker is repudiating when he refers to the "growth of flesh" as "but a blister," is mature sexuality. See, e.g., Pearlman, "George Herbert's God," 107; and Schoenfeldt, *Prayer and Power,* 248.

82. Nardo claims that "by the seventeenth century . . . the hierarchy of English society was being substantially realigned, and absolute truth and monolithic authority were only nostalgic myths" (*Ludic Self,* 41). The breakdown of political and religious authority was only beginning in Herbert's day, however, and to the extent such a breakdown existed, it may have bolstered rather

than undermined parental authoritarianism, as evidenced by the Puritans' approach to child rearing.

83. Cf. Shuger, *Habits of Thought*, esp. 104–5. I will note here that in her chapter on Herbert, Shuger separates the selves of *The Temple* along slightly different lines, arguing that the social self of "The Church-porch," who is self-fashioned, autonomous, and capable of manipulating others, should be distinguished from the speaker of the poems of "The Church," a "pneumatic self" who is "dependent, passive, and private" (*Habits of Thought*, 93). Shuger's subsequent description of the "pneumatic self" resembles Winnicott's description of a true self who has been displaced by a false self early in life and therefore remains infantile. Her description of the social self has much in common with Winnicott's description of the false self.

84. Delumeau, *Sin and Fear*, 167.

85. deMause argues that poor treatment of children is perpetuated over generations ("Evolution of Childhood," 41); Alice Miller develops the thesis extensively (e.g., *For Your Own Good*); Stone, on the other hand, questions how historical change occurs if parents merely repeat the mistakes their own parents made (*Family, Sex and Marriage*, 178).

86. Winnicott, *Home*, 57.

87. On Renaissance ambivalence toward individualism, see Braden, "Unspeakable Love: Petrarch to Herbert," esp. 268.

88. Winnicott himself cites Polonius' words in discussing the concept of the true self, though he does not stop to analyze the irony in depth (*Home*, 66).

89. On Polonius' double messages to his children, see Nardo, *Ludic Self*, 25.

90. Nardo emphasizes that Hamlet's madness is a form of play designed to cope with the double binds inherent in his environment. My emphasis is on how *being* itself constitutes a double bind in the mad world in which Hamlet finds himself (*Ludic Self*, 15–34).

91. These readings of the line do not originate with me, but I have been unable to locate my source.

92. See Strier, *Love Known*, 35.

93. Also, in Renaissance usage "coursing" was "a common term for denoting the movement of a verse line" (Pahlka, *Saint Augustine's Meter*, 149).

94. Lull claims that the circle "excludes God" (*Poem in Time*, 123). Singleton claims that it "isolates the speaker" (*God's Courtier*, 158). However we construe the fact, the speaker mentions God only in the first and last lines, just as he mentions "I" only in these lines (See Strier, *Love Known*, 35).

95. For three approaches to form in "Sinnes Round," see Stein, *George Herbert's Lyrics*, 145; Pahlka, *Saint Augustine's Meter*, 149–52; and Elsky, *Authorizing Words*, 163–65.

96. Elsky, *Authorizing Words*, 163–64.

97. Lull, *Poem in Time*, 131.

98. Schoenfeldt, whose reading of the poem focuses on sexual overtones, also sees the assonance between "sin" and "ascend" as significant (*Prayer and Power*, 243).

99. I am agreeing with Elsky that the poem undoes itself, but I do not fully agree with his reasoning: "The last line rejects the circular sinfulness of the poem and erases the hieroglyph of the circle even as it completes it" (*Authorizing Words*, 164). I am convinced that the "offenses" constituted by the hieroglyph are clear by the second line. The erasing, which Elsky correctly intuits, results from the contradiction between downward and upward motion and, as

Elsky himself implies, between the horizontal and the vertical circling. Spatially, the tower collapses.

100. On the eye/I pun, see Shuger, *Habits of Thought*, 94.

101. Chauncey Wood points out that the Son (or sun) is both "efficient and final cause of what the poet has been talking about," in "A Reading of Herbert's 'Coloss 3.3,'" *George Herbert Journal* 2 (1979): 22–23.

102. William B. Bache, "A Note on Herbert's 'Coloss 3.3,'" *George Herbert Journal* 6 (1982): 28.

103. On the personalization of the Bible verse, see Wood, "Reading of Herbert's 'Coloss 3.3,'" 21; Bloch, *Spelling the Word*, 35; and Edmund Miller, *"Drudgerie Divine"*, 91.

104. The poem not only explicates the Bible verse but also "[engages] in a dialogue" with it, illustrating both sermon method and one Protestant meditation technique, according to Lewalski (*Protestant Poetics*, 171).

105. Others also compare two or more of these poems. See, for instance, Pahlka, *Saint Augustine's Meter*, 189; and Sherwood, *Herbert's Prayerful Art*, 133–34.

106. Judy Z. Kronenfeld, "Herbert's 'A Wreath' and Devotional Aesthetics: Imperfect Efforts Redeemed by Grace," *ELH* 48 (1981): 298.

107. Veith perceives a pattern. Though in the first three repetitions, no new knowledge is gained, "when God's knowledge is being described, the repeated term becomes qualified or even inverted . . . showing an increase and even a reversal of self-knowledge at the confrontation with God" (*Reformation Spirituality*, 169). On the variation of these repetitions, see also Stein, *George Herbert's Lyrics*, 144.

108. On the speaker's move toward dependence, see Kronenfeld, "Herbert's 'A Wreath,'" 299.

109. On the workings of form in the poem, see George Klawitter, "The Problem of Circularity in Herbert's Wreath," *George Herbert Journal* 6.1 (1982); Veith, *Reformation Spirituality*, 169; Stein, *George Herbert's Lyrics*, 143–45; Edmund Miller, *"Drudgerie Divine"*, 90; Asals, *Equivocal Predication*, 54; Gallagher, "Rhetoric, Style and George Herbert," 506–7; and Elsky, *Authorizing Words*, 166.

110. For others who argue that God redeems the speaker's imperfect efforts, transforming the speaker's crooked winding ways into a "crown of praise," the finished artifact, see Kronenfeld, "Herbert's 'A Wreath'"; Nardo, *Ludic Self*, 97–98; and Sherwood, *Herbert's Prayerful Art*, 133.

111. Some critics argue that the contradiction between the speaker's repudiation of crookedness and the artifact's final circularity means that form and content in "A Wreath" must be understood as existing in two separate realms (e.g., Gallagher, "Rhetoric, Style and George Herbert," 506–7; and Todd, *Opacity of Signs*, 177). I am arguing, in contrast, that the speaker and the prosodic subject are different, even contradictory, agencies who are inextricably intertwined.

112. For those who argue that the finished artifact remains emblematic of crookedness even as it becomes a "crown of praise," see Schoenfeldt, *Prayer and Power*, 175; and Lull, *Poem in Time*, 123 and 130. For a critic who reads the poem as ending on an apology for "this poor wreath" and therefore negating itself, see Elsky, *Authorizing Words*, 165–66.

113. Erich Fromm, *Psychoanalysis and Religion* (New Haven: Yale University Press, 1950), 21–64.

114. That Renaissance social conventions are implicit in the self-Other dynamics of *The Temple* is a fundamental premise of some excellent recent studies. E.g., Schoenfeldt, *Prayer and Power*, and Singleton, *God's Courtier*.

115. On regression as part of the treatment for false self problems, see Winnicott, *Maturational Processes*, 150–52; and *Psychoanalytic Explorations*, 44.

116. On the ordering of the poems in, and other information regarding, various manuscripts of *The Temple*, see Hutchinson, l-lxxvii.

117. Shuger, *Habits of Thought*, 96.

118. For another critic who compares this speaker to Polonius, see Michael McCanles, *Dialectical Criticism and Renaissance Literature* (Berkeley and Los Angeles: University of California Press, 1975), 77.

119. Singleton claims that the speaker is addressing a courtly audience whose language has become hollow, an audience "whose *inner* surface must be restitched into substance" (*God's Courtier*, 168). She does not perceive the speaker's self-contradiction, however.

120. Herbert's advice here resembles a passage from Erasmus quoted and analyzed by Norbert Elias in which the notion that angels are watching becomes a way of instilling shame and hence self-control in small children (*History of Manners*, 130, 134).

121. Benet argues that the speaker, though ungrateful in the past and probably in the future, is presently grateful and hence not implicated (*Secretary of Praise*, 42).

122. The speaker does not "merit" salvation, of course, but merit and value are two different things. On the centrality of the issue of merit (or lack of merit) in the poem, see Veith, *Reformation Spirituality*, 148–50; Fish, *Self-Consuming Artifacts*, 122; McCanles, *Dialectical Criticism*, 84–85; and Lewalski, *Protestant Poetics*, 294.

123. There is much questioning among critics about how sincere the speaker's resignation is in the third stanza of the poem. Most critics argue that he is still refusing Christ's offer, though Strier disagrees. Like Strier, I see the speaker as giving up, fully complying, but without any understanding of or claim to the plan to which he is surrendering himself. For various readings of this stanza, see Benet, *Secretary of Praise*, 154; Stein, *George Herbert's Lyrics*, 124; Edmund Miller, *Drudgerie Divine*, 45; Seelig, *Shadow of Eternity*, 22–23; Mulder, *Temple of the Mind*, 78; McCanles, *Dialectical Criticism*, 85; Vendler, *Poetry of George Herbert*, 125; Lewalski, *Protestant Poetics*, 294; Lull, *Poem in Time*, 15; Todd, *Opacity of Signs*, 187; Pahlka, *Saint Augustine's Meter*, 102; and Strier, *Reformation Theology*, 81.

124. On Christ as maternal in the poem, see Pearlman, "George Herbert's God," 111–12; on Christ as feminine but more eroticized than motherly, see Schoenfeldt, *Prayer and Power*, 256–58; on Christ as initially feminine but ultimately masculine in the poem, see Lull, *Poem in Time*, 47–49.

125. Quite a few critics note the tension between approaching and withdrawing, but none I have run across discuss the human subject as divided in the poem. On the approach-withdraw conflict, see, for instance, Vendler, *Poetry of George Herbert*, 276; Singleton, *God's Courtier*, 194; Benet, *Secretary of Praise*, 188; Martz, *Poetry of Meditation*, 319; Fish, *Living Temple*, 131; and Bloch, *Spelling the Word*, 103.

126. As Westerweel notes, the poem depicts a "scene" which "could easily be staged" (*Patterns and Patterning*, 225).

127. Cf. Richard Strier, who argues that Christ's asking whether the speaker lacks anything is "more a gesture than a question" (*Love Known*, 75).

128. Winnicott, *Maturational Processes*, 152.

129. On the I/eyes pun, see, for instance, Schoenfeldt, *Prayer and Power*, 204; Cook, *Seeing Through Words*, 50; Westerweel, *Patterns and Patterning*, 244; and Edmund Miller, *"Drudgerie Divine"*, 136.

130. Strier's claim that the speaker "would rather be damned than have his sense of propriety so deeply offended" assumes a more profound level of feeling (or at least moral sense) than I think is evident in this ludicrously self-defeating request (*Love Known*, 80). The false self is sheer surface here.

131. The issue of manners is not to be taken lightly, of course. In a Renaissance social context, knowing how and when to accept or refuse hospitality from a superior was an important means of advancing one's interests without losing oneself. For an excellent discussion of Renaissance social conventions in the poem, see Schoenfeldt, *Prayer and Power*, 199–229.

132. Fish, *The Living Temple*, 134–35.

Chapter 5. Counting One, Taking Part

1. Winnicott, *Home*, 56.

2. Ibid., 56.

3. Ibid., 58.

4. Ibid., 148.

5. On the way personal integration facilitates social participation, see ibid. 27, 60, and 222.

6. Ibid., 143.

7. Ibid., 148–49.

8. Ibid., 143 and 148–49.

9. Rudnytsky, *Psychoanalytic Vocation*, 111; and Stephen A. Mitchell, *Relational Concepts in Psychoanalysis: An Integration* (Cambridge: Harvard University Press, 1988), 2 and 129–30.

10. See esp. *Civilization and Its Discontents,* where Freud discusses the way that civilization evolved historically to limit individual demands for self-gratification, the way that the socialization of each individual child parallels that process, and the way that the superego emerges from the child's internalization of the father.

11. On the child's jubilance during the mirror stage, see esp. Lacan, *Ecrits*, 1–7.

12. Ibid. See also Ellie Ragland-Sullivan, *Jacques Lacan and the Philosophy of Psychoanalysis* (Urbana: University of Illinois Press, 1986), esp. 1–67.

13. Flax, *Thinking Fragments,* e.g., 94; and Winnicott, *Maturational Processes*, 39, n. 1.

14. Winnicott, *Maturational Processes*, 44–45.

15. Lacan, *Ecrits*, 1–7; and Winnicott, *Playing and Reality*, 111. See also Rudnytsky, *Psychoanalytic Vocation*, 78–79.

16. Flax, *Thinking Fragments*, 98–107.

17. Ibid., 106.

18. For Freud's ideas, see *Civilization And Its Discontents.* On Lacan's ideas, see Flax, *Thinking Fragments*, 98–107.

19. "Illusion" is a broad category, encompassing art, religion, play, and the infant's primary narcissistic connection to the mother and to the world. Lacan talks more about "desire" than "illusion," but his theory as a whole implies that the objects of human desire—for totality of being, for meaning, for recognition or gratification from the Other, for self-knowledge from One who is supposed to know (God/Other/analyst) and so forth—are illusory. In general, Freud sides with the reality principle against individual desire and views illusions as infantile. Winnicott's ideas about religion, play, culture, and the mother-infant relationship suggest that desire and illusion have socially adaptive functions and should, in some contexts, be indulged rather than quelled.

On Lacan's usage of the word *desire,* see Jane Gallop, *Reading Lacan* (Ithaca: Cornell University Press, 1985), 149–53. See also Lacan, e.g., *The Four Fundamental Concepts of Psycho-Analysis,* ed. Jacques-Alain Miller, trans. Alan Sheridan (New York: Norton, 1978), 30–32, 214–15, 217–19, 235–36 and 251–55. On the contrast between Freudian and Winnicottian approaches to religion, see Rudnytsky, *Psychoanalytic Vocation,* 97–99 and 180–81. Also see Sigmund Freud, *Moses and Monotheism: Three Essays,* in vol. 23 of *The Standard Edition of the Complete Psychological Works of Sigmund Freud,* ed. and trans. James Strachey, et. al. (London: Hogarth Press, 1937–39), esp. 66–137; and his *The Future of an Illusion,* in vol. 21 of *Works of Sigmund Freud.* Cf. Winnicott, e.g., *Home,* 142–49; and *Maturational Processes,* 93–105. On the contrast between Freudian and Winnicottian approaches to primary narcissism, see Mitchell, *Relational Concepts,* 175–234. On the contrast between Freudian and Winnicottian attitudes toward play, see Flax, *Thinking Fragments,* 116. For Winnicott's most complete elaboration of his theory of the importance of play and illusion, see *Playing And Reality.* For his discussion of the importance of creative living as a basis for the self's capacity to cope with the Reality Principle, see *Home,* 39–54. Cf. Freud, e.g., *Civilization and Its Discontents.*

20. Schoenfeldt also reads the pollution imagery as figuring sexual revulsion. See *Prayer and Power,* 251.

21. Some critics, like Joseph Summers and Strier, believe that the speaker of "Man" consciously includes himself in his indictment of man from the very beginning. Others, among them Singleton, Harman, Veith, and Fish, read the last line as an epiphany in which the speaker discovers that he is as guilty of man's faults as others are. Critics in both groups imply that the speaker's judgment of man is appropriate at the point and to the extent that he includes himself in the judgment. Theologically speaking, I believe they are right. Yet at the end of the poem, the speaker's identification with others whom he has represented as alien produces not empathy toward them but rather alienation from himself. Harman argues that the speaker ends up alienated from a self-representation which has failed to proceed as such. I believe that he ends up alienated from an actual self because his ostracizing mode of representation (originally aimed at others) remains unrevised (in the end rendering even the self other). Although as Fish argues, the speaker progresses beyond the Pharisee-like stance he has previously maintained—that is, he overcomes the defense of projection—the way he does so renders the imperative to "love thy neighbor as thyself" virtually meaningless. Instead, this speaker comes to hate himself as much as he hates his neighbor. See Summers, *Herbert: His Religion and Art,* 106; Strier, *Love Known,* 11; Singleton, *God's Courtier,* 95 and 138–

39; Veith *Reformation Spirituality*, 62; Fish, *Self-Consuming Artifacts*, 180–81; and Harman, *Costly Monuments*, 75 and 78–79.

22. Benet discusses the centrality of these lines to "The Sacrifice," claiming that, "Herbert wants the reader to feel Christ's sorrow as keenly as possible" since such empathy may yield insight about Christ's love (*Secretary of Praise*, 109). Such empathy, I believe, is the very nature of Christ's love in *The Temple*, just as lack of it is the very nature of sinful humankind. Paradoxically, "if sinful man *could* feel"—if the human heart were not hard, if people were not dull—Christ's sacrifice would be unnecessary.

23. On the way that the Lord's treatment of the speaker's heart parallels Renaissance torture of traitors, see Schoenfeldt, *Prayer and Power*, 130. On the way that allegory as a narrative mode makes the events the speaker discusses seem less real, see Vendler, *Poetry of George Herbert*, 89.

24. Regarding the speaker's lack of insight, see, e.g., Bloch, *Spelling the Word*, 214; Strier, *Love Known*, 159; Ira Clark, "'Lord in Thee the *Beauty* Lies in the *Discovery*': 'Love Unknown' And Reading Herbert," in Roberts, *Essential Articles*, 490; Robert L. Montgomery Jr., "The Province of Allegory in George Herbert's Verse," in Roberts, *Essential Articles*. 123–24; and Dickson, *Fountain of Living Waters*, 118.

25. On the speaker's desire for sympathy rather than help, see Summers, *Herbert: His Religion and Art*, 177; and Clark, "'Love Unknown' and Reading Herbert," 488.

26. For arguments that the friend is the speaker's self, see Strier, *Love Known*, 161; Skulsky, *Language Recreated*, 130; and Vendler, *Poetry of George Herbert*, 90–91.

27. For arguments that the friend is Christ or the Holy Spirit, see, e.g., Asals, *Equivocal Predication*, 39; Nardo, *Ludic Self*, 84 and 96; Clark, "'Love Unknown' and Reading Herbert," 488 and 492; Montgomery, "Province of Allegory," 124; Martz, *Poetry of Meditation*, 309; and Seelig, *Shadow of Eternity*, 10. Vendler also seems to entertain this possibility, though she later reads the poem as an internal dialogue. See Vendler, *Poetry of George Herbert*, 7 and 90–91.

28. On the speaker's wordiness and his "pedantic" narrative style, see Vendler, *Poetry of George Herbert*, 88; and Strier, *Love Known*, 160. Strier also notes that the speaker's tale is not finally as sad as the speaker claims.

29. Regarding the pun on *tender*, see, e.g., Rickey, *Utmost Art*, 83; Strier, *Love Known*, 164; Skulsky, *Language Recreated*, 129; Clark, "'Love Unknown' and Reading Herbert," 487; and Dickson, *Fountain of Living Waters*, 118.

30. Summers emphasizes the way that the poet achieves a "conversational tone" by making the poem's quatrain pattern more subtle through the device of enjambment and thereby achieving the "effect of an extraordinarily flexible blank verse" (*Herbert: His Religion and Art*, 178). Rickey claims that with the dimeter lines Herbert "injects a note of intensified dissonance" (*Utmost Art*, 144). My reading of the prosody differs from Summers' in that I hear the speaker as engaging, to all effects and purposes, in a monologue rather than a conversation. While I agree with Rickey that the dimeter lines add intensity, I see this departure less as a sign of "dissonance" than as a sign of quickening and of otherwise absent affect.

31. According to Todd, the speaker's claim that most of himself is gone is Herbert's way of disclaiming his or the speaker's suffering. Suffering does not count as long as he is not present to experience it (*Opacity of Signs*, 54). I see

the lines as figuring the intensity of the speaker's suffering; while the speaker stays and groans, his thoughts and joys are elsewhere, pleading just as he is for reunion. We may conclude that the speaker's thoughts and joys are with or in the absent Other. The image is of intense desire, and the speaker's capacity to feel such desire indicates that he is more present than he might like to be.

32. Michael Balint, *The Basic Fault: Therapeutic Aspects of Regression* (London: Tavistock, 1968).

33. Winnicott, *Psycho-Analytic Explorations,* 191.

34. Winnicott, *Maturational Processes,* 37–55, 83–92 and 140–52.

35. On the ways of learning, honor and pleasure *contributes* to rather than merely opposes his love of God (a position to which I subscribe), see Schoenfeldt, *Prayer and Power,* 7 and 240–41. For critics who imply that the speaker's knowledge is useless except to the extent that it indicates how much he is willing to give up for God, see, e.g., Edgecombe, *"Sweetnesse Readie Penn'd",* 88; Rickey, *Utmost Art,* 151; Bloch, *Spelling the Word,* 14 and 40–41; Strier, *Love Known,* 87–90; Stein, *George Herbert's Lyrics,* 33; and Wall, *Transformations of the Word,* 220. For one who argues that even the speaker's assertion that he loves God is sinful because it is founded on a misguided sense of personal agency, see Fish, *Self-Consuming Artifacts,* 178–79.

36. On the Augustinian allusion, see, e.g., Vendler, *Poetry of George Herbert,* 33; and Strier, *Love Known,* 11. Cf. William Flesch, who argues that the poem is anti-Augustinian, "not about an everlasting rest but about everlasting exile from rest and about the preterit consolationless comfort of sharing that exile," in his *Generosity and the Limits of Authority: Shakespeare, Herbert and Milton* (Ithaca: Cornell University Press, 1992), 83.

37. Some critics claim that "The Pulley" concerns not prelapsarian humankind but, in Edmund Miller's words, "the story that might have been if God had set out to create imperfect man, man already fallen" (*"Drudgerie Divine",* 49). See also Vendler, *Poetry of George Herbert,* 34. Cf. Summers, *Herbert: His Religion and Art,* 18; and Mary Theresa Kyne, *Country Parsons, Country Poets: George Herbert and Gerard Manley Hopkins as Spiritual Autobiographers* (Greensburg, Pa.: Eadmer Press, 1992), 52. For a more positive understanding of man's incompleteness in the poem, see Benet, *Secretary of Praise,* 94–95.

38. Related to the holding imagery is the speaker's representation of God as maternal in the poem, especially in the third stanza. See Edmund Miller, *Drudgerie Divine,* 51; and Richard Strier, "Ironic Humanism in *The Temple,*" in Summers, *Too Rich,* 44.

39. Cook, *Seeing Through Words,* 94.

40. Harman comments on self-organization in "The Pulley":

> The values and characteristics associated with structured selves and structured scenes—the preservation of boundaries, the projection and fulfillment of desire, the development of character, the interest in psychic coherence and in the relation of part to whole—have necessarily been abandoned. (*Costly Monuments,* 149)

I agree that "The Pulley" represents the human self as neither independent the way the mature Freudian self is nor solipsistic the way the infantile Freudian self is; rather the self is relational the way the Winnicottian self is. However, this fact need not imply that the self altogether lacks structure, only that relatedness is intrinsic to the self's structure; healthy boundaries, a sense of agency and ongoing identity, psychic coherence and so on are to be maintained dialectically.

41. Harold Toliver, *Lyric Provinces in the English Renaissance* (Columbus: Ohio State University Press, 1985), 178.

42. Singleton, *God's Courtier,* 92.

43. For a Calvinist reading of the poem, see Veith, *Reformation Spirituality,* 49–50.

44. For a very different but viable reading of form in the poem, see Freer, *Music For a King,* 179–83.

45. See Pahlka, *Saint Augustine's Meter,* 95–96.

46. For critics who address the ironies of the speaker's praise of man, see for instance, Strier, "Ironic Humanism in *The Temple,*" passim; Fish, *Living Temple,* 85–87; Lull, *Poem in Time,* 41–43; Bloch, *Spelling the Word,* 258; and Benet, *Secretary of Praise,* 89–91, 143–44.

47. Benet argues that the speaker is "unaware" that he is undercutting his "grand claim" in these and other lines (*Secretary of Praise,* 143).

48. See Skulsky, *Language Recreated,* 77–78.

49. A. L. Clements, "Theme, Tone, and Tradition in George Herbert's Poetry," in Roberts, *Essential Articles,* 44.

50. Rickey, *Utmost Art,* 93 and 122.

51. Skulsky, *Language Recreated,* 83.

52. Skulsky argues of these lines that "what the speaker asks God to abolish . . . aren't individual selves, but only their private ownership; get rid of Thine and Mine, not Thee and Me. From now on, let each of us belong equally to both" (*Language Recreated,* 84). Though I can follow this argument linguistically, I cannot conceptualize what the abolition of private ownership of selves could mean beyond the speaker's prior assertions of absolute interdependence unless it connotes a self-Other merger—where there is no mine and thine because the me and thee to whom these possessive terms refer no longer exist as separate entities. While I agree with Skulsky that the speaker's separateness from the Lord is crucial in this poem, I think the speaker's *desire* for a more primitive form of relatedness is very strong in the end.

53. For critics who argue that the sonnet's logical form parallels the speaker's illusion of self-agency, see Cook, *Seeing Through Words,* 63–64; and Strier, *Love Known,* 56.

54. For critics who comment on how the Lord in the end undermines the speaker's attempts to fend for himself, see Veith, *Reformation Spirituality,* 69–70; Harman, *Costly Monuments,* 81; and Bloch, *Spelling the Word,* 150. Schoenfeldt agrees but qualifies: "Even as the opportunity for human supplication is precluded by divine omniscience . . . the possibility of significant human activity towards the divine is reasserted in the notion of a lease, however "small" the rent (*Prayer and Power,* 81).

55. Virginia Mollenkott observes that the speaker's "objectivity becomes all the more pronounced by being set within the ordinarily lyrical form of the sonnet in her "George Herbert's 'Redemption,'" in Roberts, *Essential Articles* 506). Mulder notes that "A sonnet is normally lyrical, but the language of this particular one is surprisingly cold and legalistic" (*Temple of the Mind,* 76). Neither pursue the implication I am suggesting: the personal, lyrical resonances of sonnet form do not merely contrast the speaker's impersonal diction and tone; they register the self-Other relationship with the *right* decorum.

56. Edmund Miller, *"Drudgerie Divine",* 46–47.

57. Flesch, *Generosity*, 80. Edgecombe may also be right that "the couplet ... shows ... a resolution which is only dimly apprehended"—that even at the end of the poem, the speaker remains only vaguely aware of the connection between his suit and his Lord's death (*"Sweetnesse Readie Penn'd"*, 175).

58. For critics who claim that "Affliction" (I) is biographical, see, for instance, Charles, *Life of George Herbert*, 84–87; Sherwood, *Herbert's Prayerful Art*, 107; White, *"This Book of Starres"*, 23; Miller, *"Drudgerie Divine"*, 6; Freer, *Music For a King*, 217–18; Singleton, *God's Courtier*, 26; and Summers, *Herbert: His Religion and Art*, 86. For two who maintain that it is necessary to keep the persona of the poem separate from the author, see Lull, *Poem in Time*, 69; and Fowler, "'With Care and Courage,'" 130. For one who argues that the poem both "invites and frustrates biographical speculation," see Schoenfeldt, *Prayer and Power*, 70.

59. Benet, *Secretary of Praise*, 116.

60. Bill Smithson notes that the poem divides thematically into three sections, though his divisions differ from mine ("Herbert's Affliction Poems," 126).

61. White claims that the speaker's wish to be a tree indicates a desire to be "less than human, without a will and without language" (*"This Book of Starres"*, 28). This reading, though different from mine, seems commensurate with a possible allusion to Dante or Ovid; however, White does not make the connection, instead linking the tree symbol to Eden and to the tree of knowledge of good and evil, which produced the forbidden fruit.

Most critics emphasize either the tree's intrinsic usefulness or its lack of suffering (e.g., Benet, *Secretary of Praise*, 118; Toliver, *Lyric Provinces*, 132; Christopher Hodgkins, *Authority, Church, and Society in George Herbert: Return to the Middle Way* (Columbia: University of Missouri Press, 1993), 202; and Vendler, *Poetry of George Herbert*, 45). Veith sees the image as an allusion to the Christian symbol of the mustard seed, which signifies a measure of faith (*Reformation Spirituality*, 113).

62. As others assume, *just* may also be intended in the legal sense. Eg., Toliver, *Lyric Provinces*, 134; Vendler, *Poetry of George Herbert*, 45; and Veith, *Reformation Spirituality*, 113.

63. Vendler, *Poetry of George Herbert*, 45; and Skulsky, *Language Recreated*, 181.

64. See, e.g., Empson, *Seven Types of Ambiguity*, 184; Martz, *Poetry of Meditation*, 270–71; Lewalski, *Protestant Poetics*, 295; Benet, *Secretary of Praise*, 118; and Fowler, "With Care and Courage," 144.

65. Freer reads this clause as contradicting the last line, since "if the poet feels that God has clean forgotten him, there would be no point in asking God anything" (*Music For a King*, 217). It seems to me that the clause is subjunctive in meaning; for "though I am," read "though I be."

66. Many of the critics who argue that the speaker is asking God to let him not love God (or even asking God not to let him love God) if he does not love God, hear the line as turning on the word *love*, which means one thing in the first clause and another in the second; the speaker wants not to love God in one way (as a lover, partially, in feeling, etc.) if he does not love God in another ("truly," wholly, in behavior, etc). These readings are very different from mine, though they also define *let* as *allow*. See, e.g., Todd, *Opacity of Signs*, 47; Smithson, "Herbert's Affliction Poems," 130; Ilona Bell, "Revision and Revelation in George Herbert's 'Affliction I,'" *John Donne Journal* 3 (1984): 90; and Harman, *Costly Monuments*, 101.

67. Schoenfeldt, *Prayer and Power*, 77.

68. Bloch, *Spelling the Word*, 95.

69. Veith, *Reformation Spirituality*, 111.

70. Mulder, *Temple of the Mind*, 118.

71. White, *"This Book of Starres"*, 27.

72. Martz, *Poetry of Meditation*, 297; and Singleton, *God's Courtier*, 124.

73. Edgecombe, *"Sweetnesse Readie Penn'd"*, 6–7.

74. Fowler, "With Care and Courage," 144.

75. Shuger, *Habits of Thought*, 114.

76. Ibid., 114.

77. Cf. Fish's reading of "The Holdfast," *Self-Consuming Artifacts*, 175–76.

78. Chodorow, "Toward a Relational Individualism," 203.

79. Rickey claims that the speaker is addressing a "second, and invisible, person" (*Utmost Art*, 126). Wall sees the doubt as originating "both from within and from without the speaker" (*Transformations of the Word*, 214). Strier claims that the speaker's own thought is represented as "a conscious and independent agent" (*Love Known*, 105). Others tend to concur with this third position. See, for instance, Skulsky, *Language Recreated*, 120; Bloch, *Spelling the Word*, 274; and Benet, *Secretary of Praise*, 51.

80. Strier points out that the poem may be understood in Lutheran terms as reflecting a "scorn for legalism" (115). I agree completely and believe further that the Reformation contrast between the new man empowered by love and the old Adam both subject to and convicted by the law accords in key ways with Winnicottian ideas about true and false selves.

81. Several critics assume that the allegorical figures of the poem represent aspects of the speaker rather than attributes of others. Clearly these figures could be either internal or external, and in some complex psychological sense, they have to be both. The speaker's paranoid sense of being jeered at by the merry world strongly suggests to me that some (possibly introjected) other is involved, however. See especially Vendler, *Poetry of George Herbert*, 184–85; Singleton, *God's Courtier*, 139; and Skulsky, *Language Recreated*, 149.

82. On Beautie as representing "a tempting female," see Schoenfeldt, *Prayer and Power*, 251.

83. On the speaker as "the little boy asking his father to help in confronting the bullies," see Bloch, *Spelling the Word*, 17.

84. Joseph Summers comments on the "marvellous wit and playfulness of the poem" (*Herbert: His Religion and Art*, 189).

85. See Vendler, *Poetry of George Herbert*, 185.

86. Bloch draws a firm line here: "Herbert asks God not to punish his persecutors but rather to love him" (*Spelling the Word*, 18).

87. For a contrasting argument, see Fish, who implies that the action is "prepossesst" by the Other, so that the poem refutes personal agency: "the act not only belongs to God, but it always has" (*Living Temple*, 160. Cf. *Self-Consuming Artifacts*, 190).

88. Vendler views the first stanza as "obdurately heavy-footed and choppy," claiming that it is "pure versified catechism, with banal rhymes, an awkward repetition of 'things—thing,' and an infantile vocabulary" (*Poetry of George Herbert*, 270). I view it as a song of innocence, childlike and playful; these are, of course, value judgments.

89. See Schoenfeldt, *Prayer and Power*, 179.

90. If my emphasis on *charity* as action seems superfluous, I should point out that in I Corinthians 13, where Paul compares the virtue of charity to the virtues of faith and hope, he is careful to characterize charity by the spirit as well as the letter: "though I bestow all my goods to feed the poor, and though I give my body to be burned, and have not charity, it profiteth me nothing" (13.3). If the point is that charitable acts are meaningless when divorced from a completely giving attitude, some contemporary paraphrases of the King James (E.g., The Living Bible) outPaul Paul, translating *charity* as *love* and thereby erasing the implication that a Christian is supposed to *do* anything. In Herbert, the ethical imperatives of Christianity remain intact, though the capacity to "do good" is grounded in the Other's sanctification of the believer.

91. Herbert, *Works,* ed. Hutchinson, 244.

Works Cited

Aries, Philippe. *Centuries of Childhood: A Social History of Family Life.* Translated by Robert Baldick. New York: Knopf, 1962.

Aristotle, "Generation of Animals." Vol. 1 of *The Complete Works of Aristotle: The Revised Oxford Translation.* Edited by Jonathan Barnes, 1111–1218. Princeton: Princeton University Press, 1984.

Asals, Heather A. R. *Equivocal Predication: George Herbert's Way to God.* Toronto: University of Toronto Press, 1981.

Attridge, Derek. *The Rhythms of English Poetry.* London: Longmans, 1982.

Augustine. *On Music.* Translated by Robert Catesby Taliaferro. Vol. 2, *The Fathers of the Church,* edited by Ludwig Schopp et. al., 153–379. New York: Cima Publishing, 1947.

Bache, William B. "A Note on Herbert's 'Coloss 3.3.'" *George Herbert Journal* 6 (1982): 27–30.

Balint, Michael. *The Basic Fault: Therapeutic Aspects of Regression.* London: Tavistock, 1968.

Bell, Ilona. "The Double Pleasures of Herbert's Collar." In Summers, *Too Rich,* 77–88.

————. "Revision and Revelation in George Herbert's 'Affliction I.'" *John Donne Journal* 3 (1984): 73–96.

Benet, Diana. *Secretary of Praise: The Poetic Vocation of George Herbert.* Columbia: University Press of Missouri, 1984.

Bergmann, Martin S. "Psychoanalytic Observations on the Capacity to Love." In *Separation-Individuation: Essays in Honor of Margaret S. Mahler,* edited by John B. McDevitt and Calvin F. Settlage, 15–40. New York: International Universities Press, 1971.

Bloch, Chana. *Spelling The Word: George Herbert and the Bible.* Berkeley and Los Angeles: University of California Press, 1985.

Bollas, Christopher. "The Aesthetic Moment and the Search for Transformation." In Rudnytsky *Transitional Objects,* 40–49. First published in *The Annual of Psychoanalysis* 6 (1978): 385–94.

Bowlby, John. *Separation Anxiety and Anger.* Vol. 2 of *Separation and Loss.* New York: Basic Books, 1973.

Braden, Gordon. "Unspeakable Love: Petrarch to Herbert." In Harvey, *Soliciting Interpretation,* 253–72.

Brown, C. C. and W. P. Ingoldsby. "George Herbert's 'Easter-Wings.'" In Roberts, *Essential Articles,* 461–72. First published in *Huntington Quarterly* 35 (1972): 131–42.

241

Burckhardt, Jacob. *The Civilization of the Renaissance in Italy*. 5th ed. Translated by S. G. C. Middlemore. New York: Macmillan, 1904.

Bush, Douglas. *English Literature in the Earlier Seventeenth-Century, 1600–1660*. London: Oxford University Press, 1945; reprint 1946.

Bynum, Caroline Walker. "The Body of Christ in the Later Middle Ages: A Reply to Leo Steinberg." *Renaissance Quarterly* 39 (1986): 399–439.

———. *Holy Feast and Holy Fast: The Significance of Food to Medieval Women*. Berkeley and Los Angeles: University of California Press, 1987.

———. *Jesus as Mother: Studies in the Spirituality of the High Middle Ages*. Berkeley and Los Angeles: University of California Press, 1982.

Castiglione, Count Baldesar, *The Book of The Courtier*. Translated by Leonard Eckstein Opdycke. New York: Horace Liveright, 1929.

Charles, Amy M. *A Life of George Herbert*. Ithaca NY: Cornell University Press, 1977.

Chodorow, Nancy. *The Reproduction of Mothering: Psychoanalysis and the Sociology of Gender*. Berkeley and Los Angeles: University of California Press, 1978.

———. "Toward a Relational Individualism: The Mediation of Self Through Psychoanalysis." In Heller, *Reconstructing Individualism,* 197–207.

Christensen, Philip Harlan. "The Sonnets from Walton's Life: Sonnets of the Sonne." In Miller, *Like Seasoned Timber,* 169–80.

Clark, Ira. "'Lord in Thee The *Beauty* Lies In The *Discovery*': 'Love Unknown' And Reading Herbert." In Roberts, *Essential Articles,* 473–93. First published in *ELH* 39 (1972): 560–84.

Clements, A. L. "Theme, Tone, and Tradition in George Herbert's Poetry." In Roberts, *Essential Articles,* 33–51. First published in *ELR* 3 (1973): 264–83.

Cook, Elizabeth. *Seeing Through Words: The Scope of Late Renaissance Poetry*. New Haven: Yale University Press, 1986.

Crews, Frederick. *Skeptical Engagements*. New York: Oxford University Press, 1986.

Crews, Frederick, et. al. *The Memory Wars: Freud's Legacy in Dispute*. New York: The New York Review of Books, 1995.

Daalder, Joost. "Herbert's Poetic Theory." *George Herbert Journal* 9 (1986): 17–34.

Dauber, Antoinette B. "Thomas Traherne and The Poetics of Object Relations." In Rudnytsky, *Transitional Objects,* 135–60.

Delumeau, Jean. *Sin and Fear: The Emergence of a Western Guilt Culture, 13th-18th Centuries*. Translated by Erick Nicholson. New York: St. Martin's Press, 1990.

deMause, Lloyd. "The Evolution of Childhood," In deMause, *History of Childhood,* 1–73.

deMause, Lloyd, ed. *The History of Childhood*. New York: Psychohistory Press, 1974.

Dickson, Donald R. *The Fountain of Living Waters: The Typology of the Waters of Life In the Poetry of Herbert, Vaughan, and Traherne*. Columbia: University of Missouri Press, 1987.

Dollimore, Jonathan. *Radical Tragedy: Religion, Ideology and Power in the Drama of Shakespeare and his Contemporaries.* Chicago: University of Chicago Press, 1984.

Donne, John. *The Complete English Poems of John Donne.* Edited by C. A. Patrides. London: Dent, 1985.

———. In Vol. 4 of Potter, *The Sermons of John Donne,* 45–62.

Edgecombe, Rodney. *"Sweetnesse Readie Penn'd": Imagery, Syntax, and Metrics in the Poetry of George Herbert.* Edited by James Hogg. Salzburg: Salzburg Studies in English Literature, Elizabethan and Renaissance Studies 84.2, 1980.

Elias, Norbert. *The History of Manners.* Vol. 1 of *The Civilizing Process.* Translated by Edmund Jephcott. New York: Urizen Books, 1978.

Eliot, T. S. *T. S. Eliot: The Complete Poems and Plays 1909-1950.* San Diego: Harcourt Brace Jovanovich, 1971.

———. "The Metaphysical Poets." In *Selected Essays,* New ed. 241–50. Harcourt Brace Jovanovich: San Diego, 1950.

Elsky, Martin. *Authorizing Words: Speech, Writing and Print in the English Renaissance.* Ithaca: Cornell University Press, 1989.

Elyot, Thomas. *A Critical Edition of Sir Thomas Elyot's the Boke Named the Governour.* Edited by Donald W. Rude. New York: Garland Publishing, 1992.

Empson, William. *Seven Types of Ambiguity.* London: Chatto and Windus, 1930.

Ferguson, Margaret W., Maureen Quilligan and Nancy J. Vickers, eds. *Rewriting the Renaissance: The Discourses of Sexual Difference in Early Modern Europe.* Chicago: University of Chicago Press, 1986.

Fish, Stanley. "Letting Go: The Reader in Herbert's Poetry." *ELH* 37 (1970): 475–94.

———. *The Living Temple: George Herbert and Catechizing.* Berkeley and Los Angeles: University of California Press, 1978.

———. *Self-Consuming Artifacts: The Experience of Seventeenth-Century Literature.* Berkeley and Los Angeles: University of California Press, 1972.

Flax, Jane. *Thinking Fragments: Psychoanalysis, Feminism, and Postmodernism in the Contemporary West.* Berkeley and Los Angeles: University of California Press, 1990.

Flesch, William. *Generosity and the Limits of Authority: Shakespeare, Herbert, Milton.* Ithaca: Cornell University Press, 1992.

Forsyth, Donelson R. *An Introduction to Group Dynamics.* Monterey, Calif.: Brooks/Cole Publishing Co., 1983.

Foucault, Michel. *Discipline and Punish: The Birth of the Prison.* Translated by Alan Sheridan. New York: Pantheon Books, 1977.

Fowler, Anne C. "'With Care and Courage': Herbert's 'Affliction' Poems." In Summers, *Too Rich,* 129–45.

Freer, Coburn. *Music For a King: George Herbert's Style and the Metrical Psalms.* Baltimore: Johns Hopkins University Press, 1972.

Freud, Sigmund. *Civilization and Its Discontents.* In Vol. 21 of *The Standard Edition of the Complete Psychological Works of Sigmund Freud (Standard Edition).* Translated and edited by James Strachey, et. al., 64–145. London: Hogarth Press, 1927–31.

————. *The Future of an Illusion.* In Vol. 21, *Standard Edition,* 5–56.

————. *Moses and Monotheism: Three Essays.* In Vol. 23, *Standard Edition,* 7–137.

Fromm, Erich. *Psychoanalysis and Religion.* New Haven: Yale University Press, 1950.

Fussell, Paul. *Poetic Meter and Poetic Form.* 1965. Rev. ed. New York: Random House, 1979.

Gallagher, Michael P. "Rhetoric, Style and George Herbert." *ELH* 37 (1970): 495–516.

Gallop, Jane. *Reading Lacan.* Ithaca: Cornell University Press, 1985.

Garner, Shirley Nelson, Claire Kahane and Madelon Sprengnether, eds. *The (M)other Tongue: Essays in Feminist Psychoanalytic Interpretation.* Ithaca: Cornell University Press, 1985.

Gascoigne, George. "Gascoignes Lullabie." In *A Hundredth Sundry Flowers.* Edited by C. T. Prouty. *The University of Missouri Studies* 17 (1942): 150–51.

George, Charles H. and Katherine George. *The Protestant Mind of the English Reformation, 1570–1640.* Princeton: Princeton University Press, 1961.

Gilman, Ernest B. *The Curious Perspective: Literary and Pictorial Wit in the Seventeenth Century.* New Haven: Yale University Press, 1978.

Greenblatt, Stephen. "Fiction and Friction." In Heller, *Reconstructing Individualism,* 30–52.

————. *Shakespearean Negotiations: The Circulation of Social Energy in Renaissance England.* Berkeley and Los Angeles: University of California Press, 1988.

Greene, Robert. *Menaphon.* Vol. 6, *The Life and Complete Works in Prose and Verse of Robert Greene, M.A..* Edited by Alexander B. Grosart. New York: Russell & Russell, 1964.

Hall, Edward T. *The Silent Language.* New York: Doubleday, 1959.

Halli, Robert W. Jr. "The Double Hieroglyph in George Herbert's 'Easter-Wings.'" *Philological Quarterly* 63 (1984): 265–72.

Harman, Barbara Leah. *Costly Monuments: Representations of the Self in George Herbert's Poetry.* Cambridge: Harvard University Press, 1982.

Hart, Jeffrey. "Herbert's *The Collar* Re-read." In Roberts, *Essential Articles,* 453–60. First published in *Boston University Studies in English* 5 (1961): 65–73.

Harvey, Elizabeth D. and Katherine Eisaman Maus, eds. *Soliciting Interpretation: Literary Theory and Seventeenth-Century English Poetry.* Chicago: University of Chicago Press, 1990.

Haydn, Hiram Collins. *The Counter-Renaissance.* New York: Charles Scribner's Sons, 1950.

Hayes, Albert McHarg. "Counterpoint in Herbert." In Roberts, *Essential Articles,* 283–97. First published in *Studies in Philology* 35 (1938): 43–60.

Helgerson, Richard. *Forms of Nationhood: The Elizabethan Writing of England.* Chicago: University of Chicago Press, 1992.

Heller, Thomas C., Morton Sosna and David E. Wellbery, eds. *Reconstructing Individualism: Autonomy, Individuality, and the Self in Western Thought.* Stanford: Stanford University Press, 1986.

Herbert, George. *George Herbert The Complete English Poems*. Edited by John Tobin. London: Penguin, 1991.

———. *The English Poems of George Herbert*. Edited by C. A. Patrides. London: Dent, 1974.

———. *The Works of George Herbert*. Edited by F. E. Hutchinson. Corrected ed. Oxford: Oxford University Press, 1945.

Hester, M. Thomas. "Altering the Text of the Self: The Shapes of 'The Altar.'" In Maleski, *A Fine Tuning*, 95–116.

Higbie, Robert. "Images of Enclosure In George Herbert's *The Temple*." In Roberts, *Essential Articles*, 268–79. First published in *Texas Studies in Literature and Language* 15 (1974): 627–38.

Hill, Christopher. *Society and Puritanism in Pre-Revolutionary England*. New York: Schocken Books, 1964

Hill, D. M. "Allusion and Meaning in Herbert's 'Jordan I.'" *Neophilologus* 56 (1972): 344–52.

Hodgkins, Christopher. *Authority, Church, and Society in George Herbert: Return to the Middle Way*. Columbia: University of Missouri Press, 1993.

Holland, Norman. *The Brain of Robert Frost*. New York: Routledge, 1988.

———. *5 Readers Reading*. New Haven: Yale University Press, 1975.

———. *Poems in Persons: An Introduction to the Psychoanalysis of Literature*. New York: Norton, 1973.

Hollander, John. *The Untuning of the Sky: Ideas of Music in English Poetry 1500–1700*. 1961. New York: Norton, 1970.

———. *Vision and Resonance: Two Senses of Poetic Form*. New York: Oxford University Press, 1975.

Hopkins, Brooke. "Jesus and Object Use: A Winnicottian Account of the Resurrection Myth." In Rudnytsky, *Transitional Objects*, 249–60. First published in *International Review of Psychoanalysis* 16 (1989): 93–100.

Hughes, Richard E. "George Herbert and the Incarnation." In Roberts, *Essential Articles*, 52–62. First published in *Cithara* 4 (1964): 22–32.

———. "George Herbert's Rhetorical World." In Roberts, *Essential Articles*, 105–13.

Hunter, Jeanne Clayton. "With Wings of Faith: Herbert's Communion Poems." *Journal of Religion* 62 (1982): 57–71.

Huttar, Charles A. "Herbert and the Emblem: Herbert and Emblematic Tradition." In Miller, *Like Seasoned Timber*, 59–100.

Illick, Joseph E. "Child-Rearing in Seventeenth-Century England and America." In deMause, *History of Childhood*, 303–50.

Jankowski, Theodora A. "As I Am Egypt's Queen: Cleopatra, Elizabeth I, and the Female Body Politic." *Assays* 5 (1989): 91–110.

Kahn, Coppelia. "The Absent Mother in *King Lear*." In Ferguson, *Rewriting the Renaissance*, 33–49.

———. "The Hand That Rocks the Cradle: Recent Gender Theories and Their Implications." In Garner, *(M)other Tongue*, 72–88.

Kerrigan, William. "Ritual Man: On the Outside of Herbert's Poetry." *Psychiatry* 48 (1985): 68–82.

King, Margaret L. *Women of the Renaissance*. Chicago: University of Chicago Press, 1991.

Klawitter, George. "The Problem of Circularity in Herbert's Wreath." *George Herbert Journal* 6.1 (1982): 15–20.

Kohut, Heinz. *The Search For the Self: Selected Writings of Heinz Kohut: 1950–1978*. 2 vols. Edited and with an Introduction by Paul H. Ornstein. New York: International Universities Press, 1978.

Kristeva, Julia. *Revolution in Poetic Language*. Translated by Margaret Walker. New York: Columbia University Press, 1984.

———. *Tales of Love*. Translated by Leon S. Roudiez. New York: Columbia University Press, 1987.

Kronenfeld, Judy Z. "Herbert's 'A Wreath' and Devotional Aesthetics: Imperfect Efforts Redeemed by Grace." *ELH* 48 (1981): 290–309.

Kyne, Mary Theresa. *Country Parsons, Country Poets: George Herbert and Gerard Manley Hopkins as Spiritual Autobiographers*. Greensburg, PA: Eadmer Press, 1992.

Lacan, Jacques. *Ecrits: A Selection*. Translated by Alan Sheridan. New York: Norton, 1977.

———. *The Four Fundamental Concepts of Psycho-Analysis*. Edited by Jacques-Alain Miller. Translated by Alan Sheridan. New York: Norton, 1978.

———. *The Seminar of Jacques Lacan: Book I Freud's Papers on Technique, 1953–54*. Edited by Jacques Allain Miller. Translated by John Forrester. New York: Norton, 1988.

Laqueur, Thomas Walter. *Making Sex: Body and Gender From The Greeks To Freud*. Cambridge: Harvard University Press, 1990.

Lewalski, Barbara K. *Protestant Poetics and the Seventeenth-Century Religious Lyric*. Princeton: Princeton University Press, 1979.

Lodge, Thomas. *Scillaes Metamorphosis*. In Vol. 1 of *The Complete Works of Thomas Lodge*. Edited by Edmund W. Gosse. 1883; New York: Russell & Russell, 1963.

Low, Anthony. "Herbert's 'Jordan' (I) and the Court Masque." *Criticism* 14 (1972): 109–18.

Lull, Janis. *The Poem in Time: Reading George Herbert's Revisions of "The Church"*. Newark: University of Delaware Press; London and Toronto: Associated University Presses, 1990.

Luther, Martin. *Luther's Works*. 55 vols. Edited by Jaroslav Pelikan and Helmut T. Lehmann. St. Louis: Concordia Publishing House, 1955.

Macfarlane, Alan. *The Family Life of Ralph Josselin, a Seventeenth-Century Clergyman: An Essay in Historical Anthropology*. Cambridge: Cambridge University Press, 1970.

Maclean, Ian. *The Renaissance Notion of Woman: A Study in the Fortunes of Scholasticism and Medical Science in European Intellectual Life*. Cambridge: Cambridge University Press, 1980.

Maleski, Mary, ed. *A Fine Tuning: Studies of the Religious Poetry of Herbert and Milton*. Binghamton, N.Y.: Medieval and Renaissance Texts and Studies, 1989.

Marcus, Leah Sinanoglou. "George Herbert and The Anglican Plain Style." In Summers, *Too Rich*, 179–93.

———. *Childhood and Cultural Despair: A Theme and Variations in Seventeenth-Century Literature.* Pittsburgh: University of Pittsburgh Press, 1978.

Marshall, Sherrin. "Childhood in Early Modern Europe." In *Childhood in Historical and Comparative Perspective: An International Handbook and Research Guide,* edited by Joseph M. Hawes and N. Ray Hiner, 53–70. New York: Greenwood Press, 1991.

Martin, Louis. "The Trinitarian Unity of *The Temple:* Herbert's Augustinian Aesthetic." *George Herbert Journal* 13 (1989/90): 63–77.

Martz, Louis. *The Poetry of Meditation: A Study in English Religious Literature of the Seventeenth-Century.* New Haven: Yale University Press, 1954.

Marvick, Elizabeth Wirth. "Nature versus Nurture: Patterns and Trends in Seventeenth-Century Child-Rearing." In deMause, *History of Childhood,* 259–301.

McAuley, James. *Versification: A Short Introduction.* Detroit: Michigan State University Press, 1966.

McCanles, Michael. *Dialectical Criticism and Renaissance Literature.* Berkeley and Los Angeles: University of California Press, 1975.

McColley, Diane. "The Poem as Hierophon: Musical Configuration in George Herbert's 'The Church.'" In Maleski, *A Fine Tuning,* 117–43.

Melanchthon, Philippe. *On Christian Doctrine.* Translated and Edited by Clyde L. Manshrek. Introduction by Hans Engelland. New York: Oxford University Press, 1965.

Miller, Alice. *For Your Own Good: Hidden Cruelty in Child-Rearing and the Roots of Violence.* Translated by Hildegarde and Hunter Hannum. New York: Farrar, Straus and Giroux, 1983.

———. *Prisoners of Childhood.* Translated by Ruth Ward. New York: Basic Books, 1981.

———. *Thou Shalt Not Be Aware: Society's Betrayal of the Child.* Translated by Hildegarde and Hunter Hannum. New York: Farrar, Straus and Giroux, 1984.

Miller, Edmund. *Drudgerie Divine: The Rhetoric of God and Man in George Herbert.* Salzburg: Salzburg Studies in English Literature: Elizabethan and Renaissance Studies 84, 1979.

Miller, Edmund, and Robert DiYanni, eds. *Like Seasoned Timber: New Essays on George Herbert.* New York: Peter Lang, 1987.

Milton, John. *Complete Poems and Major Prose.* Edited by Merritt Y. Hughes. New York: Macmillan, 1957.

Minkova, Donka. E-mails to the author. 10, 12, 13 February, 1997.

Mitchell, Stephen A. *Relational Concepts in Psychoanalysis: An Integration.* Cambridge: Harvard University Press, 1988.

Mollenkott, Virginia. "George Herbert's 'Redemption.'" In Roberts, *Essential Articles,* 503–7. First published in *ELN* 10 (1973): 262–67.

Montgomery, Robert L. Jr. "The Province Of Allegory In George Herbert's Verse." In Roberts, *Essential Articles,* 114–28. First published in *Texas Studies in Language and Literature* 1 (1960): 457–72.

Montrose, Louis Adrian. "*A Midsummer Night's Dream* and the Shaping Fantasies of Elizabethan Culture: Gender, Power, Form." In Ferguson, *Rewriting the Renaissance,* 65–87.

Mulder, John R. *The Temple of the Mind: Education and Literary Tastes in Seventeenth-Century England.* New York: Pegasus, 1969.

Nardo, Anna K. *The Ludic Self in Seventeenth-Century English Literature.* New York: State University of New York Press, 1991.

Nashe, Thomas. "A Reply to Harvey." In Vol. 2 of *Elizabethan Critical Essays.* Edited and with an Introduction by G. Gregory Smith, 239–44. Oxford: Clarendon, 1904.

Nestrick, William V. "'Mine and Thine' in *The Temple.*" In Summers, *Too Rich,* 115–27.

Nuttall, A. D. *Overheard by God: Fiction and Prayer in Herbert and Milton, Dante and St. John.* London: Methuen, 1980.

Ormerod, David. "Number Theory in George Herbert's 'Trinity Sunday.'" *George Herbert Journal* 12 (1989): 27–36.

Ostriker, Alicia. "Song and Speech in the Metrics of George Herbert." In Roberts, *Essential Articles,* 298–310. First published in *PMLA* 80 (1965): 62–68.

Ozment, Steven. *When Fathers Ruled: Family Life in Reformation Europe.* Cambridge: Harvard University Press, 1983.

Pahlka, William. *Saint Augustine's Meter and George Herbert's Will.* Kent, Ohio: Kent State University Press, 1987.

Paster, Gail Kern. "'In the Spirit of Men There is No Blood': Blood as Trope of Gender in *Julius Caesar.*" *Shakespeare Quarterly* 40 (1989): 284–98.

Patrick, John Max. "Critical Problems in Editing George Herbert's *The Temple.*" In *The Editor As Critic and The Critic as Editor.* John Max Patrick and Alan Roper. Introduction by Murray Krieger, 3–24. Los Angeles: William Andrews Clark Memorial Library, University of California, 1973.

Pearlman, E. "George Herbert's God." *ELR* 13 (1983): 88–112.

Pollock, Linda A. *Forgotten Children: Parent-Child Relations from 1500 to 1900.* Cambridge: Cambridge University Press, 1983.

Ragland-Sullivan, Ellie. *Jacques Lacan and the Philosophy of Psychoanalysis.* Urbana: University of Illinois Press, 1986.

———. "Seeking the Third Term." In *Feminism and Psychoanalysis.* Edited by Richard Feldstein and Judith Roof, 40–64. Ithaca: Cornell University Press, 1989.

Randall, Dale B. J. "The Ironing of George Herbert's 'Collar.'" *SP* 81 (1984): 473–95.

Rickey, Mary Ellen. *Utmost Art: Complexity in the Verse of George Herbert.* Lexington: University Press of Kentucky, 1966.

Roberts, John R., ed. *Essential Articles for the Study of George Herbert's Poetry.* Hamden, Conn.: Archon, 1979.

Rollin, Roger B. "Self-Created Artifact: The Speaker and the Reader in *The Temple.*" In Summers, *Too Rich,* 147–61.

Ross, Malcolm MacKenzie. *Poetry and Dogma: The Tranfiguration of Eucharistic Symbols in Seventeenth-Century English Poetry.* New Brunswick, N.J.: Rutgers University Press, 1954

Roston, Murray. *Renaissance Perspectives in Literature and the Visual Arts.* Princeton: Princeton University Press, 1987.

Rudnytsky, Peter L. *The Psychoanalytic Vocation: Rank, Winnicott, and the Legacy of Freud.* New Haven: Yale University Press, 1991.

Rudnytsky, Peter L., ed. *Transitional Objects and Potential Spaces: Literary Uses of D. W. Winnicott.* New York: Columbia University Press, 1993.

Scarisbrick, J. J. *The Reformation and the English People.* Oxford: Blackwell, 1984.

Scarry, Elaine, ed. *Literature and the Body: Essays on Populations and Persons.* Baltimore: Johns Hopkins University Press, 1988.

Schleiner, Louise. "Jacobean Song and Herbert's Metrics." *SEL* 19 (1979): 109–26.

Schoenfeldt, Michael C. *Prayer and Power: George Herbert and Renaissance Courtship.* Chicago: University of Chicago Press, 1991.

Seelig, Sharon Cadman. *The Shadow of Eternity: Belief and Structure in Herbert, Vaughan and Traherne.* Lexington: University Press of Kentucky, 1981.

Severance, Sybil-Lutz. "Numerological Structures in *The Temple.*" In Summers, *Too Rich,* 229–49.

Shakespeare, William. *William Shakespeare: The Complete Works.* Edited by Alfred Harbage. New York: The Viking Press, 1969.

Sherwood, Terry G. *Herbert's Prayerful Art.* Toronto: University of Toronto Press, 1989.

Shuger, Debora Kuller. *Habits of Thought in the English Renaissance: Religion Politics and the Dominant Culture.* Berkeley and Los Angeles: University of California Press, 1990.

———. *The Renaissance Bible: Scholarship, Sacrifice, and Subjectivity.* Berkeley and Los Angeles: University of California Press, 1994.

Sidney, Philip. "A Defence of Poetry." In *Miscellaneous Prose of Sir Philip Sidney.* Edited by Katherine Duncan-Jones and Jan van Dorsten, 73–121. Oxford: Clarendon Press, 1973.

Singleton, Marion White. *God's Courtier: Configuring a Different Grace in George Herbert's Temple.* Cambridge: Cambridge University Press, 1987.

Skulsky, Harold. *Language Recreated: Seventeenth-Century Metaphorists and the Act of Metaphor.* Athens: University of Georgia Press, 1992.

Smithson, Bill. "Herbert's 'Affliction' Poems." *SEL* 15 (1975): 125–40.

Spenser, Edmund. *Spenser's Poetical Works.* Edited by J. C. Smith and E. De Selincourt. London: Oxford University Press, 1912.

Stein, Arnold. *George Herbert's Lyrics.* Baltimore: Johns Hopkins University Press, 1968.

Stern, Daniel N. *The Interpersonal World of the Infant: A View from Psychoanalysis and Developmental Psychology.* New York: Basic Books, 1985.

Stewart, Stanley. *The Enclosed Garden: The Tradition and the Image in Seventeenth-Century Poetry.* Madison: University of Wisconsin Press, 1966.

———. *George Herbert.* Boston: Twayne, 1986.

Stone, Lawrence. *The Family, Sex and Marriage In England 1500–1800.* New York: Harper and Rowe, 1977.

Strier, Richard. "Ironic Humanism in *The Temple.*" In Summers, *Too Rich,* 33–52.

————. *Love Known: Theology and Experience in George Herbert's Poetry.* Chicago: University of Chicago Press, 1983.

Summers, Claude J. and Ted-Larry Pebworth, eds. *Too Rich to Clothe the Sunne: Essays on George Herbert.* Pittsburgh: University of Pittsburgh Press, 1980.

Summers, Joseph H. *George Herbert: His Religion and Art.* London: Chatto and Windus, 1954.

Swan, Jim. "Difference and Silence: John Milton and the Question of Gender." In Garner, *(M)other Tongue,* 142–68.

Todd, Richard, *The Opacity of Signs: Acts of Interpretation in George Herbert's The Temple.* Columbia: University Press of Missouri, 1986.

Toliver, Harold. *Lyric Provinces in the English Renaissance.* Columbus: Ohio State University Press, 1985.

Tucker, M. J. "The Child as Beginning and End: Fifteenth and Sixteenth-Century English Childhood." In deMause, *The History of Childhood,* 229–257.

Tuve, Rosemond, *A Reading of George Herbert.* Chicago: University of Chicago Press, 1952.

————. "On Herbert's Sacrifice." In Roberts, *Essential Articles,* 434–52. First published in *Kenyon Review* 12 (1950): 51–75.

Veith, Gene Edward Jr. *Reformation Spirituality: The Religion of George Herbert.* Lewisburg, Pa.: Bucknell University Press; London and Toronto: Associated University Presses, 1985.

Vendler, Helen. *The Poetry of George Herbert.* Cambridge: Harvard University Press, 1975.

Wall, John N. *Transformations of the Word: Spenser, Herbert, Vaughan.* Athens: University of Georgia Press, 1988.

Weatherford, Kathleen J. "Sacred Measures: Herbert's Divine Wordplay." *George Herbert Journal* 15.1 (fall 1991): 22–32.

Westerweel, Bart. *Patterns and Patterning: A Study of Four Poems by George Herbert.* Amsterdam: Rodophi, 1984.

White, James Boyd. *"This Book of Starres": Learning To Read George Herbert.* Ann Arbor: University of Michigan Press, 1994.

Wilcox, Helen. "Herbert's Musical Contexts: Countrey Aires To Angels Musick." In Miller, *Like Seasoned Timber,* 37–58.

Willbern, David. "Phantasmagoric Macbeth." In Rudnytsky, *Transitional Objects,* 101–34. First published in *ELR* 16 (1986): 520–49.

Winnicott, Donald W. *Babies and Their Mothers.* Edited by Clare Winnicott, Ray Shepherd, Madeleine Davis. Reading Mass: Addison-Wesley Publishing Company, 1986; paperback, 1988.

————. *The Child and the Outside World: Studies in Developing Relationships.* Edited by Janet Hardenberg. New York: Basic Books, 1957.

————. *Home Is Where We Start From: Essays by a Psychoanalyst.* Edited by Clare Winnicott, Ray Shepherd, Madeleine Davis. New York: Norton, 1986.

————. *The Maturational Processes and the Facilitating Environment: Studies in the Theory of Emotional Development.* New York: International Universities Press, 1965.

————. *Mother and Child: A Primer of First Relationships.* New York: Basic Books, 1957.

————. *Playing and Reality.* London: Tavistock Publications, 1971; 1982.

————. *Psycho-Analytic Explorations.* Edited by Clare Winnicott, Ray Shepherd, Madeleine Davis. Cambridge: Harvard University Press, 1989.

Wood, Chauncey. "A Reading of Herbert's 'Coloss 3.3.'" *George Herbert Journal* 2 (1979): 15–24.

Woods, Susanne. *Natural Emphasis: English Versification From Chaucer to Dryden.* San Marino, Calif.: Huntington Library, 1984.

————. "The Unhewn Stones of Herbert's Verse." *George Herbert Journal* 4 (1981): 30–46.

Zemon Davis, Natalie. "Boundaries and the Sense of Self in Sixteenth-Century France." In Heller, *Reconstructing Individualism,* 53–63.

Index

abandonment, 65, 79, 81, 87, 90; of child by mother, 114; child's experience of loss as, 134; of God by poet, 112; infantile fears of, 138

absence: and effect on transitional object, 116; of externality, 149; of God, 74, 79, 85, 86, 87, 91, 114, 115, 117, 118, 121; of an Other interested in calling forth the true self, 158; in small child's experience, 116, 106; of Christ, 102–3, 170; of maternal holding, 187; of mother, 101; of Other, 194. *See also* separation

actualization: of human potential, 175; of true self, 153

Adam, 127

agency: of Christ, 129; personal, 123, 124, 149, 152, 193, 200; potential of true self to become, 123; prosody as, 24; sense of, 194; of speaker, 152

alchemy, 37, 47

alien: role of, in self-fashioning, according to Greenblatt, 124

aliveness: spiritual, of new man; 26, experience of, 145

allegory, 166–67, 197

ambivalence: of toddler toward other, 101, 102; regarding selfhood in the Renaissance, 125, 146; of self toward Other, 159, 188–90

anaclitic: depression, 139; tendencies: of King James I's subjects, 107

anamorphic form, 31

androgyny: of King James I, 56, 107; of Herbertian self, 65; of God, 60, 65; of Queen Elizabeth, 54, 56; of Renaissance courtiers, 54; of trinity, 59. *See also* gender

annihilation: of personal being in infant, 61; panic, 138; self–enclosed self doomed to, 174

anxiety, 25

approach–withdrawal conflict: in "Love" (III), 158–59

Aquinas, Thomas: on male and female contributions to embryo, 66

Arianism, 76

Aries, Phillippe, 135

Aristotle, 68, 72; on male and female contributions to embryo, 57, 66; on *pneuma* and equation between mother and matter, 57; and form, 66–67

Aristotelean, 67

arms: encircling infant, 62; of God as enclosure, 66

art, 109; function of, 121; religious, 108

Asals, Heather, 12, 23, 218 n. 77

as–if attitude, 101; and madness in *Hamlet*

attunement, 131, 184

Augustine, 23, 72, 76; discussion of form, 67–70; on reunification of flesh and spirit, 29; on self, 125

authoritarian: Calvin's God as, 153; child rearing practices in the Renaissance as, 124, 134; ideology in the Renaissance, 134; interpersonal and intra-personal dynamics in the Renaissance, 107; Milton's God as, 147, 153; relational model as one cause of false-self organization, 124; religion, and Calvinism, 125, 153

authority: prosody as, 24; dependence on, 107; cooperative versus hierarchical models, 58; of elders, 134; of fathers in history, 137; figure and false-self interactions, 167; of God, 145; imaginary surveillance by, as a means to self-control, 156; legiti-